WAY TOO MUCH FUN

The story of my life

DON E. PERKINS

Way Too Much Fun
The story of my life

ISBN 0-9759198-0-6

Printed in the United States by Morris Publishing
3212 East Highway 30
Kearney, NE 68847
1-800-650-7888

DEDICATION

I dedicate this collection of sketches to all of those folks who made my life and its many adventures possible.

You know who you are!

My heartfelt appreciation and thanks to each one of you whether you're living or dead. You've made all of my life *Way Too Much Fun.*

Don E. Perkins

CONTENTS

WAY TOO MUCH FUN

The Story of My Life

INTRODUCTION

A six year-old boy sat stiffly staring down at the melted snow dripping from his four-buckle overshoes. He was barely able to hold back his tears so he welcomed any distraction that took his mind off his sadness. For the first time in his life someone he knew and loved had died.

He sat between his father and his mother in Dunn's Funeral home. His grandma sat on the other side of his mother. She was crying and held a handkerchief to her eyes. Many of his aunts, uncles, and cousins were there, too, for his grandpa's funeral. And there were scores of other people. Some were family friends and some were from church, but he had never seen many of the others. They were dressed in their best Sunday clothes. All behaved in a strange, awkward way. When they talked they spoke only in whispers.

An organ played many of the familiar hymns he heard on Sundays, but they sounded muted and less vigorous than usual. Finally the organ stopped and Reverend Clifton Rash, the pastor from First Federated church, walked slowly to the lectern. It was reassuring to hear his familiar voice as he read from the Bible. But he, too, seemed sad and spoke more softly than usual. He talked about the promises God made in the Bible and told everyone that the boy's grandpa was indeed now in Heaven as God had promised.

After he finished everyone drove their cars with headlights turned on to Woodland Cemetery. The pastor once more spoke words of reassurance and delivered a long prayer. Then the funeral was over. Walking through the snow to their cars folks loosened up and began talking out loud rather than in whispers.

On the way home the boy thought about all of the good times he'd had with his grandpa. He had gotten to know a few things about this man with the auburn hair, the freckles, and the large calloused hands, but there was so much more he didn't know. And there were so many things he thought he could have learned from him. Now it was too late.

I was that six year-old boy at the funeral of my maternal grandpa Edwin W. Bowlsby. Over the years I have retained many fond memories of this wonderful man who spoke so kindly to me as he showed me many amazing things. He was the man who frequently stopped by on Saturday afternoons in his Model T Ford and took me home to stay with him and my grandma for the weekend. I got to help Grandpa in his huge vegetable garden, maybe pick strawberries, or watch him smoke his beehives and take out the frames of honey. Then sometimes we'd just sit on the porch steps and talk.

My grandma thought that boys should know how to sew on buttons and embroider doilies. She began teaching me. Before long I could sew on a button and make French knot embroidery stitches well enough to please her. For breakfast she made the tastiest pancakes I've ever eaten. She also served me coffee. My parents did not allow me to drink coffee at home so I thought this was a real treat. No doubt Grandma diluted my coffee with a lot of water.

Grandma was the one who took me to the Iowa State Fair every year. She was a tireless walker. I struggled to keep up as she marched around the grounds looking at the animals, the vegetables, the quilts, and the canned food. I believe we always covered everything there was to see except I noticed she always detoured us around the girly show on the Midway. Before we left she always bought me a souvenir.

Although I remember some things it appalls me how much I don't know about Grandpa and Grandma, my other grandparents, or many of my relatives. I think about the good times and the bad times through which they lived and the changes that happened in the world during their lifetimes. How did World War I affect them; did they worry during the flue epidemic of 1918; how did they earn a living; what health problems did they face; and how did they feel about their lives? I don't even know how far they went in school, what their favorite subjects might have been, or if they knew how to swim? I regret that I did not get a chance to find out.

Perhaps one day my family will have questions about my life. They may want to know how I became a bugler in the Navy during World War II; about my summer job in a mental hospital; how Gladys and I met, or how I felt when each of our children was born.

With this in mind I have written the following sketches describing a few of the events and people that shaped my life. I want you to feel the joy I've felt and absorb the insights I may have gained. And maybe, just maybe, these sketches will provoke a laugh or two along the way. ENJOY!

Don E. Perkins
Des Moines, Iowa
July 1, 2004

Chapter 1

THE EARLY YEARS

Until I was four years old we lived on Twenty-Second Street a block north of Washington Street in Des Moines. I have a hazy picture of our house, its yard, and the house next door where Charlie McCarty and his German shepherd, Fritz, lived. When we were outside Fritz was always with us ready to run and wrestle. Charlie and I rode our tricycles on the sidewalk in front of our houses. Our mothers warned us that we were not to ride beyond our houses or in the street. One day I rode my tricycle to the corner. Mom marched me home and tied a rope around my waist. She tied the other end to the clothesline post. I could range out only ten or fifteen feet so that didn't give me much room for playing. I did not like being tied up like a dog, but when Charlie urged me to untie the rope I decided that would just lead to even greater punishment so I served my time and she eventually untied me.

Bob, another chum, lived three blocks away. He and his family were friends from church. My mother forbade me to ride my tricycle or walk to his house by myself. When my mother visited there we walked over together. Then Bob and I could have an afternoon of play. He was a year older and I thought he was much more experienced because his father had taken him rabbit hunting. That was something my father had not done so I was eager to hear about it. Even though Bob was too young to shoot a gun I thought just going hunting would be exciting. I wanted to go hunting some day, too, but it was several years before my older cousin Ivan took me on my first hunt.

One day Bob and I were with our mothers in the small neighborhood grocery about four blocks from home. While our mothers shopped we explored the store. Bob decided he wanted a banana from the bunch hanging from a hook suspended from the ceiling. He climbed on top of a counter and at the same time he reached up and broke off a banana the storeowner saw him, grabbed him, and pulled him away from the bananas. His mother was mortified to see Bob shoplifting. I just felt sorry for Bob because the shopkeeper hollered at him and I thought his mother might spank him when they got home.

Occasionally my mother visited one of her friends from high school. The lady had no children so there was no one to play with. While they talked I tried to amuse myself with a toy or two. The most memorable thing about these visits was that I often heard Debussy's "Clair de Lune" on the radio. It was the theme music for the popular soap opera "Mary Marlow." I suppose that my mother and her friend were fans of that show. One time the friend offered me a piece of her homemade chocolate fudge. I really didn't feel very well and didn't want any so I declined by saying, "It looks too good to eat." I probably had heard a grownup say that at some time. The friend and my mother insisted so I ate a piece. Not long afterward I lost the fudge and my lunch as well. I was so embarrassed that I didn't want to visit there again.

Other times my mother and I rode the streetcar downtown to Younkers department store. Grandma Bowlsby worked in the basement yard goods department. If we arrived at lunchtime Grandma took us upstairs to the employees' cafeteria. It was near the top of the building and I liked looking out at the other downtown buildings from that height. I suppose the lunchroom menu listed many tasty things to eat, but two items were favorites of mine. My mother always ordered egg custard in a little white cup and whole wheat bread for me. I looked forward to seeing my grandma, but I believe I probably was equally excited about the custard and whole wheat bread.

In addition to eating lunch at Younkers my mother did most of her shopping there. If I needed to use a restroom while we were in the store my mother took me to the ladies room. That was customary in those days. Once while we were in the ladies rest room I saw a woman sit down on the sofa and light a cigarette.

My folks strongly opposed smoking and considered it especially immoral for women to smoke. All of the adults that I knew considered women who smoked "bad, loose, or fast" women. I grabbed my mother by the hand and pulled her in front of the sofa. I pointed to the sinner I had discovered and shouted, "There's a **bad** woman, Mom!" My mother was so embarrassed that she rushed me out of the rest room as quickly as possible.

We shopped for some of our food at the old City Market downtown on the northwest corner of Second and Locust Streets. This building was essentially a large roof held up by steel beams and open on all sides. Anyone could rent a stall and sell fresh vegetables, fruit, eggs, milk, or bakery goods.

Italian truck gardeners from the south side of town rented most of the stalls. As we strolled through the aisles it was not unusual to come upon two or more of these vendors screaming at each other in Italian while wildly waving their arms and gestured with their hands as though they were ready to fight. My mother reassured me and said, "Don't worry they won't hurt each other. They're just very excitable people." Although I saw many noisy arguments I never saw anyone actually strike a blow.

If I behaved while we were at the Market my mother rewarded me with a half-pint bottle of chocolate milk. That was a special treat because we didn't have chocolate milk at home. We sat on a bench beside the milk vendor's stall while I sipped the delicious milk through a straw. When I finished slurping the last drops we walked to the corner to wait for a Number 7 Urbandale streetcar to take us home.

We Leave The Old Neighborhood

In 1929 when I was four years old my folks bought a house at 3407 Forty-seventh Street, in the part of Des Moines known as Beaverdale. With the assortment of stores and shops in its business district along Beaver Avenue I thought of Beaverdale as a small town separate from Des Moines. My parents said they wanted to move away from the near downtown area to where the air was better and where I would have more room for playing. Because I had chronic ear infections, many colds, and other illnesses, they considered my health fragile. They expected the fresh air, sunshine, and outdoor exercise to make me healthier.

The new place had a large lot with apple, pear, and cherry trees; raspberry and current bushes; grape vines; a strawberry bed; large garden space; and a chicken house. Every one in the neighborhood raised chickens and several of our neighbors had cows. The family next door had draft horses. To me it seemed like we'd moved to the country and I liked that.

I remember leaving Charlie, Fritz, and Bob, but I don't remember much about packing and loading our belongings. It was dark when my parents, grandparents, and Uncle Willie unloaded the last of our things into the house. My uncle Willie, who did live in the country where he had a herd of Jersey dairy cows, used his truck for moving us. It was comforting to discover the bright full moon rising over our apple trees looked the same as it had on Twenty-Second Street.

In their campaign to improve my health my folks made me sleep on a day bed in our screened in front porch at the new place. They thought that sleeping in the fresh air was good for me. After the worst of winter was over and until it got quite cold in late October I slept on the porch. In the summer it was pleasant sleeping outside because it was always cooler than in the house. During the colder nights in the spring and in the fall I had heavy quilts to snuggle into. On cold mornings when I pushed my face up out of the warmth of the quilts and inhaled that first breath of frigid air I was immediately jolted wide-awake. Then I jumped out of bed and scampered for the living room. Here I stood with my back to the heat register soaking up the warmth and put on my clothes.

School Begins

My folks explained that starting school would be exciting. As Mom drove me to Byron Rice elementary school and enrolled me in kindergarten, I wasn't so sure. She stayed in our classroom for a time along with several other mothers, but after several minutes the teacher asked the mothers to leave. Now she had us to herself. She reminded me of my Grandma Bowlsby and read stories to us most of the morning.

At noon the mothers returned to take us home. Before leaving the building I insisted that my mother come with me so I could show her what impressed me most about my first morning in school. I took her by the hand and led her to the basement of the building. I wanted her to come with me into the boys' bathroom for I had discovered the urinal. I assumed she would want to see my discovery, but she deferred and I had to be content with describing it to her.

I don't recall much about the rest of my kindergarten year, but I remember the day we began first grade. For me that was much more exciting than beginning kindergarten. Now we would be in school all day rather than just half a day. It also meant we would learn to read. Then we could read books to ourselves rather than having someone read to us. On the first day of school we reported to the kindergarten room as we'd done every day the year before. Our teacher lined us up and marched us to the first grade room next door. Miss Alexander the first grade teacher welcomed us. She assigned us seats at real school desks with inkwells. Then she explained how she expected us to behave. I felt like a big kid now that I was in first grade sitting at a real school desk with a real ink well protruding from its top.

The rest of my experiences in grade school drift by like a series of vignettes. In third grade our classroom was in the basement. It was always dark and perhaps it smelled musty for Miss Price, our teacher, kept a small bottle of perfume on her desk. From time to time she squirted a drop or two onto the light bulb in her desk lamp. When it hit the hot light bulb it sizzled and gave off a pleasant perfumy odor. Possibly another reason for the perfume was that this classroom was directly across the hallway from the boys' and girls' bathrooms.

Miss Hall, the music teacher, was a large mean looking woman. She wasn't fat, just tall, large boned, and very muscular. She looked like the woman shot putter I'd seen pictured on the sports' page. One look at Miss Hall and you immediately knew she would tolerate no foolishness. She held her classes in the auditorium where we sat in the first two rows. Miss Hall stood in front of us or sat at the piano while teaching us songs such as "John Peel," and "Green sleeves." At Christmas time we sang carols, but not modern songs like "Rudolph," or "Frosty the Snowman." Later when we were in the upper grades I thought it was especially thrilling to hear our class sing in two-part harmony.

Miss Hall said we must buy a simple 10-hole harmonica in the key of C. Then she taught us to play them. I don't believe we sounded good, but when we played as a group I liked to imagine I was playing in a symphony orchestra. Our harmonica repertory included old time favorites such as, "Old Susanna," "The Bear Went Over the Mountain," and "Old Folks at Home." Certainly it was not Brahms or Beethoven, but to me it was every bit as grand.

Accidents and Disability

During recess and over lunch hour the playground was alive with youthful exuberance. One morning Dick Schultz fell off the climbing bars. He screamed and cried as he got up from the ground. Both bones in his forearm were broken just above the wrist and his left hand hung limply. I looked toward the building and saw Miss Hall racing toward us looking unusually grim. "Oh Dick's going to get it now," I thought. "Surely she will scold him for being so clumsy," but I was wrong. She picked Dick up and cradled him in her strong arms. She reassured him, wiped the tears and dirt from his face, and carried him into the building for first aid. The next day Dick was back in school with his left arm in a plaster cast supported by a sling and enjoying the attention the cast earned him. Miss Hall continued to conduct her classes in the same no-nonsense manner, but now I saw her differently. I knew that beneath her tough appearance and hard-boiled manner there lived a caring and compassionate person.

One noontime there was a more serious accident. After lunch kids began to ask, "Did you hear what happened to Martin Hanslick?" Martin was a grade level below me, but I knew him. His sister Jean Ann was in my grade. From rumors we learned that over the lunch hour Martin was riding his bicycle in the Beaverdale business district when a car hit him severely injuring his leg. An ambulance took him to the hospital. The doctors amputated his leg above the knee. In almost no time Martin was back in school walking with crutches. Later he was fitted with a wooden leg and soon walked with only a slight limp. To all of us he was the same boy he'd always been since he did not allow the loss of a leg to keep him from any of our fun and games.

Another of my classmates walked with crutches. Vesper Lee was a year older than most of us and was in our class because she had missed a year of school while doctors treated bone infections in her legs. Long scars ran down both of her legs. She wore braces and used crutches to get around. Perhaps it was because she was a year older that she seemed to feel the rest of us we were childish. Unfortunately that attitude held us at a distance and we never got to know her.

How To Tame A Bully

During recess on the playground we worked off the energy that built up while sitting quietly in the classroom. We ran, tumbled, wrestled, played softball or football, and fought. Alvie was the playground bully. He was taller than most of us and enjoyed pushing, shoving, and challenging every boy to a fight. He usually got the fights he wanted. These encounters escalated from name calling, to pushing and shoving, and finally to the savage flailing of arms and fists. When a fight began all the other kids gathered around to watch the excitement. They hollered, "Fight! Fight! Fight!" The teacher monitoring the playground that day usually came running to break it up. Any boy fighting

Alvie hoped the teacher came quickly to end it before Alvie could do serious damage.

I had my share of fights with Alvie and didn't like them. It upset me that he always was able to hit me and take me to the ground. One day Alvie swaggered up began shoving and called me names. It was clear he wanted to fight. Finally I got angry and decided I was tired of this big bully picking on me. I swung at him repeatedly with both fists trying to smash his face and bloody his nose. I felt good every time I landed a solid blow. Alvie was surprised. Next I rushed at him throwing him to the ground. He landed on his back with me astride his chest pounding my fists hard into his face. Shortly after that one of the teachers ran up and pulled me off Alvie. With one of us on each side she marched into the building, sat us down in her classroom, and made us miss the rest of recess. I looked across at Alvie's bloody nose and grinned. I had beaten the playground bully. After that he never gave me a hard time on the playground or did he seek a rematch.

A Boy And His Bike

I don't remember a time when I didn't have wheels. First it was a wooden "KiddieKar" which I rode inside the house about the time I was learning to walk. Next I had a tricycle when we lived on Twenty-Second Street. Shortly after we moved to Forty-seventh Street I received my first two-wheeler. It looked like a "big boy's" bike except its wheels were only ten inches tall. I was excited as I confidently put one foot on a pedal and pushed off with the other as I had seen big boys do. My ride ended abruptly with me on the lawn and the bike on top of me. I got up and tried again. Again I spilled on the grass.

After a few more spills I cried in frustration and slammed the bike down "You're no friend of mine," I shouted. I had no idea that riding a two-wheeler would be so hard. It looked so easy when the big boys did it. I was ready to quit.

Dad watched all of this and told me to rest a while on the porch steps then try again. He said, "You can ride that bike – I know you can." This time he held on to the back of the seat while I pedaled and tried to balance. Off I went with Dad holding on while I pedaled and steered. I rode back and forth across the yard and each time felt more confident. Gradually I began to sense that subtle feel of my body and the bike working cooperatively to achieve balance.

After another brief rest I tried again. Then on one stretch, I felt everything was going well. I looked around to tell Dad and saw he was still standing at the far side of the yard where we started. After he got me going I rode across the yard by myself! From then on my bike and I were great friends. I was grateful to Dad for helping me learn to ride like the big boys.

After I became more experienced my mother suggested, "Maybe you'd like to ride over to visit Grandma Bowlsby." Would I? It sounded great! Grandma lived twelve or fourteen blocks away on Fifty-fourth Street. Most of the way I would travel on busy Douglas Avenue, but I would ride on the sidewalk and not in the street.

It was the kind of summer day intended for outdoor fun like bike riding. I rode out our driveway and down the street toward Douglas. Immediately I felt the satisfaction of riding alone away from the close supervision of an adult. At least it felt that way. Although I never saw her I sensed my mother was somewhere behind me in the car. Undoubtedly she watched my entire journey, but not wanting to shatter my illusion of independence she kept out of sight. It was a short trip and I arrived at Grandma's house without mishap. Shortly afterward my mother drove in and joined us for lunch

I Get A Big Boy's Bike

After I outgrew my sidewalk bike I got a full size bike in an unexpected way. One day I was with Dad in the east side business district. I don't know what he was trying to buy, but his usual approach was to price the item at several stores before buying. In canvassing these stores he took every short cut possible – in front doors, out back doors, and down alleys. A shopping trip with Dad always covered many blocks.

As we hurried down the sidewalk on east Grand Avenue I spotted a coin purse. Inside we found $5.70, but no identification. We kept it and searched the lost and found ads in the newspaper for several days. Finally Dad felt we had made an honest effort to find the owner of the purse and now we had the right to keep it. He suggested perhaps we could use the money to buy that bicycle I wanted. I rode a friend's bike home to show my parents. My friend wanted to sell it, but my folks were unable to pay his asking price of $25.00.

A few days later I told my cousin Ivan that I was looking for a bike. Ivan was four or five years older than I and many times I relied on his experience for information. He said he had a friend who had a bike for sale. Dad said we'd look at it. When his friend retrieved the bike from the shed I was disappointed. The tires were flat, the wheels wobbled, the paint had deteriorated, the seat was torn, and the chain hung limply. Apparently Dad saw more potential in this wreck than I did. From the money I found he paid the boy's asking price of seventy-five cents and I had a bike even though it was not ridable.

I believe Dad enjoyed taking on this bicycle restoration project. First he took off the wheels and removed the tires from the rims. He had to make the rims run true. Dad replaced the missing or bent spokes, soaked the wood rims in water, then clamped the wheels, and tightened the spokes. He ended up with two wheels which wobbled only slightly as they turned. Finally he painted the rims with aluminum paint. He removed the bearings, repacked them in new grease, and cleaned and oiled the coaster brake. He bought new tires from the found money and used gasket cement to mount them onto the rims. Finally he had two rather nice looking serviceable bicycle wheels.

He removed the pedal hanger and pedals from the frame, sanded what was left of the old paint on the frame, and repainted it a brilliant red trimmed with cream. I helped with this restoration as much as I could, but a five-year has limited mechanical skills. I began to feel, however, that perhaps I'd eventually have a ridable bicycle after all.

From the money Dad bought a new seat, handlebar grips, and a big red reflector for the rear fender to complete the restoration. Now the bike was ready for a spin. First Dad rode it up and down the street to make sure everything held together and to see that the brake worked. Then it was my turn. I put one foot on a pedal and confidently pushed off with the other foot. This bike was indeed different from my little sidewalk bike. It radiated more power, speed, and potential for carrying me anywhere I wanted to go. I just knew that this bike would take me on many adventures. I was grateful to Dad for his work in converting a wreck of a bike and $5.70 into my wonderful riding machine.

After a few weeks to gain more experience and riding skill my parents gave their permission for me to ride to school, however, they established strict rules that severely limited the length and breadth of my bike-riding world. During the rest of my time at Byron Rice School I rode my bike to and from school.

Chapter 2

OUR SCHOOLYARD UNION CALLS A STRIKE

My grade school classmates and I had never seen any workers on strike. But we'd heard about strikes because there was considerable labor unrest in the 1930's. The rebelliousness of these strikers grabbed our attention. Maybe we could call our own strike on the school playground. We weren't sure just how to go on strike, but we decided we'd just sit down and not go back in the building after recess.

One afternoon the weather was so warm and sunny that no one wanted to go inside. "This is the day for our strike," I declared. When the bell rang for us to go to class we planned to sit down on the playground and refuse to move. We talked as many of the younger kids into joining us as we could. They held back saying that we'd all get in trouble. But when they saw that the older boys agreed to strike they joined us. Then we all waited for the bell. This was the first time we'd ever wanted recess to end. Finally old Mr. King, the school janitor, came to the door and rang his big brass bell.

"Sit down! Sit down!" We all sat down and told everyone to stay down. We were on strike! Several of the younger kids waited a second or two and then ran for the door. "Sissy! Sissy! Come back here!" we yelled. Others seemed determined and sat down. We all looked very serious and kept encouraging one another, "Yeah, we'll sit here 'til school's out and then go home. That'll show 'em."

The last of the little kids now disappeared into the building. We tried to encourage one another. "Boy, I bet the teacher sure wonders where we are," I yelled. "Stay down, guys. It'll be fun!" Somehow I didn't sound as confident as I had earlier.

Several minutes passed and a few more kids ran to the building. Now some of the older kids grew uneasy. Then guys in my own grade, my closest buddies, began leaving. After a few more minutes just me and three or four of my classmates remained. Eventually we, too, decided, "Hey, maybe this isn't the day for our strike after all." We ran for the door ending our strike.

In the days that followed we discussed strategy. Someone said, "All the real union guys have union cards." Bob hung out at the local print shop. He replied, "I can get us some cards printed up."

A day or so later Bob had the cards and we were ready. I don't remember everything printed on the card, but it looked official and did say the cardholder was a member of the "Byron Rice School Union Pushing for Nicer Teachers." As we understood it having a union card gave you permission to strike.

We each had a union card and wrote our name in the space where it said, "Name." We gave a card to any kid on the playground who was willing to join us in another strike. Before long most of the boys in school were union members.

One sunny spring afternoon at recess we began organizing our strikers on the playground. I reminded everyone, "Remember, we want nicer teachers. That's what this strike is all about. This time we really will stay on the playground all afternoon. No matter what happens don't go in."

At last old Mr. King rang his big brass bell and some of the little kids ran for the door. "Hey, look at the sissies go!" we yelled. Somebody hollered, "Hey you scabs. You're nothing but dirty scabs!" We'd read that "scab" was what a union member called a strikebreaker.

All the boys in our class as well as most of the older boys and a few of the younger ones stayed seated. "Yeah, we're staying here all afternoon," I cried. Then we all hollered, "We want nicer teachers! Nicer teachers! Nicer teachers! Strike! Strike! Strike!"

Several minutes passed before clusters of kids here and there broke away and ran for the door. It did no good to plead with them. Finally all of the other boys in our class left, too. Just Bob and I stayed. We sat and talked quietly. "They sure were a bunch of sissies," we agreed. "Wonder if the teacher misses us yet."

We also wondered what punishment we might get for going on strike. We sensed it might be serious. "Hey, we've got union cards. They can't do anything to us," I said. After several minutes our strong resolve began to ebb. We reluctantly called off our strike and slowly walked toward the door.

We started up the long stairway to our second floor classroom. Miss Anderson, the principal, was waiting for us at the head of the stairs. With arms folded across her chest she looked down sternly as we slowly climbed the steps. Bob was ahead of me and when he reached her she stepped aside and let him pass. Then she stepped back and blocked the stairs again. Even if you were not misbehaving, Miss Anderson's glance made you feel that she was going to punish you. Now she looked like an executioner ready to go to work. She said, "Come with me, Donald." I followed the executioner into an empty classroom and we both sat down.

I didn't know exactly what she was going to do to me, but I felt my union card would do me little good now. I thought she might give me a thorough tongue-lashing, take away all recess time, and make me stay after school every day for the rest of the year. Or she might have some horrible punishment in mind much worse than I could imagine.

She began in a soft voice without any anger, "Donald, Donald. I'm so disappointed in you. You've used your leadership skills in the wrong way. I expected greater things from you and I'm terribly upset by what you've done." I was not prepared for that.

She seemed truly sad. Then she took me to my class. I did not lose recess nor did I have to stay after school, but her calm shaming words touched me in a way that a scathing tongue-lashing and detention could not.

A few days later Miss Anderson showed me that she believed I was a reliable student by naming me the Byron Rice courier. This was a prestigious assignment, but it also got me out of class for a couple of hours every Tuesday morning. I was to report to her office promptly at 9:00 o'clock. She then gave me a cardboard tube containing a bottle of water taken from the boiler by old Mr. King. I was to carry the water sample to the School Board office downtown. They would analyze it. She gave me two tickets for my trip down and back on the streetcar. Riding by myself on such a mission made me feel important.

Because of Miss Anderson's confidence in me, I was determined not to disappoint her again. I never even thought about organizing another schoolyard strike. Besides our first strike had been successful after all, hadn't it? It gave us at least one "nicer teacher."

.

Soccer Scores Big

Miss Schoenburger, the physical education teacher, decided to organize our random playground activities by introducing us to soccer. She lined out the playing field, stuck up poles to mark the goals, and recruited several of us to play. She demonstrated the fundamentals and explained the rules. After all of her effort we felt compelled to play soccer during most of our recesses. The school didn't have regulation soccer balls so Miss Schoenburger gave us basketballs. They were harder to control and kick and doing a header with a basketball was a jolting experience that we did as infrequently as possible.

After several weeks of playing among ourselves Miss Schoenburger decided we should experience some other competition. Several of the city's grade schools had fledging soccer teams so she scheduled some inter school games. Those of us who played thought it was great fun to be bussed to the different schools around town. I thought that hearing the crowd cheer when we made a good play was thrilling. The games must have looked rather ragtag, however, since none of us had uniforms or wore proper shoes. For identification each team member wore a piece of red or yellow cloth around his waist.

The WPA Digs Up Our Playground

About this time construction began on our north playground. That large area had the usual ups and downs of a former cow pasture, but was not actually hilly. The School Board decided, however, that it should be level. One day trucks hauled men, shovels, and wheelbarrows onto our playground. The men put a snow fence around the area and erected a sign saying it now was a project of the WPA. (Works Progress Administration.) The federal government established the WPA during the Great Depression to provide jobs for unemployed workers. They did not use bulldozers and other motorized earth-moving equipment on our playground; one or two teams of horses pulling earth moving scoops and many men using shovels and wheelbarrows tackled the job.

We had to spend recesses on the small playground on the south side of the building. It was congested, but that didn't dampen our activities. Every day we walked to the north side to check on the rebuilding of our playground. One of the first things the workers did was build two out houses. One of our classmates told us what he'd heard his dad say. "For every six workers on a WPA project you will find two of them shoveling, two wheeling barrows, and two sitting in the out house." Whether true or not the workers did a good job leveling our playground. Over summer the grass grew so thick that when school began again in the fall we had a grassy field for soccer and other outdoor fun. What's more our playground was level.

Outside Of School

Although school occupied a large part of my time during these early years other things were going on as well. Following my

Grandpa Bowlsby's death Grandma remained in their house on Fifty-fourth Street south of Douglas. This acreage with its orchard, garden, berries, and bees, in addition to her full time job at Younkers, was too much for her. What's more everything around the place reminded her of Grandpa. Not many months after his death she sold the acreage and bought a newly finished Beaverdale brick house at 2512 Thirty-seventh Street.

My parents decided we would move into this house with Grandma. I don't know the reasons, but it was during the Great Depression so I suspect it was to save money. My folks rented our place on Forty-seventh Street to the Harry and Frances Kolk family. They attended our church and their son Bob was my old chum from the Twenty-second Street neighborhood.

The cut limestone fireplace in Grandma's new house was an attractive focal point in the living room. I looked forward to seeing a fire in it. But Grandma intended to keep the fireplace in its pristine condition. She didn't want a fire to blacken its walls and announced that we should never light a fire in her fireplace. The kitchen with its handy built-in cupboards and counter tops covered with tile would not be used either. Instead my father had to hook up a gas hot plate and a sink in the basement. All our meals were prepared and eaten there.

Mom Has Twenty-six Children

Mom continued to work as a foster mother for the Iowa Children's Home Society during the two years that we lived with Grandma. Years later she often said that counting my sister and I she had cared for twenty-six children. She did this to earn money for household expenses, as a way to pay for my piano lessons, and because I believe she truly loved to look after babies. Usually she cared for newborn infants, but on two occasions she cared for older children.

The nurse from the Society told my mother about two year old Dickey's epilepsy when she brought him to our house. The nurse instructed Mom what to do should he have a seizure. Dickey's first seizure frightened all of us. He fell down, started twitching, jerking, and frothing at the mouth. Following the nurse's instructions Mom swooped him up and ran for the bathroom. She filled the tub with warm water, ripped off his clothes, and laid him in the tub being careful to hold his head above water. Because of Dickey's wild threshing most of the water was splashed out of the bathtub. Eventually Dickey stopped convulsing and relaxed. My mother couldn't relax until she mopped up the soggy bathroom and changed her soaked clothes.

A few days later Dickey had a second seizure, but this time Mom let him lie on the rug while she watched to make sure that he didn't hurt himself. By not following the nurse's instructions both Dickey and my mother stayed drier and he survived his seizure just fine.

Another time Mom cared for Alice a four-year-old girl with a harelip. She was well behaved, intelligent, and got along fine with all of us. I thought she was a fun kid to have around. After living with us for several months the nurse took her away. I don't know why she took her, but I hope it was for restorative surgery. After that I hope she found good adoptive parents.

A Special Baby

Patricia was one of the new born infants the nurse brought to live at our house. Each child was special, but Patricia stood out from all of the others. She was always happy, smiled a lot, and took an interest in everything going on around her. She was just two weeks old, but had long, dark hair that curled into ringlets. My folks liked each of the children the Society brought for them to care for, but I sensed that they felt differently about Patricia. As time passed they talked about adopting her. Finally they became serious about it and filed adoption papers when she was two years old.

For our family vacation that summer we all went to Colorado. We saw the Garden of the Gods, Seven Falls, and drove to the top of Lookout Mountain. We had fun, but my folks were preoccupied wondering whether the final adoption papers were ready to be signed. They thought they should be home in case a problem came up. Their speculation finally got so intense that they cut short the vacation and we went home. A few days after we arrived the papers were final. I was now eight years old and felt good having Patty, a two-year-old kid sister.

Bicycle Accidents

While we lived on Thirty-seventh Street with Grandma a part of my ride back and forth to school took me down Thirty-eighth Street and across Urbandale Avenue. As Thirty-eighth approaches Urbandale from the north it goes downhill for half a block. There is a stop sign at the bottom. It's impossible to see oncoming traffic on Urbandale until you are in the intersection.

Every day I dutifully stopped at the stop sign to look for oncoming cars. Not once was there any traffic on Urbandale. Besides you gained considerable speed going down the hill and had to waste it by stopping at the bottom. One day on the way home for lunch I thought, "Hey, I'm not going to stop at that ol' stop sign. Never any cars coming anyway." I let the bike go as fast as it would downhill and made no attempt to stop at Urbandale. I shot into the intersection. Suddenly from the corner of my eye I saw a sedan coming from the left. The driver had a horrified look on his face as he tried to miss me. His tires screeched, but it was too late.

He hit me. I flew off my bike and landed on the railroad tracks running down the middle of Urbandale. Streetcars used these tracks and two or three times a week the interurban train hauled freight cars loaded with lumber or livestock feed to the lumberyard and the feed store in Beaverdale. Today was one of the days for the train to deliver its cars. It was getting close and then I heard the screech and hiss of its air brakes. I managed to get bike and myself off the tracks and out of the way as the train rolled to a stop.

The worried sedan driver rushed up and asked me, "Are you all right? Where are you hurt?"

I wasn't sure, but I didn't think I was badly hurt just scared. "I think I'm just bruised."

"Here, get in the car. I'll take you on home."

He loaded my bike and me into his car and drove me home. He explained to my startled mother what had happened. I guess Mom felt I had already learned my lesson because she did not lock up my bike like I thought she might. That evening Dad repaired the bike's damage and the next day I rode it again. But from then on I always stopped at the Thirty-eighth Street crossing.

My second bicycle accident happened three blocks from the first. While returning to school one noon I caught up with some of my classmates who were walking. As I passed them a good-natured chase began. They ran after me and we hollered and laughed at each other. Once I glanced back at them and the next instant I had stopped suddenly when I ran into the rear of a parked car. I flew off the bike and into the pavement mouth first. As I got up from the pavement I must have looked horribly injured since my friends suddenly became somber and solicitous. Then I noticed blood dripping from my mouth onto my shirt.

We went to school trying to act nonchalant, but the first teacher who saw me grabbed my arm and asked, "What in the world happened!" She rushed me to the nurse's office. A cut on the inside of my mouth was bleeding profusely. Apparently there was no other damage. The nurse stopped the bleeding, cleaned me up, and asked, "Do you want to go home?" I was not anxious to go home since I feared that my mother would punish me for reckless bike riding. I stayed for the afternoon classes. When I went home after school I reported that I merely had fallen off the bike and bit my lip.

A Special Awakening

In seventh grade I became intensely interested in our science class. An attractive, energetic young lady fresh out of teacher's college taught it and that probably helped to spark this interest. She didn't seem much older than I was. I suspect certain hormones that had begun cruising through my body may have contributed to my enthusiasm. I studied more for this class than for any other. I wanted to impress her by being first to volunteer for extra credit work. When we studied radio I built a crystal set at home brought it to school and demonstrated it to the class. Another time we studied weather. I built a weather vane. During class each day two or three of us took the weather vane and a thermometer outside to the playground to record wind direction and temperature. Somehow this beginning teacher managed to kindle in me an interest in science that has continued all my life.

Mysterious Discussions

Several times I found my folks in earnest conversation, but they always stopped talking when I came into the room. I never heard enough to learn what they were talking about, but I feared I'd done something wrong and now they were deciding what my punishment should be.

One day we visited Grandpa and Grandma Hoare. When I came inside from playing Dad and Grandpa were having a serious conversation. I heard Grandpa say, "I understand, Robby. It's ok with me whatever you want to do." Then they both stopped talking. It really must be serious because Dad's asking for Grandpa's advice.

Not long after Aunt Agnes, my Dad's sister visited us from Colorado. I overheard her say, "But it's not spelled the same. That begins with w, h." I still didn't know what I'd done, but now they've got Aunt Agnes involved, too. I thought, "Oh, this is looking bad."

Not long afterward Dad and Mom sat me down for a serious discussion. I sensed they were about to explain what the mysterious conversations of the past few weeks were all about. I wasn't sure I wanted to hear what my punishment would be. Dad began, "We want to tell you about an important decision we've made. It won't change who we really are, but I think you'll be happy with what we've done."

"That didn't tell me much. Why doesn't he just come right out with it?" I thought.

"I've talked with Grandpa and Grandma, Aunt Agnes, and Aunt Bertha. I even phoned Uncle Art."

"They've gotten everyone in on it. That can't be good."

"All of them said it'd be ok"

"Oh what's he going to do to me?"

"So your mother and I went to the Courthouse and we've changed our family's last name from Hoare to Perkins. That was your Grandma Hoare's last name before she married Grandpa."

So that was what all the discussions were about. I hadn't done anything wrong after all. I felt relieved and said, "So I'll be Donald Perkins and not Donald Hoare?"

"That's right. And Patty will be Patty Perkins and your mother and I will be Mr. and Mrs. Perkins."

"Will Grandpa and Grandma Hoare be Grandpa and Grandma Perkins?" I asked.

"No, they'll still be Grandpa and Grandma Hoare," Dad said.

I wasn't sure I liked the new name. Hoare was the only last name I'd ever known and not once had I wanted to change it. I saw nothing wrong with it. But Dad said, "We changed it because some kids and grownups may make nasty remarks about the name Hoare. There's a word that sounds the same that means something bad. We especially didn't want Patty to have to live with that."

So on July 21, 1937 we became the Perkins family. Dad had business size cards printed saying the family name was legally changed. Mom gave Patty and me cards to give to our teachers so they'd know about the name change. When my buddies heard that I was now Donald Perkins they asked, "What happened? Did your folks get divorced?"

When I got older I understood more precisely why Dad changed our name. He said that his sisters Agnes and Bertha had endured nasty comments about the name when they were in school. I was glad that now Patty would not hear such things said about her.

Chapter 3

FAMILY TRIPS

Chicago World's Fair

When the Chicago World's Fair opened in 1933 it received so much good publicity my folks decided to see it the following year. We drove to Chicago and stayed with my Uncle Art and Aunt Josie in their apartment in Blue Island. Uncle Art was the oldest child in my father's family and Dad was the youngest. There was a twenty-one year difference in their ages. Art was a baker like his father (Grandpa Hoare). Since my sister Pat had a birthday while we were there he baked her a fantastic cake with more sugary bows, ribbons, and roses than I had ever seen on a cake. Aunt Josie was a Scandinavian and spoke with an accent that I thought was quite pleasant. Other than the Italian produce vendors at our City Market I had not talked with anyone with an accent.

The Fair had many spectacular attractions, but the orange flavored ice cream served at the state of Florida exhibit was the most memorable for me. It tasted like they had mixed a juicy orange into creamy homemade ice cream. I wondered if that's what they did.

While in Chicago we went to Jackson Park beach. Swimming in a lake so large that I could not see across it was a little fearsome, but when I noticed other kids enjoying it I was reassured. A girl about my age playing in the water near us wanted to know where I lived. When I said, "Iowa," she acted as though she'd never heard of it. I asked where she lived and she said, "Cicero." When I told my folks they said, "Her father is probably a gangster. You better be careful around her." I didn't know what I should do to be careful so I simply played down the beach away from her.

South Dakota Vacation

The following year we drove to South Dakota to visit my great aunt and uncle Bessie and Ed Shoemaker on their farm near Canning. Bessie, one of Grandma Bowlsby's sisters, was my mother's favorite aunt. Susie, Grandma's other sister, also lived in South Dakota, but because Susie had played a trick on my mother many years earlier she did not like her and did not plan to visit her. The trick somehow involved breaking a rotten egg on my mother's forehead.

The Shoemaker family consisted of my aunt and uncle, two boys about my age, and their sister. The rolling hills in this part of the state seemed to stretch on forever. The only trees grew along the creek banks. I saw so few houses along the highway I wondered where the people lived.

South Dakota and most of the upper Midwest was in a drought that year. Uncle Ed's cornfields looked sick. The stalks were only about three feet high because of the drought and grasshoppers. The ears tried to form, but were stunted. Now grasshoppers were eating the leaves, the ears, and the stalks as well. Dad asked Uncle Ed how much corn he would harvest. "About seventy-five bushel," Uncle Ed replied.

"Seventy-five bushels per acre?" Dad asked.

"No, for the whole damn farm," Uncle Ed responded emphatically.

The well at the farm was dry so Uncle Ed hauled water for the house and his livestock from an artesian well two miles away. One morning he hitched the team to a wagon, loaded several large metal barrels, and asked if I wanted to ride with him to get water. I had never ridden in a wagon before. I climbed in and we bumped along the dirt road causing the water barrels to bounce rhythmically. After several minutes Uncle Ed gave me the reins and said, "Here, you drive for a while." It was a thrill to be in control of two large horses as their harness jingled and their hooves kicked up dust in the dry dirt of the road. He showed me where to turn in, but I turned too sharply and the wagon teetered, about to upset. The frightened horses lunged not knowing what was happening. Uncle Ed grabbed the reins and brought everything back under control. After we filled the barrels we each had a long drink of the cool water before starting back along the dusty road.

The next day everyone got into our 1929 Pontiac four door car and lumbered down the road. Uncle Ed wanted to show us some colorful rock cliffs. We drove for several miles, turned off the dirt road, and bounced across a dusty field. Clouds of grasshoppers flew up as the car passed. Many flew in the windows and landed in our laps, on our arms, and on our faces. Several times we crossed through gates in the barbed wire fences and then came to a creek. When it had water this was a ford, but now it was dry. Dad shifted to low gear and we pulled across. As we came up out of the creek bed we felt a bump like running over a rock, but thought no more about it. At the next stop, however, one of my cousins smelled gasoline when he got out to open the gate. The gas tank was leaking. Apparently the drain plug had scraped a rock and ripped off as we came out of the creek bed.

Someone grabbed a kettle from our camping supplies to catch what gasoline was left. Dad found a cork bobber in his fishing tackle box and shaped it with his pocketknife to plug the hole in the gas tank. He twisted a length of bailing wire to hold the bobber to the tank. It looked like a serviceable repair, but we caught only about a quart of gasoline in the kettle. That wouldn't take us far and we were miles from any town. "I know some folks on a farm a couple miles that way," Uncle Ed said as he pointed toward some low hills covered with brown grass. I looked, but saw nothing that looked like a farm.

"Maybe they won't mind giving us some gas." Dad and Uncle Ed left for the farm to find out.

We sat on the dry dusty ground in the shade of the car and waited. The sound of the wind blowing dust devils through the dry prairie grass and the whirring of grasshoppers' wings as they flew were the only sounds I heard. Even with my family nearby this was a lonely place. After about an hour someone hollered, "Here they come." When they got closer I saw Uncle Ed was carrying a can of gasoline.

The grownups decided we wouldn't go on to the painted cliffs, but would head back to Uncle Ed's farm. Unfortunately I never saw the one scenic attraction that my aunt and uncle wanted to show us. And the fishing bobber repair? It held just fine. In fact we got all the way to Iowa without it leaking.

Cub Scouting Begins In Des Moines

The Boy Scouts of America announced a new program called the Cubs for boys ages nine, ten, and eleven years old. Our church sponsored Boy Scout troops 29 and 76 and now was interested in sponsoring a Cub Pack also. Through the efforts of Mom, Dad, and several others, the Boy Scouts of America chartered a Cub pack at our church. It was designated Cub Pack #1 since it was the first in the Tall Corn Council. Dad was one of the committeemen and Mom became a den mother. The dens consisted of six to twelve boys who met once a week at the home of the den mother. When I was nine years old I joined the Cubs and became a member of the den that met at our house.

A boy scout called a den chief led the meetings. The program required the mastery of certain outdoor skills much like the Boy Scouts. The den chief and the den mother received some guidance in planning the den's activities, but they were free to plan almost any kind of activity they wanted. Mom planned trips for our den to visit the State Historical Building, the Colonial Bakery, the State Capitol, and a radio station. But the longest trip of all was to the Boy's Training School at Eldora, Iowa.

Mom was a strict disciplinarian. Whenever I misbehaved it almost always resulted in punishment such as confinement in my room or a spanking. But when I really exasperated her she threatened to have me sent to the Boys' Reform School at Eldora. With this in mind I had misgivings about our trip to Eldora. For several days prior to the trip I tried hard not to misbehave. I didn't want her to leave me there. Perhaps she planned this field trip as a way to get me to Eldora so she could leave me. I didn't think she would leave me, but then I wasn't so sure.

The tour through the buildings at Eldora surprised me. The way my mother described the place I expected a dark, clammy, dungeon-like prison, but this place was airy, clean, and inviting. Nowhere did I see the mean guards with clubs and guns she had warned me about. The classrooms looked like those at Byron Rice School. And the wood working shop was larger and better equipped than ours. Outside softball games were underway on well-kept softball diamonds. I liked what I saw. After that trip my mother discovered her threats to send me to Eldora no longer bothered me.

Homesick

As a Cub Scout I went to Camp Mitigwa, near Boone, Iowa, for a week in 1936. This was my first time away from home over night without my parents. Our first day was busy. We hiked, we went swimming in the camp's pool, we had huge meals served family style, and that evening we had a campfire. An adult leader nicknamed Johnny Inkslinger told us about the thrilling adventures of Paul Bunyan and Babe his blue ox.

After the campfire it was bedtime. The bugler blew Taps. Someone turned the lights off. As I lay in my bunk I looked across the yard and watched the dying embers of the campfire for a long, long time. As I watched I felt a kind of sadness I had never felt before. I could not drift off to sleep. I discovered what I really wanted was to be home in my own bed. Briefly I thought about waking up the den chief and ask him to arrange for me to go home. But that would be embarrassing. I didn't want to be a sissy baby. I watched the embers grow fainter. The next thing that I remember the bugler was blowing Reveille. That night was the only time in my life I remember being homesick.

Most of the boys in our den were at Mitigwa that year. We sold mixed nuts at Thanksgiving and Christmas time to earn money to pay our way. When I got the bags of nuts I went door-to-door trying to sell them, but was not successful. I came home discouraged. My mother gave me a pep talk and sat me down by the telephone. She insisted that I phone everyone I knew at church and in the neighborhood. "Tell them you're selling mixed nuts to earn your way to camp. Ask them to buy a pound or two," she said. I tried and was amazed that in a short time I sold enough mixed nuts to pay for two boys to go to camp.

Merritt Dwiggins

Our den got to know one another better as we lived and worked together during our week at camp. The den became a close-knit group. That was helpful since not long afterward tragedy struck and we needed each other's support. Merritt Dwiggins, one of our den members, failed to show up for a den meeting one afternoon. That evening we heard a car hit and killed him near Beaver and Allison as he was riding his bike to the den meeting. We heard that the craft project he was bringing to the meeting had been broken and was scattered beside him where he lay on the pavement.

It was a sad time for each of us as we walked past Merritt's open casket at his funeral. It looked like he was just asleep. His blond hair was slightly stained by blood from his head injuries. At the end of the service at the cemetery we stood as a group and said the closing that we always used at the end of our den meetings, "May the great Father watch over us until we meet again."

A few days after the funeral my mother visited Merritt's parents and asked if it would be all right for us to rename our den the Merritt Dwiggins Den. They felt that was a thoughtful and a fitting tribute indeed.

To Mitigwa A Second Time

When I turned twelve I graduated from Cub Scouts to Boy Scouts. That summer I went to Camp Mitigwa with my troop. It didn't seem different than the year before when I was there as a Cub Scout except everyone was a year older and a little taller. Perhaps the major difference was we could do more challenging activities. A week at camp was an excellent time to work on merit badges. I worked on swimming, first aid, and nature, but the most memorable was canoeing.

Canoe activities took place on the Des Moines River down the hill from the camp. To qualify for a canoeing merit badge you had to deliberately upset the canoe, slosh as much water out of it as possible while treading water, then climb back in. All of this while you and the canoe drifted downstream. You had to learn different paddle strokes and demonstrate them to the satisfaction of the instructor. You had to learn to portage a canoe by yourself or with others. And the final requirement was a fourteen-mile canoe "hike." This "hike" would cap our week's canoe activities. If we successfully completed it we would get our canoeing merit badge.

The morning of the trip we wore swim trunks, carried a bath towel, and took a little spending money. Three scouts rode in each canoe. While two paddled the third rested in the center. Then he would relieve one or the other of the paddlers. Altogether we had a flotilla of five or six canoes.

We eagerly pushed our canoes into the river and headed for the Ledges State Park seven miles upstream. Our goal was to reach the park by noon. We were fresh and excited so the paddling went well. We soon found that we'd have to walk some of the way because the river was low. In places it was too shallow to float a canoe loaded with three boys. When we ran aground we hopped out and walked while pushing the canoe. When the bottom dropped off to deeper water we got back in and paddled on. We must have walked a good part of the way to the Ledges.

Around noon we got to the Park and pulled the canoes onto the sandbar. The camp truck was there with lunch. We were hungry and thirsty so it didn't take us long to start eating. After lunch we rested and looked around the park. It was good to stretch after sitting in the canoe most of the morning. With our pocket change we bought ice cream bars, candy, and pop from the concession stand.

The instructor blew his whistle and hollered, "It's time to go back. Come on!" We soon found it was easier to make progress on the river for now we were paddling with the current, but of course we had to walk our canoes many times like we'd done on the trip up.

I noticed that almost all of my body not covered by swim trunks had turned bright red. I had extreme sunburn. By the time we reached camp I felt miserable. The corpsman at sickbay gave me a lotion that eased the pain enough so I could sleep that night. But even with painful sunburn it was a great finish for the week. I had earned my canoeing merit badge

Fourteen Cents Worth of Hamburger

As a kid growing up during the Great Depression I didn't know anyone who had much money. Many men and women were out of work and all our relatives, friends, and neighbors had to repair, make do with what they had, or do without. I heard other people described as being "poor" so often that I asked my mother, "Are we poor, too?" Mom didn't give me a definite answer, but tried to reassure me that everything would be all right. Dad told me, "Childhood is the best time of your life. Just enjoy it. Don't worry about such things." From all of this I concluded that we, too, were poor.

Although we were poor we were fortunate to have space for a large vegetable garden and fruit trees including two productive cherry trees. During the summer our meals consisted of whatever vegetables were ripe at the time. Mom canned what we couldn't eat for winter. All of the garden produce that we didn't eat and that wasn't canned became my responsibility. I hauled beans, peas, strawberries, cherries, corn and whatever surplus we had at the time in my red coaster wagon around the newly developed housing areas on Maryland Pike, Sheridan Avenue, and Beaver Crest Drive, all in Beaverdale. I sold a lot of produce and was pleased that many of the people I called on became repeat customers. Before long I had a regular route. It did not bring in much money, nevertheless, these sales helped pay for some of our needs. One side benefit of this job was that before age ten I knew how to count change back to a customer.

My folks earned extra money however they could. One time they worked for many weeks making clothes pin bags shaped like ducks. They used white cloth for the body and yellow cloth for the bill and feet. They stuffed the bill, head, neck, and feet with cotton. Small black buttons served as eyes. I don't know where they sold them, but they made several dozen.

While I didn't like weeding the garden or picking vegetables I really hated picking cherries. I believed that his dislike for picking cherries was probably the real reason George Washington chopped down his father's cherry tree. It was my job to keep our two prolific trees picked. Often my father phoned my mother from work to say that he'd sold a peck or two of cherries to one or another of his coworkers and that I should pick them so she could deliver them downtown at quitting time. I had to spend most of my day in the trees rapidly picking cherries to meet the afternoon deadline.

We wore our patched clothes until the patches wore out. My cousin Ivan was three or four years older than me and I frequently got some of the shirts and pants he'd outgrown. My sister was not so lucky with hand-me-downs, but my grandmother was an excellent seamstress and made many of my sister's dresses. We both got new shoes each fall when school began. They were always a size or two large so we would not outgrow them so soon. Usually they'd last until the following summer. By then school was out, it was warm, and we could go barefoot except when we went to church or on other special occasions.

When the house needed repairs my father salvaged lumber or other materials wherever he could. We picked up the broken and blemished bricks discarded by the brick works at the north end of Harding Road to rebuild a small root cellar that opened off one of the basement walls. I thought the bricks made a grand looking little cave for the potatoes, apples, and other produce we wanted to store over the winter.

As often as she could afford it Mom sent me to the butcher shop to buy fifteen cents worth of hamburger. That bought enough hamburger to give our family a fine meal especially if she extended it by making it into a meat loaf. But now the state instituted a two percent sales tax on all purchases beginning at fifteen cents. However the state charged no tax on sales below fifteen cents.

Mom decided she would pay no such tax if she could find a way around it. She had an easy solution. From then on she sent me to the butcher shop to buy fourteen cents worth of hamburger thereby saving a penny and it was hard to tell the difference between fourteen and fifteen cents worth of meat.

In the weeks that followed the butcher seemed to enjoy seeing me come into his shop. He'd always smile broadly and ask, "And what can I do for you today, young man?" knowing full well that my answer would be "Fourteen cents worth of hamburger, please."

Of course as a child I did not experience the loss of a job, foreclosure on my home, nor did I have to stand in a soup line to keep from going hungry, but I absorbed from my parents and the adults around me many of their traits. Their attitudes, habits, and views of the world became my attitudes, habits, and views of the world. Frugality, inventiveness, and thrift were their survival skills. Yet life didn't seem harsh at the time, nor does it seem harsh in retrospect. The amazing part is that our lives were not bleak at all. We did not feel deprived. Instead there was a warm feeling of togetherness and a sense of family and of community that was comforting. It was as though everyone was saying, "We will experience these difficult times together as a family, as a neighborhood, and as a nation. Better times will come. We will survive and be better people for it."

When better times came most of us were experienced survivors. But as we moved into better times some of us did not shed the old skills and attitudes learned during the lean years. Those skills and attitudes got my parents and a whole generation of us through a difficult time. I would not recommend an economic depression as a desirable learning experience for children, but I believe it sparked the development of many positive traits.

Chapter 4

NEVER UNDERESTIMATE YOUR FATHER

Our Mine Pond Boat

During the Great Depression we moved in with Grandma Bowlsby on Thirty-seventh Street. This neighborhood was new territory for me to explore with several new kids to get to know. One neighborhood attraction was the Mine Pond along Urbandale Avenue near Thirty-fourth Street. It had been a coalmine, but now all that remained were a few low mounds of shale and a pond covering about an acre. The rumor held that the mine's main shaft was somewhere near the middle of the pond.

Most of the neighborhood boys believed the pond was bottomless especially over the old shaft. From time to time some of the older boys hammered a raft together and cautiously poled themselves across the water searching for the shaft. I don't remember that anyone ever found that fearsome spot, but the pond remained an enticing challenge nevertheless. My parents admonished me repeatedly, "Under no circumstances are you ever to get on a raft and go out on the pond." They didn't forbid me from poking around its edges, however, looking for frogs, crawdads, and other creatures.

One day Dick Williamson and I found a rowboat in the willows at the edge of the pond. It was in good shape except the board on one side was cracked where it had fallen over. We were excited for here was the means for transporting us in grand style onto the pond.

"This'll be better than any ol' raft," Dick said. "Yeah, let's try it out." I replied.

I had promised never to go out onto the pond on a raft, but this was different. It was a regular boat and not a ramshackle raft. But we discovered that it was much too heavy for us to move. Then I thought, “Hey, maybe my dad will help us drag it into the water. Maybe he’ll even haul it home on the car. Then we can fix that side and paint it.”

We both were excited thinking about going out onto the Mine Pond in our boat. But I doubted that Dad would help us with our plans. He’d probably say that it was too dangerous for us to be fooling around the Pond in a boat and make us leave it where it was.

We rushed home and I told Dad we found a good boat and that we wanted him to help us bring it home so we could fix it up. He was not enthusiastic about the idea so I was surprised when he said, “Well, ok. Let’s have a look, but I’m not promising to bring it home.” With that I knew we had the battle half won.

At the pond he found the boat was made of cypress wood and put together with brass screws. The screws countersunk then covered with red lead filler. Someone had built it with care. After examining the boat for several minutes he said, “Well let’s see if we can load it on the car and get it home in one piece.” Dick and I grinned from ear to ear as we helped him with our boat. We were still grinning when we pulled into our driveway and unloaded it in the backyard.

We sat the boat on two sawhorses. Dad told us to pour water inside to see if it leaked. What a disappointment to see water dripping from every joint and seam in the bottom. Dad suggested we caulk every place that leaked. After we did that we poured tar over the caulking. This time when we poured water inside it didn’t leak. We found a can of gray enamel in the garage and gave it a new coat of paint. It began to look seaworthy.

But now we wondered how we’d propel the boat. No oars were with it when we found it. Dad was resourceful and carved two serviceable paddles. A few days later he came home with some old life jackets he’d found in a second hand store. Now it seemed the boat and its occupants would be seaworthy.

Dick and I were anxious to launch our boat and enjoy the results of our labor. One day Dad said, "Today's the day. Let's put it in the water." We tied it onto the car, put paddles, and lifejackets in the back seat, then headed for the grand launching. The closer we got to the Mine Pond the more excited Dick and I became, but Dad drove past the Pond without slowing down. I shouted, "Stop, dad! You missed it!"

He smiled and said; "We're not going to put *our* boat in just a little muddy pond. We're going to put it in some real water – the river."

Now this was much more than we had expected. He drove to the Euclid Avenue Bridge and we put in below the bridge. When I saw how fast the water was flowing, though, I felt a little afraid. I would have been more comfortable on the calm waters of the Pond, but Dad was confident so I thought he must know what he was doing. We put on the life jackets and shoved ourselves away from the bank.

Finally Dad, Dick, and I were afloat on a grand body of water. This was far more than I'd expected. The boat moved nicely and only a few spots of water seeped through our repairs. We paddled across the river, got out on a sandbar to rest a while, then back into the boat, and paddled up and down the river before easing back to the landing. We loaded the boat onto the car and our cruise had been successful. It was a shorter ride than Dick and I hoped for, but paddling a rowboat was harder than we expected.

As the three of us headed home with our boat tied firmly onto the car our muscles were tired, but we were pleased with our launching and boat ride. We all grinned, but I saw my Dad's grin was the broadest of all.

The Ol' Fishing Hole

My father grew up in a house at 1149 Thirteenth Street, Des Moines. His father James Travis Hoare was an avid fisherman.

To reach his favorite fishing spot on the Des Moines River north of town he first caught an Urbandale streetcar in front of his house and rode it north to Beaver Junction on Harding Road just south of Euclid Avenue. Here he transferred to a northbound Ft. Dodge, Des Moines, and Southern Interurban.

Grandpa rode the interurban through Johnston Station, the Camp Dodge military base, and got off at the little town of Herrold at the north end of the base. From Herrold he walked roughly five miles to the river south of an area he called Toonerville. Today that is the area at the west end of the mile-long bridge over Saylorville Lake. Grandpa fished at Red Banks so called because of the red shale banks. The lake now covers his fishing spot, but a sign on the road marks Elliot's Crossing. That is close to where he fished.

When my father was big enough to walk from Herrold to the river and back he went fishing with Grandpa. As I grew up Dad took me to Red Banks for fishing as his father had done with him. The river bottom there was rocky. You could expect to catch channel cat and bass. In later years silt began to cover the bottom and fishing deteriorated until all you could catch were carp.

Even if the fish weren't biting Red Banks was a wonderful place for rock hunting or for exploring in the woods. The timber was dense on the slope from the road down to the river. There were several springs along this slope. Some flowed little rivulets while others were just damp and spongy. These spongy springs were deceptive since ferns and other plants covered them. Several times I walked into one believing it was solid ground and sloshed in above my ankles. It was messy work cleaning the gunky mud off my shoes.

Murray's Camp

Murray's Camp was a half-mile down river from Red Banks. A few picnic tables were scattered across a relatively flat grassy area along the bank. Water was available at a well and a wooden outhouse stood on top of the pit toilet. That was Murray's Camp. In 1937 our family could not afford to take a vacation trip, but Dad thought it would be great fun for the two of us to camp at Murray's for a week. Mom and my sister Pat would stay home and do womanly things.

We packed food, cooking utensils, gasoline cooking stove, fishing gear, army cots, clothes, and a big, old 9' x 12' tent that belonged to my Uncle Ernest. We decided to take the restored Mine Pond boat. It might be useful for fishing and at the end of the week we'd just load our gear in the boat and float down river to Des Moines.

We loaded up the 1936 Plymouth 2 door, stood the stern of the boat on the rear bumper, and tied it securely. Mom and Pat delivered us to Murray's then left for home. We set up camp and soon the place looked livable. The tent had plenty of room for two cots and all of our gear.

We carried the boat down to the landing and tied it up. Now we were ready for a week of boating, swimming, fishing, and loafing. During the week we did all of that. We had plenty of fish to eat, did some boating up and down the river, and got in lots of rock hunting. The swimming part, however, didn't live up to my expectations. I had never gone swimming in water with a current so I was surprised when I jumped in intending to swim across the river to a sandbar and found that for every foot I swam toward the sandbar I drifted two feet down stream. That was a jolt. It took a lot of effort to swim across to the sandbar. After that I didn't swim much.

One night the wind came up while we slept. When parts of the tent began to flap we woke up and tied everything down then got back in our cots. Soon it began raining. Lightning lit up the camp and we saw the trees bending in the wind. The thunder was deafening. A thunderstorm is much louder when you're outdoors and surrounded by it. A strong gust of wind suddenly lifted the tent, poles, and all off the ground. The violence ripped the canvas from the ridgepole down to the sidewall. Rain was soaking everything. Dad was always prepared. From somewhere in his duffel he got out a large needle and heavy thread and began sewing up the rip in the tent while I held the canvas together as best I could. After the repair the rain did not come in as much. We draped anything that had gotten wet over boxes or from a line running between the tent poles on the inside of the tent. We climbed back into our cots and gradually drifted off to sleep as the thunder, wind, and rain rumbled on down river.

Two backwaters in the river near the camp held debris delivered there by the current. I saw a dozen or more bottles trapped among the other debris and salvaged them without any clear idea why. Later Dad suggested we make a bottle xylophone. We suspended the bottles from a rope tied between two trees. Then we tuned the bottles to the scale by partially filling them with water. With a little work we soon had a fair sounding instrument. We took turns playing tunes on it to liven up our leisure time.

River Float Trip

On the appointed day Mom and Pat drove into camp. It had been an enjoyable week, but now I looked forward to the float trip down the river. We loaded everything we didn't need for the trip into the car even our rustic bottle xylophone. We put water, food for lunch, and snacks in the boat for the trip and pushed off.

As she drove away Mom called back, "I'll wait on Hanley Bridge to see if you're ok." It took about ten minutes for us to float to the bridge. Mom and Pat were waiting. As we drifted by we hollered up, "We're ok! See you at Euclid. Maybe around 4:00." We waved and drifted on.

Leisurely floating down a slow moving river with your Dad on a glorious summer day has to be one of the most enjoyable and relaxing activities I can think of. We didn't talk much, but sat back and watched the shoreline inch past. Mostly it was thick timber, but occasionally a farm field planted in corn came almost to the riverbank. Herons fished in the shallows. Turtles sunned themselves on logs, but quietly plopped into the water as our boat approached. I hoped to see a deer or fox, but none showed up. Now and then we dipped a paddle into the water to keep the boat in the current.

At noon we pulled onto a large sandbar and built a driftwood fire to cook lunch. Everything tasted delicious. After lunch and a bit of rock hunting we got back in the boat and drifted on. The closer we got to Des Moines the more signs of civilization we heard and saw. There were farmhouses, barns, cattle, people working in the fields, and roads with cars and trucks. This was a change for us since we hadn't seen another person all week at Murray's Camp.

The river makes many twists and bends as it flows toward Des Moines. It was exciting waiting to see what would be new around each bend. As we floated around a final bend there it was – the Euclid Avenue Bridge a mile ahead. We paddled toward a makeshift landing cut into the bank near the bridge. As we drifted closer we saw Mom and Pat. They waved and shouted, "Glad you made it." They looked relieved and perhaps a little surprised that we made it safely.

Armed and Semi-Dangerous

Dad gave me a BB gun when I was eight or nine years old. He laid down strict rules about shooting and supervised me while I learned to use it. I was not to shoot at: songbirds, streetlights, windows, and people. Other things such as tin cans, targets, and sparrows, were ok. And finally Dad emphasized that I was to make sure there was nothing behind my target that could be hurt if I missed.

For the most part I obeyed these rules. However at times his rules seemed too restrictive. I was not to shoot at our chickens, but one day I thought, "What's the harm," and shot at a chicken's wing anyway. It squawked and jumped almost three feet. I thought that was fun and it didn't seem to damage the chicken. Its thick wing feathers protected it. One day my aim was off. My shot hit Mom's best layer in the head. I panicked, picked up the limp bird, and threw her under the hen house. Later when Mom missed the hen and went looking for it she found it and guessed what had happened. She was extremely angry and said, "If you'd let me know right away I could have dressed it out and at least the meat wouldn't have been wasted!"

After a few years with a BB gun I wanted a .22 rifle. Finally my folks consented and I bought a used Mossberg bolt-action rifle from a school acquaintance for $7.50. Except for a minor split in the stock it was in excellent condition. My father gave me a carton of shells – 12 boxes with 50 shells in each box. I built a wooden box, filled it with sand, and propped it against the south basement wall. I stuck a target on the front of the box and blazed away from the far end of the basement. The noise was deafening, but no one told me I should protect my ears.

The sand box did an excellent job of stopping the bullets, but after several dozen shots the force of the bullets shifted the sand until little remained behind the target. By the time I noticed this several bullets had gone through the box into the tile basement wall making a hole about three inches across. I mixed up some cement and patched it. From then on I tried to do my shooting outdoors.

Usually I took my rifle with me to Red Banks when we went fishing. One day Dad took Pat and me fishing. We baited our lines, put the lines in the water, but the fish weren't biting. We took the gun to the sandbar and sat empty clamshells upright in the sand at the edge of the river to use as targets. We sat down about 30 feet away and took turns shooting. As we passed the gun between us we were careful to keep it pointed toward the river and not at each other. But once as Pat passed the gun back to me she apparently still had her finger on the trigger and had not put the gun on the safety. It fired kicking up sand at our feet.

We were stunned and for a moment said nothing. Then suddenly Pat screamed, threw the gun into the sand, and grabbed her right foot. I looked down and saw a hole in the outside edge of the sole of her shoe. Pat had shot herself in the foot. I quickly ripped off her shoe and sock expecting to see blood and maybe some mangled toes. Fortunately there was only a little red mark on the outside edge of her foot near her little toe. The bullet only grazed her foot not even breaking the skin. Dad ran up wanting to know what happened. "Pat shot herself in the foot," I said. He exclaimed, "Pat, you might have shot Don!"

He later explained he was thinking that most people who accidentally pull the trigger shoot someone else rather than themselves. Since I was the only person nearby it was more likely that she'd shoot me and not herself. But he never lived that down. "Pat, you might have shot Don," became a family catch phrase.

I Go On The Radio

My folks heard that in celebration of Boy Scout Week the Iowa Barn Dance Frolic was looking for a boy scout to perform on the show. The Barn Dance, much like Nashville's Grand Ole Opry, aired live on WHO radio every Saturday night. They thought that it would be different and interesting for me to go on the show and play the bottle xylophone Dad and I strung together at Camp Murray. I auditioned at the station and the producer selected me for the show. My folks were probably more excited than I was.

The show originated at the Shriner's Auditorium. Later the Auditorium became the KRNT Radio Theater. Around 2,000 people filled the Auditorium every Saturday night. I remember arriving with my wacky looking xylophone clanking from a frame that Dad made for it from an old ironing board stand. A producer led us to a space where I could wait.

I had never seen so many people with guitars; in fact I'd never been close to anyone who played such an instrument. At that time country music held no interest for me. But here were dozens of country musicians tuning up and rehearsing. I felt out of place. I didn't have a guitar, didn't know anything about country music, and didn't even care for it. I waited patiently in this alien world with my folks.

Finally two stagehands came for me. They carefully carried my clinking xylophone out onto the stage where a country band was playing their number. Up close they were awfully loud. They finished and now it was my turn. The announcer smiled and asked who I was, where I was from, what school I went to, and how I came up with such an instrument. I answered and told him about the camping trip with Dad and how I fished the bottles out of the river. Then he announced, "And now Donald will play for us 'When The Bear Comes Home'". I quickly corrected him and said, "I'm going to play 'When The Bear Comes Over The Mountain'".

Correcting his slip-up made the audience laugh and that put me at ease. I began playing just the way I'd practiced all week. When it was over I was surprised how much the audience clapped and how loud it sounded. The stage hands carried my clanking bottles off the stage and my moment on the "50,000-Watt, Clear Channel Voice of the Middle West" was over. It didn't seem like a big deal after all, but I could see my folks were pleased.

Shortwave Radio Sparks My Interest

For several years I was keenly interested in shortwave radio. My friend Keith Slack who lived on Forty-fourth Street a block north of Hickman shared this interest. Whenever we could we talked about receivers, transmitters, and what projects we currently wanted to try. We did considerable experimenting trying to build a workable shortwave transmitter. One or the other of us would phone asking the other to listen on his receiver to see whether or not the signal was reaching across the mile and a half that separated us. Usually we heard nothing.

One day I found a spark coil from an old Model T Ford. We both had read that the early day Morse code transmitters were little more than an electric spark coil hooked up to an antenna. I hooked up the coil to an antenna and ground wires and used a car battery for power. When my telegraph key turned on the current a robust blue spark leaped between the terminals of the coil. I phoned Keith and asked him to listen while I keyed the spark.

After several minutes he called back and excitedly said he could hear me. The dots and dashes were not the clear tones of the radio telegraph stations we both were accustomed to hearing. Instead it sounded more like a gravel voice "Burrap! Burrap!" every time the key was depressed, but it really could be used to send a message.

I soon found, however, that Keith was not the only one who could hear my ruckus "Burraps." Anyone in the neighborhood who had a radio on heard them as well. It was heard on shortwave radios and was interfering with programs on regular radios as well. So before my crude transmitter triggered the wrath of my mother and the entire neighborhood of soap opera fans I retired it.

I studied further and one Saturday when I was twelve years old my mother drove me to the old West High School building where I took the examination for an amateur radio license. Representatives of the FCC came to Des Moines every three months to administer the examination. It had three parts: sending and receiving Morse code at the rate of at least thirteen words a minute; a technical section requiring a working knowledge of transmitters, receivers, etc.; and the third section testing your knowledge of the rules and regulations governing amateur radio station operations.

I was extremely nervous since I felt poorly prepared in all three areas. The code came first. I had no difficulty sending, but receiving gave me real trouble. The letters came too fast and they kept coming relentlessly. I was overwhelmed trying to field and make sense of this barrage of dots and dashes. As a result I failed to copy enough of the message to qualify. For me the examination was finished. I felt low, but my Mom and Dad gave me a good parental pep talk saying now that I knew what the test was like I could prepare better and go back another time. That other time did not happen for nine or ten years. In 1947, shortly after I got out of the Navy, I went back. This time I sailed through all three sections and became amateur radio station WØDBR.

Most of the time I worked on the forty-meter band using Morse code. My first receiver was a war surplus BC-348 that I modified to operate from house voltage rather then the 24 volt D.C. it had used in the military. I built my transmitter, but used tubes and modern circuitry this time rather than a Model T Ford spark coil. It was great fun talking to people all around the country. I particularly remember a New Year's Eve when I talked to a ham in New Jersey when it was midnight in the Eastern Time zone; to someone in Illinois when it was midnight in the Central Time zone; and finally to someone in California when it was midnight there. What made it particularly challenging was that I used a small two tube twenty-watt transmitter that I built as a standby in case my bigger 75-watt transmitter was down for repairs. But gradually ham radio gave way to other interests and obligations.

Chapter 5

BILLY SUNDAY COMES TO OUR CHURCH

In the 1930's First Federated Church invited Billy Sunday to Des Moines, Iowa, to hold services. Our congregation was excited. Grown ups talked about the way he carried on while preaching. "You can be sure Rev. Sunday will holler, pound his Bible, and stomp around the stage," a lady said. "And you should hear him tongue-lash the Devil," another added. "He might even take it in his head to climb up and stand right on top the pulpit."

Most of the children thought it would be exciting to see a minister doing all those things. I wanted to see how he'd get on top of the pulpit. Would he do it in one gigantic leap?

Little wonder that everywhere he preached crowds came to see his energetic performances and to hear his message. From 1896 to 1935, when he died, Billy Sunday was one of the most charismatic evangelists in the country. Everywhere he went huge crowds turned out to hear him. And now he was coming to our church.

Preparations began. Committees formed and got to work. Rev. Sunday liked large choirs so the adult choir recruited new members. A children's choir was organized and began practicing. The larger choirs would sit on bleacher seats built on the stage. An orchestra was organized and began rehearsing. Several men constructed a special pulpit for Rev. Sunday in case he decided to climb during his sermon. They made it of pine, heavily reinforced it, and then bolted it to the floor. Our finely varnished oak pulpit was safely stored out of sight.

Billy Sunday's music director arrived before Rev. Sunday. He rehearsed the choirs until they sounded almost perfect. Some of the music was new and not in our regular hymnals. As a member of the children's choir I sang from a small songbook with a bright red paper cover. Most of these songs were lively, rhythmic, and fun to sing. Both of my parents sang in the adult choir.

On January 15, 1933, Billy Sunday arrived and the evangelistic services began. So many people came that scores of them could not squeeze into the sanctuary. Loud speakers in the basement let the overflow crowds hear the services.

When it was time for the sermon Rev. Sunday lived up to his reputation. He shouted – mostly at the Devil. He stomped around the stage. Frequently he raised his Bible high in the air with one hand and thumped it hard with the other to emphasize the point he was making. Finally he didn't disappoint me; he climbed on top of the pulpit.

One night during his sermon Rev. Sunday leafed through a book. He looked over a few pages and said, "No, I don't like the sound of that." Then he ripped out those pages and threw them on the floor. He leafed further in the book and shouted, "This just won't do either," and tore out the offending pages. He leafed through the entire book ripping out most of its pages.

Holding the book with its few remaining pages high above his head he shouted, "That, my dear friends, is the way many Christians treat their Bibles. They throw out parts they don't like or disagree with. You are not to do that! The entire Bible is the word of God and must be obeyed." I was so shocked to see someone deliberately rip pages out of a book that I almost missed the point he was making.

All services closed with an altar call. While the organ and piano played quietly and the choirs sang softly or hummed, "Just As I Am," or "Have Thine Own Way Lord," Rev. Sunday stood on the stage pleading for people to, "Come forward and accept Jesus Christ as your personal savior, before it's too late." Or he'd call out, "Come forward, and renew your commitment."

Many people went forward. He walked down from the stage and shook their hands and spoke briefly to each one. Our church elders and others stood close by. They also talked with them and gave each one a tract or Bible. Then the service ended and everyone felt they had witnessed preaching like they didn't see at regular Sunday services.

Billy Sunday preached each night and on Sundays for four weeks. After he left the exuberance and excitement of the services lingered for many weeks. For all of us who already were Christians it was as though we'd heard a vigorous pep talk. I resolved to live more Christ-like each day.

Chapter 6

AND NOW JUNIOR HIGH SCHOOL

Byron Rice Era Ends

Byron Rice served grades Kindergarten through seventh. Now we wanted to move on to the more sophisticated experiences of junior high school, but we still felt reluctant. We would move from a school where we were the biggest kids to a school where we were the smallest, youngest, and most inexperienced.

In those days Roosevelt High School was also a junior high school. Our principal arranged a tour of Roosevelt so it wouldn't be so new to us when we began eighth grade in the fall. The size of the building overwhelmed us. "I bet I get lost," a girl moaned. "Yeah, and never be seen again," someone replied. We laughed, but most of us thought we probably would get lost and never find our way to classes. The Byron Rice teachers and the mothers of our class arranged a farewell luncheon at Younkers Tea Room downtown. We all dressed up for the occasion. I'd never seen my classmates so well groomed.

Halfway through lunch Miss Anderson our principal told me that as class president I should say a few words to the group after we finished eating. I was terrified, but managed to string together a few sentences that I hoped were coherent. Most of us had been together since kindergarten. I suggested that we should all be thankful for our time at Byron Rice and that we should work conscientiously at Roosevelt to bring honor on our parents, our teachers, and ourselves. That fall a new chapter began in junior high school.

Junior High

The first days at Roosevelt began almost as I expected except I didn't get lost. The building was large with hundreds of other students (I believe there were about 1800 students in both junior and senior high). Everyone seemed in a hurry to get somewhere.

It was fast-paced, but finding my way around to classes wasn't difficult. There were many new kids in our class and getting to know them came easily since all of us were beginning from scratch in a building new to us. As I thought about it I liked being in junior high.

There were some differences, however. Just getting to school was different. Byron Rice was ten blocks from home while Roosevelt was two and a half miles. Because I lived over two miles from school I received free tickets to ride the city buses to and from school during eighth and ninth grades. Students in tenth, eleventh, and twelfth grades were not eligible for free bus tickets. You could not use these tickets if you went to school early or stayed late. I used them only during the coldest part of the winter. Whenever possible I rode my bike.

Another difference Roosevelt had a cafeteria where you could buy a hot lunch. At Byron Rice most kids walked home for lunch or else brought sack lunches. At Roosevelt I usually bought my lunch in the cafeteria. I didn't think the food was tasteless as some claimed and I especially liked socializing with my friends over lunch. Five or six of us boys regularly ate at the same table.

Music Lessons

When I was six years old my mother arranged for Mrs. Karthause, a neighbor on Fortieth Street, to give me piano lessons. She was such a talented piano player I assumed she had hoped for a career as a concert pianist, but now she had to deal with piano students like me. I wasn't the most willing student and many times my mother literally dragged me to the piano, sat me on the stool, and stood over me while I practiced. Forcing me to learn to play the piano was one of those things my folks believed they were doing for my own good. "There'll come a day, when you're older, that you'll thank us for making you practice," they said.

At the time I was not thankful at all. After being dragged through the John Thompson Beginners, First, Second, and Third Grade lesson books I knew all I cared to know about piano playing. Besides, I needed to save face with my buddies. They thought boys who took piano lessons were sissies. What I really wanted to do was play the trumpet. It's loud, brash, and just seemed better suited to my temperament. Now that's a boy's instrument and none of my buddies would tease me about playing it.

Harold Thompson, who played with Dad in the army band at Camp Dodge during World War I, had a trumpet for sale. He bought it for his daughter, but she didn't want to play "a boy's instrument." I knew exactly how she felt. Mr. Thompson was a trumpet player and perhaps that influenced his choice of instrument for his daughter. Dad bought the trumpet for $5.00. That was a bargain price since Mr. Thompson bought it new from Sears & Roebuck for $29.00. It was no surprise that it showed no wear, but it didn't have a case. Dad built a case, lined it with red felt, and covered the outside with black imitation leather. It also sported a padded handle and two brass clasps for holding the lid closed.

My parents found a talented young trumpet player who was an instructor at Drake University. They bought the beginner's lesson book he recommended and I became his student. Whenever he assigned a new lesson I hoped he would play it for me so I could hear how it should sound. It was a thrill for me to hear his clear smooth notes and it gave me a sound to try for.

This time my music lessons flowed along much better. The trumpet, not the piano, was my instrument of choice. And I'm sure Mom was relieved that I practiced without her having to threaten, drag, or coerce me. There was one area of tension between us, however, and that was the trumpet's volume. At first I practiced in the living room, but that was too noisy so she banished me to my room with the door closed. That didn't work so I had to go to the basement. The noise was still too loud. Finally in desperation she sent me to the far end of our sweet corn field almost a block from the house. It was the best she could do unless she sent me completely out of the neighborhood.

So during warm weather I practiced in the cornfield. On cold or rainy days I practiced in the garage. It was not as far away as the cornfield, but still it was detached from the house.

Band Musician

While in grade school I played in the all-city grade school band. At our first practice we played among other selections, "The Crusaders Hymn." Hearing the familiar notes of that tune coming from my horn and blending with the sounds from dozens of other instruments was so thrilling that I broke out in goose bumps. When I got to Junior High School I knew I had to be a part of the Roosevelt band. Fortunately I had no difficulty joining the band. No auditions were required, but the director held auditions periodically to determine whether to assign you first, second, or third trumpet parts.

The band rehearsed in the auditorium's orchestra pit. Roosevelt's auditorium seats about 2.000. It was huge when compared to the auditorium at Byron Rice. During rehearsals the auditorium was empty so the sound of the band bounced around unabated. Sometimes the echo sounded as though another band was up in the balcony playing a half beat behind us.

I don't know why, but Mr. Tessler, the band instructor, designated me student director for one semester. My job was to tune the band and I conducted it if someone called Mr.Tessler away during a rehearsal. I liked this assignment and felt I was a good conductor. One day while we rehearsed a march Mr. Tessler had to go to the office. I took over and we began playing the march from the beginning. I gradually increased the tempo until most everyone was breathless trying to keep up. Then I gradually decreased the tempo turning the march into a dirge. Having such control was a heady feeling. Next I moved the tempo back to the usual cadence, but stopped the march saying, "Woodwinds, I don't believe you're playing it quite right. Let's hear just the woodwinds in the Trio section." After they played it through I said, "Much better. Now everybody together in the Trio." Just knowing that I was in control and could order the behavior of about 50 band members made me feel powerful. Finally my common sense and better judgment returned. I stopped these antics and may even have apologized to the band for being so self-indulgent.

Our Junior High band played with the High School band at football games on Friday nights. To look like we belonged to Roosevelt we wore the high school band's old uniforms. During the late 1930's Roosevelt played its home games at the Drake University stadium. The field had lights for night games then. Being a part of the band during the excitement of a football game, marching onto the field, and marching through formations for the half time show always thrilled me. Each time we marched onto the field playing the school song or a rousing Susa or Karl King march I got my familiar goose bumps from the excitement.

One year the band marched in Des Moines' Memorial Day parade. We formed at the State Capitol building and marched west through the downtown business district to the Woodland Cemetery. At the cemetery we played the National Anthem as Legionnaires raised the flag over the veterans' plot. It was a long march, it was hot, and it was humid. Our woolen uniforms were better suited for the crisp fall evenings of the football season and not for the hot humid days of summer. At the end of the march we were soaked, we were tired, and we felt we might never march again. And the following year we didn't.

Hormones Awaken

Students in our eighth grade class came to Roosevelt from several grade schools. All of us were in classes with students we did not know. Getting acquainted with one another was part of the process of adjusting to a new school. This simply happened when you saw one another in the hallways, the cafeteria, the study hall, or in class. But the hormones that had started to cruise through our eighth grade bodies no longer allowed social encounters to be simple.

One day I discovered just how complicated life had become. A girl in my class whom I had not met walked past my desk and dropped a folded piece of paper on it. She had written, "Hi cutie. I'd sure like to get to know you. How about meeting after school and you can walk me home and be my boyfriend."

I was flattered that she noticed me and apparently thought favorably of me, but it also made me nervous. "Girls aren't supposed to be that brazen and forward, are they?" I asked myself. She seemed to be looking for a boy friend, but I was not looking for a girl friend. Apparently more hormones cruised through her body than cruised through mine.

I answered her note since I didn't want to be rude. I suggested that I had many after school obligations and that walking her home would not be possible. I was hoping that my lack of enthusiasm would discourage her. It did not. In the days that followed she dropped a flurry of notes on my desk. Her notes showed she knew a lot about my family and me. I concluded that she had talked with some of the girls from our church who also went to Roosevelt. Then one night she phoned me at home. When I answered she sang a popular song of the day, "You Must Have Been A Beautiful Baby." She sang it all the way through then hung up. She had a fine singing voice, but even her serenade failed to spark my interest.

When leaving class one day it finally happened. We came together face to face. We had never spoken to one another, but now we were side by side walking down the hallway to our next class. We made small talk as we walked. She was an intelligent nice looking girl. In time I might have come to consider her a friend perhaps even a special friend, but she overwhelmed me by asking me to be her boy friend right away. Besides I really didn't know what obligations a boy friend had to assume. This close encounter did not change my attitude toward her, but the whole episode opened my eyes to how complicated social intercourse had become. Eventually she began leaving notes on the desk of another boy and I was relieved.

Stage and Sound Crews

The public address system in Roosevelt's auditorium was state of the art in the 1920's, but by the 1940's it was antique. Its loud speakers hung in a fancy gold painted wrought iron cage suspended from the ceiling high above the front edge of the stage. On its front were large letters "T R H S" for Theodore Roosevelt High School. There were three or four microphone jacks in the orchestra pit at the front edge of the stage for the old style carbon microphones.

The amplifier and control panel for the system was in the movie projection booth high up behind the last row of the balcony. They filled a six-foot tall relay rack at the rear of the projection booth. When you faced the relay rack to operate the system your back was to the stage so you couldn't see what was happening there. To overcome this problem a large mirror hung at an angle from the ceiling of the booth. By tilting your head back you could look up into the mirror and see when a speaker walked to the microphone. Then you could switch on the microphone and adjust the volume. A turntable for playing records sat beside the relay rack.

The system was cumbersome to operate. It was necessary to thump the microphones hard several times to distribute the carbon granules evenly inside them before they'd pick up sound. It was almost impossible to set the mikes so they could catch the dialog of a play. Feedback squealed through the auditorium when a person spoke too loudly or sometimes for no reason at all.

Despite its shortcomings I wanted to be a part of the crew that ran this system. The sound crew operated the public address system for assemblies, plays, and other programs. They also showed the noon movie in the auditorium. The 35 mm. Simplex machine in the projection booth was the same model used in the movie theaters around town. The school rented a regular movie for showing during the lunch hour each day. Most movies were five reels in length. By showing one reel each day the movie lasted the entire week. The noon movie gave students something to do after eating lunch.

Mr. M. D. Eastman, the physics teacher, was the faculty person in charge of the sound crew. After I learned that he had been my dad's physics teacher at old West High School I thought he was extremely ancient. I asked him if I could be a member of the crew. I explained that I was interested in electronics and also considered myself quite mechanically skilled. At this point he began a lecture telling me he didn't want anyone on the crew to tinker with the equipment. He stressed the awesome responsibility a crewmember took on when he worked with this expensive and delicate movie and sound equipment. I thought he was turning me down, but instead he smiled and welcomed me to the crew.

When the drama students put on a play both the stage and sound crews were busy. We usually helped the stage crew with scenery, lighting, and curtains. We also tried to mike the stage so the audience could hear the actors, but our ancient sound system just couldn't do it. It rarely amplified an actor's voice much, but it did a superb job picking up footsteps. When an actor began to move across the stage we had to quickly switch off the mikes. Otherwise all everyone heard was the "CLOMP! CLOMP! CLOMP!" of their walking. Dialog delivered at the same time was completely lost. An actor in the play "The Corn Is Green" wore boots as a part of his costume. He never stood still when he spoke his lines. He knew we turned off the mikes when he walked so he compensated by shouting. It was hilarious to see this student actor in high top boots stomping about on the stage shouting at the top of his lungs, but the audience heard his lines never the less.

Some of the plays were musicals. During the rehearsals for one of them Louie Wertz was around the stage so much I assumed he was a Roosevelt student. Actually he was a North High student and was at Roosevelt a lot while he participated in these musicals. He was an excellent piano player and later became famous as an entertainer known as Roger Williams. Chloris Leachman, another student, participated in several plays while in school. Later she became famous on the stage, in movies, and on television. I believe she was a grade or two behind me and I did not know her.

After toiling with the old sound system as best we could for a year or so the school installed an up to date system. The electrician scrapped the old speakers, their iron cage, the carbon microphones, the old relay rack in the projection booth, and the mirror. Now everyone in the audience heard what the actors said on the stage.

Chapter 7

HIGH SCHOOL BEGINS

Adjustment and Transformation

The transition from junior high to senior high went smoothly because we were familiar with the building and knew many of the teachers. The biggest difference for me began one day when about twenty-five of us were called together for a conference with the principal and two of the teachers. The principal explained that because of our achievement test scores we were to be in a new Special Experimental Curriculum (SEC) program. SEC would affect only our English and Social Studies classes. Math, science, and all other classes would remain the same. Roosevelt was one of 30 high schools nation wide in the study.

Mr. Morgan and Miss Forkner, our English and Social Studies teachers, would work together some days and other days one or the other would teach. When reports were made, tests given, or special lectures scheduled we had to attend class. The rest of the time we pursued whatever investigations or library sources we thought necessary. During the two hours allotted each day for this combined class we could use the classroom for study although it was not required. Mr. Morgan and Miss Forkner were available for questions or consultation. Or we could go to the school library, to the city library, or to any business or individual to pursue our research in the area we were studying.

This freedom was almost overwhelming. Not having to attend classes regularly seemed wonderful, but then I realized there was a day when assignments and reports would be due. So I had to learn to exert some personal discipline to manage my time without the structure of a classroom and direct supervision of a teacher. I believe it also demonstrated to us that there are many resources for learning in the community outside of school. I interviewed the head of a chemical supply company for information I needed in one of my reports. Another time I interviewed the manager of a wholesale meat company. Some days when I was away from the building I was tempted not to go back, but I still had other classes to attend.

Out For Track

I enjoyed playing softball and touch football. This was before the days of Little League and our games were informal. Several of us simply got together and played. When I got to high school, however, and saw the football squad practicing after school each day I though, "I think I could do that. I believe I'd like to go out for football." I discussed this with my parents since their consent was required. My strategy was to ask permission to play football and if they objected, then I'd say, "OK, then can I get a motorcycle." I'm not sure what my logic was in this approach. They quickly and absolutely turned down both requests so I didn't play football nor did I get a motorcycle.

Early next spring the track guys began working to get in condition. I thought, " I'd like to go out for track and I can't imagine Mom and Dad objecting to that." After all it wasn't a contact sport so the risk of injury was slight. I went to see the track coach and said, "I want to go out for track."

Coach glanced up from his clipboard looked me over and asked, "What kind of runner are you?"

"I don't know for sure, but I think I'd be a better sprinter than a distance runner."

He wrote down my name and that was it. I asked, "Now can I check out a set of sweat pants and hooded sweat shirt?" The sweatshirt was marked "Roosevelt Track" across the front. I thought having one would identify me as an official member of the track squad.

"Not right now maybe later," he mumbled. He seemed anxious to get rid of me.

After school each day I showed up in the gym dressed in my phy ed shorts, shirt, and old sweat shirt and pants. All the others had Rough Rider sweats issued by the coach. But I worked along side the others doing calisthenics and jogging around the gym. And I got shin splints like everyone else. When the weather turned warm we went outside and ran on the cinder track. I felt as though I could compete with almost any of the sprinters. I asked the coach once again for sweats. Again he turned me down with some excuse.

Somebody set up the low and the high hurdles on the track. They were an interesting challenge. "I can jump those things," I thought. I began practicing, but had trouble getting my stride right. I asked the coach to suggest how I could improve.

"Not now. Don't have time." So I watched the other hurdlers and tried to do what they did. Every day I spent my practice time running the hurdles and the 100-yard dash. Still the coach never found time to coach me.

Soon the first track meet of the year came up: the all city high school indoor meet at the Drake University field house. I dressed in my gym clothes while all of the other runners put on the Roosevelt track uniforms. "Well," I thought, "my gym shorts are blue and my shirt is white so at least I'm wearing school colors." I began to feel maybe the coach did not want me on the team. Maybe he hoped I'd just give up and go away.

We all went up to the track and warmed up. I asked the coach which events he'd entered me in and he replied, "None of them. Go sit down."

Toward the end of the evening after asking him several times to put me in a race, Coach consented to my running the 220-yard dash. My hands shook with excitement. It felt good to jog onto the track and go to the starting line. The pistol cracked and about a dozen of us began. In the first turn we were jammed together. "Surely someone's going to get spiked," I thought. But by the time we'd circled the track once space opened up between runners. I could see the leaders up ahead and pumped my legs faster. Suddenly the race was over. I had given my best yet I didn't finished in the top three, but neither was I in the bottom three. I went to the bench where several guys on the team congratulated me. I looked at Coach, but he scowled and looked away.

After I caught my breath I asked Coach to enter me in the low hurdles. He reluctantly agreed. Again I walked onto the tack, got ready, and we were off. It was a short race, but when it was over I had placed third in the city. That was satisfaction enough for me.

I continued to work out with the track team that spring, but Coach didn't acknowledge me as a team member. He never took me with the team to track meets out of town, gave me any encouragement or coaching, or issued team sweats and uniform. The track team's picture in the school yearbook shows the others wearing their track warm-up sweats, but I stand out prominently in my gym clothes. My name appears below the picture along with the others. In my darker moods I hoped that photo would cause Coach some embarrassment, but even without sweats, uniform, or coaching, I felt like I had been a member of the Roosevelt 1940 track team.

The Roosevelt Roundup

By the time was a senior I'd decided I wanted to be a journalist. It was appropriate that I take journalism as one of my elective courses. Miss Meers, a tall, white haired, older teacher taught the class. We called her "Blue Pencil Meers" because she returned everything we wrote with numerous blue pencil corrections and comments. Regardless how carefully we wrote our news articles or checked grammar and spelling, Miss Meers found mistakes to correct. Because of this I thought she was a good teacher and believe I learned a lot about writing in her class.

The journalism class was part lectures and part laboratory. In the laboratory the class wrote, edited, proofed, and pasted up the *Roosevelt Roundup* biweekly newspaper. We had reporters, sports writers, feature writers, editorial writers, and a photographer. The class elected Gertrude Manning and me as coeditors. Everyone was encouraged to write and submit news, sports, feature, or special articles. Writing and putting out the newspaper was hectic at times, but it always was enjoyable. That year I spent more time working on the paper than on any other class project. I don't know whether all my journalism work caused it, but I had to be fitted with glasses for the first time.

It was now 1942 and a year since Pearl Harbor. America was in a shooting war. Many of last year's seniors were now in service. We began to report on them in the *Roundup.* We called the article "Rooseveltians In Service."

Drake University, in Des Moines, accepted me to begin classes as journalism major in January 1943 immediately following high school graduation. In February 1943 I'd be eighteen and subject to the draft. I didn't want drafted into the Army. I wanted to serve in the Navy so I contacted the recruiter and found they had an enlisted college reserve option called the V-1 program. After enlisting the Navy placed you on inactive duty allowing you to finish college. Then the enlistee would be called up for active duty and enter the officer-training program. My parents felt like most parents during these war years. They were reluctant to see me go into service, but since it was inevitable they were glad I was getting the branch I wanted. They gave their permission and I enlisted in the Navy at age seventeen.

Chapter 8

WORK OUTSIDE OF SCHOOL

From an early age my parents impressed upon me the need for work. I fed the chickens, weeded the garden, emptied waste paper baskets, and mowed grass. Selling vegetables door to door on my vegetable route was my earliest employment away from home. Mom and Dad praised me when I worked hard and showed initiative on the vegetable route.

At about age fourteen I got my next outside job by answering an ad in the *Beaverdale News.* "Boys with bicycles, wanted to run errands," the ad said. Errand Service was located in a storefront in the Beaverdale business district. I applied and got a job. The owner gave me two bright red shirts with "Errand Service" and a phone number in big white letters across the back. Three or four of us waited in the storefront until someone phoned to have something delivered. The boss gave the order and the address to the boy whose turn it was. The boy got the money to buy the item requested and then rode his bike to deliver it. Usually the caller needed a quart of milk, a pound of butter, a loaf of bread, or wanted a prescription picked up. When he delivered the item the boy collected its cost plus twenty-five cents for his delivery service. The caller usually gave a tip, too.

I was up next the evening a man phoned for a pack of Camel cigarettes. Since I was underage my boss wrote a note to the drug store clerk. I walked to the drug store next door, bought the cigarettes, and rode to the address on Sheridan Avenue just four blocks away. A man stood waiting on his front stoop and ran up to me as I pulled into his driveway. He grabbed the pack out of my shirt pocket, tore out a cigarette, and lit up. After two or three deep puffs he was less agitated. He smiled and handed me a dollar bill. That was much more than the cost of the smokes and the twenty-five cents delivery fee, but he insisted that he didn't want any change. That was the largest tip I ever received.

After a few months the service was not doing enough business for the owner to continue renting the storefront. He arranged with Miss Olive Cox at the Polar Pantry ice cream parlor to base his messengers there. By then I was the only messenger he had left so I began waiting for delivery calls at the Polar Pantry at the corner of Beaver and Fagen. There weren't many calls so I had time to observe the ice cream business.

Miss Cox, the owner, was about forty and came to Des Moines from Omaha. She had owned a similar shop there so was not new to the ice cream business. She purchased the shop from Ken and renamed it the Polar Pantry.

When I was a grade school kid Ken's Ice Cream Parlor was a popular place to buy candy, gum, fake tattoos, and ice cream. You could always find several boys hanging around. Ken kept punchboards, which were illegal, and this may have been the major attraction. Holes lined the boards. For a nickel a punch you could poke a wire probe down the hole of your choice and push out a small rolled up piece of paper. If the paper had a winning number you won a cash prize.

My folks were upset when they heard I was to work out of the Polar Pantry. They assumed it was still a place to gamble. I assured them that it wasn't and that Miss Cox ran a respectable shop. I soon discovered, however, a different type of illegal activity there.

Each evening Miss Cox left for supper at precisely 6:00 pm. She did not return until quitting time at 9:00 pm. Then she came back to take the money from the cash register and lock up. Jack, her only employee, was a high school student a little older than me. He reported for work at 6:00 pm and worked until closing time. I noticed that almost every evening as soon as Miss Cox left two or three of Jack's friends came to the shop. Jack gave each of them a bottle of coke that they did not pay for and took a bottle for himself. Each of them drank some of their coke and then filled the bottles up with whiskey.

Once or twice Jack offered me a coke and whiskey, but I declined. One day in confidence Miss Cox asked me what was going on in the shop each evening after she left. I didn't want to squeal on Jack; neither did I want to mislead her. She pressed me saying that the money in the till seemed to be coming up short and she felt that maybe Jack was pocketing some of it. I told her that I never saw him stealing money, but he wasn't charging his friends for their cokes. I also told her that they spiked those cokes with whiskey. This troubled her and she said she'd take care of the problem, but would not let Jack know how she learned of his drinking.

The next evening she drove away for supper at 6:00 pm, but circled the block and parked her car where she could watch the shop. Soon afterward Jack's friends came in, got their cokes, and spiked them with whiskey. She quickly returned on the pretext of forgetting some invoices she needed. She said she could smell whiskey and took the bottles to check them. She fired Jack and told him to leave immediately.

Cool Polar Pantry Days

Now she needed someone to take Jack's place. I was in the right place at the right time and began work the next day. During the school year I reported for work at 6:00 pm and worked until closing at 9:00 pm. I also worked almost all day on Saturday and some on Sunday afternoon. My starting wage was ten cents an hour. This was about standard for high school kids doing similar work. After working there for several months I asked for a raise. She took a long time to think about it and even discussed it with her brother. In the end she offered to boost my wages to $.175 per hour. I wanted $.20 or $.25, but accepted her offer.

In the summer I worked longer hours during the week and on weekends. On Saturdays I reported to work at 8:00 am. This was the day for making ice cream. Over my first summer at the Polar

Pantry I learned to operate the shop's five-gallon ice cream machine. The mix came from Miss Cox's brother's creamery. We poured the mix into the machine, added flavoring, and started the freezer. In just a few minutes when the batch was semi-frozen we opened the valve and let it run into a five-gallon metal can. We stored the can in the freezer where it hardened. After washing the machine it was ready for the next flavor. We tried to keep at least twelve flavors on hand.

At noon I finished making ice cream and was off work until 6:00 pm that evening. One summer I used that time for swimming at the Camp Dodge pool. Pat, my sister, went with me, but she didn't know how to swim. I worked with her teaching her to swim. By the end of the summer when she was able to swim the width of the pool I bought her a small plaster statue of a sea captain to commemorate the occasion.

After consulting with her brother Miss Cox installed a hamburger grill in our supply room. She asked Kennard's Bakery in Beaverdale to make special buns. This was a wise business decision because the Kennard buns tasted like homemade and not like the commercial buns the other shops used. Also we toasted the buns on the grill and that gave the Polar Pantry hamburgers another big advantage. Cooking hamburgers was new to me, but I found it wasn't difficult. As word got around our sales took off. At times I had the entire grill covered with meat and buns.

A & P Grocery Stock Boy

It became clear that Miss Cox did not intend to increase my wages. I knew I could do better so I quit and went to work as a stock boy at the Beaverdale A & P grocery. Here I earned twenty-five cents per hour. Three of us reported for work at 6:00 pm when the store closed. Then we began restocking the shelves. After we all arrived the store manager locked us inside the store and went home for supper. The only way we could get out was break a window. But we didn't worry about that.

I soon found that stocking grocery shelves is boring work. One of the other guys discovered a fringe benefit, however. He ate a few chocolate chips from each box on the shelf and then put the boxes back on the shelf. He suggested that I help myself. Baker's Semi Sweet Chocolate Chips were tempting, but I declined.

I worked at the A & P Grocery four or five months, but when I heard that Reed's Ice Cream shop in Beaverdale was looking for help I applied and got a job there. Reed's was a larger shop than the Polar Pantry and had booths and tables for its customers. The shop sold ice cream in pint, quart, and gallon packages. And of course it sold ice cream cones, sundaes, malts, and sodas, but it did not have a hamburger grill. The shop looked and felt like all of the other Reed's shops in Des Moines – too much like a school lunchroom. The middle-aged couple that ran the shop was considerate and I liked working for them; yet I missed the small cluttered, homey feel of the Polar Pantry.

Younkers – Boys' Department

While I was in high school I took a sales job at Younkers during the Christmas shopping season. I worked Saturdays and when school closed for the holiday break I worked all day. The personnel department showed us temporary help how to fill out a sales slip and operate the cash register. After that they considered us ready for the sales floor.

They sent me to the junior boys' department. We sold pants, shirts, suits, underwear, socks, belts, ties, jackets, coats, hats, and snow suits. Since this was winter, snowsuits and other warm clothing were big sellers. I enjoyed showing the merchandise to customers and was thrilled every time I made a sale. I think many of the young boys were more comfortable coming to me for sales help rather then either of the two prim, stiff, middle aged ladies who were the department's regular employees.

One day both ladies suggested that I back off and give them a chance to make more sales. "You get the same pay no matter how much you sell," they pointed out. "Our salaries are tied directly to how much we sell."

I listened thoughtfully, but did not agree to back off. Had I been naive to think that everyone should do his or her best? They were asking me to slack off and somehow that seemed wrong. So I tried not to make a show of hustling sales, but I didn't deliberately slack off.

Sears Roebuck & Company

The following Christmas season I got a job at Sears wrapping packages. Although it wasn't demanding it required ingenuity. For example a customer asked me to wrap the Flexible Flyer sled she had purchased. She wanted it wrapped so her young son wouldn't recognize it as a sled when she took it home. That took some time, but I think I disguised it fairly well.

Later that season the store's display department had an opening. I talked to Wray Johnson, the manager, and got the job. He introduced me to Jack Stitt, the artist, and Mary, a window dresser. I became the fourth person in the department. Our major responsibility was to dress the large display windows on the street level. All first-rate department stores had such windows and often there was intense rivalry between stores as each tried to produce a more appealing window scene. Our nearest competitor was the J.C. Penney's store across the street. In addition we built displays on the sales floors and printed counter top signs to describe merchandise and list the prices. I did all this printing presswork, assisted with window dressing, and helped with whatever else the department was doing.

The six story Sears store had three elevators arranged side by side. Customers rode on two of them. The third carried customers only when the store was extremely busy. The rest of the time it was available to the display department for hauling mannequins, clothing, and props from our penthouse studio to the sales floors. One day I loaded a female mannequin into the elevator and went down to the women's ready to wear floor to pick up the clothing they wanted displayed on her in the street level window I was dressing. After getting the clothes I drove down to the main floor and opened the elevator door, but before carrying a nude mannequin across the main floor sales area to the window I began to dress her. All at once I heard a little old lady scream and cry out to her adult daughter, "Look what that man is doing to that woman! Do something Eloise! Do something!"

Most of the customers on the main floor heard the lady cry out. They edged closer to the elevator and stood looking accusingly in my direction. "It's only a mannequin, Mother. It's all right," the daughter reassured her. The other customers chuckled and moved away. I closed the elevator door.

I thoroughly enjoyed working with my coworkers except I was a little uneasy around Mary. She dressed in men's clothing, walked like a man, and used coarse language. Since Mary was so different from the girls and women I knew I did not know how I should act toward her. Should I treat her like I treated most women or should I treat her like one of the boys? One day as we dressed female mannequins in one of the large street level display windows she began patting, squeezing, and feeling certain parts of the mannequin's body. She saw that I looked shocked and surprised. "Hey, I just like women's bodies. Hell, I never pass up a chance to squeeze or poke their good ol' parts," she explained in an off hand way as she grabbed a mannequin's breast.

Later I asked Jack about her and he confirmed that indeed she was a lesbian. Several months later Mary took time off and went to Texas with her girl friend. While there they persuaded a soldier to get the girl friend pregnant. Back in Des Moines several months later Mary visited people in the store showing off her very pregnant girl friend. She proudly announced to everyone, "We're going to have a baby."

Chapter 9

THE ST. AMBROSE NAVY

Uncle Sam Wants Me

One early spring day toward the end of my first semester at Drake I received a letter from the Navy notifying me they had transferred me from the old V-1 program to the new V-12 program. I had to report for active duty on July 1, 1943. I was surprised! I thought I'd finish four years at Drake then be called up. I had to report to St. Ambrose College, Davenport, Iowa, to continue my college work.

"Well," I thought, "that doesn't sound too bad. I'll still be going to college."

The letter also said I would be paid $50.00 a month as an apprentice seaman. The Navy would cover board and room at the college, books, and tuition. I thought that was a good deal and my folks were happy that I wasn't being sent to the fleet right away. They had just one question, however, "Why in the world is the Navy sending a good Protestant boy like you to a Catholic school?"

Several of us at Drake received orders to report to St. Ambrose. At least I'd be with some guys I already knew. I heard that the Navy gave new recruits ragged extremely short butch haircuts. I thought I'd outsmart them and asked my barber for a decent looking butch haircut before I left. Several other guys did, too. So in one respect at least we looked a little like sailors even while wearing our civilian clothes.

Off To War

On July 1, 1943, my parents and Pat drove me to the Rock Island train station to leave for Davenport, Iowa. The others were there with their parents, assorted relatives, and friends. On the surface those of us leaving seemed happy and excited, but most of the parents looked sad and had difficulty holding back their tears. My folks were among those on the edge of tears.

As I was ready to board the train I was surprised to see Carol and Jean, two girls from church, dash up. We all made little jokes about what life in the Navy might be like and what Des Moines might be like without me around. Then it was time to climb aboard. My mother kissed me; my dad shook my hand, my sister hugged me, and Carol and Jean stood close and said, "Goodbye, good luck, and God's speed." I took a seat where I could look out at my folks, Pat, Carol, and Jean. I smiled and waved. They waved back, but Carol, pointing to Jean, mouthed, "Why didn't you kiss her?"

At times I believe I'm totally insensitive to social convention. It's not that I don't know what might or what might not be proper it's just that I don't seem to recognize when that action moment has arrived. At least at this time in my life I was not always aware. Apparently Jean had expected a good-bye kiss and I had failed to give her one. For all she knew we might never see each other again. But now it was too late for the train had started to move.

Jean was the first girl I dated and the first girl I kissed. On my sixteenth birthday my mother picked me up after school in the 1936 Plymouth my father had purchased new with his bonus money from World War I. She took me to the driver's licensing station on the east side. I passed the written test and was a little nervous during the driving and parking tests, but I passed them, too, and received my license. The first thing I asked my mother was, "May I have the car tonight?"

I took Jean to a movie and then a coke. Afterward when I took her home we sat in the car and talked a while. Then before I took her to the door I kissed her. Carol introduced us shortly after Jean came to Iowa from Michigan three years earlier. We went to church together, we both sang in the choir, and both had been in the same graduating class at Roosevelt. We dated off and on for three years. After all of that time it was reasonable for Jean to feel a good-bye kiss was appropriate. I felt badly that I had not realized that.

St. Ambrose Goes Naval

The mood on the train heading for Davenport and the St. Ambrose Navy was festive. We were in the Navy and possibly heading into the greatest adventure of our young lives. Everyone talked and laughed excitedly. The miles flew by and before we knew it the train pulled into Davenport.

Several of us shared a cab for the short ride up the hill and out to the college. As we approached the campus it was plain to see we weren't the first to arrive. Scores of young men in civilian clothes carrying suitcases milled about on campus. It appeared the major action was at the administration building. We checked there, but learned we were to report to the gym.

The gym seemed huge yet with so many guys milling around it was congested. All of us were trying to find out where we should check in and what we should do. We could see some men in uniform and assumed they were the ship's company whose job it was to get us housed, fed, and clothed. Now they seemed ill prepared to deal with a crowd of 300 recruits bombarding them with questions. Finally one of these petty officers stood on a chair and shouted, "Knock it off, everyone! Quiet! Take a seat and we'll get underway."

An officer strode to the front of the group and began, "Good morning, gentlemen. I am Captain Blackburn your commanding officer. I want to welcome you aboard the St. Ambrose V-12 Unit." He sounded so military. "This is a newly commissioned unit of the United States Navy and you are the first men to report aboard." It was quiet. We all seemed to be sitting at attention – if that's possible. No one wanted to miss what Captain Blackburn said nor did we want to appear unmilitary.

He explained how things would be organized, how we were to be checked in, and how classes would be assigned. He reminded us, "You men now have the distinction of being in the finest Navy in the world. Remember that and act accordingly!" I sat up straighter. "Bear in mind that even though you are still wearing civilian clothes you are subject to my command and to all the Navy's rules and regulations."

We would live in the four story Davis Hall dormitory. But there was a problem. We could not move in because the college had just sanded and varnished the wooden floors. From now on the Navy would call them decks. Until the varnish on the decks cured we would sleep in bunks set up on the basketball court in the gym.

Our orders advised us to bring a minimum of civilian clothes with us because the Navy would issue shoes and uniforms on arrival. But there was a problem. "Sorry gentlemen, the railroad lost the car carrying the shoes and uniforms for this base. You will have to wear your civvies until that car is found and brought to Davenport," Captain Blackburn regretfully reported. I had one change of underwear with me. My shoes had large holes in each of the soles. I hoped they found that railroad car soon.

The Captain told us, "Classes will not start for at least two weeks. We're working out the scheduling with the college, but in a week or so each of you will have a chance to develop a class schedule."

The Executive Officer split the group into three companies of 100 men each. A chief petty officer in command of each company was to work with us in an attempt to get us looking more like sailors.

We're In The Navy Now

After Captain Blackburn's welcoming speech the routine checking in began. The staff assigned bunks and we stowed our luggage along the gym walls. Then we went to the dining hall on the ground floor of Ambrose Hall. This building looked as though it may have been the original building on campus. It now seemed like a creaking lovable relic.

Nuns cooked and served the food. They dished it out as we moved down the line with our trays. At the end of the line a diminutive nun stood on a wooden milk crate and put a half pint carton of milk on each man's tray. I noticed she gave some of the men two cartons of milk. When I got to her I asked why she gave some men two cartons. She replied with a touch of Irish brogue, "And didn't ye see how puny those wee lads looked? I want them healthy and strong." I must have looked healthy enough to suit her since she gave me only one carton.

After lunch most of us looked around the campus or loafed on the steps of the buildings talking and smoking. Smoking right out in public was a new experience for me. My folks wanted me never to smoke and the few times they smelled cigarette smoke on my clothes while I was in high school I got a lecture. They said if I was going to smoke they'd rather that I came right out in the open rather than sneak around. A few weeks before I left for St. Ambrose I told my folks that I'd probably smoke when I got in service. Most of the other guys would be smoking. With that in mind I brought a pipe and tobacco home and proceeded to light up. The next day my dad brought home a new pipe and tobacco and began smoking. He said the only reason he hadn't smoked over the years was so he would not be a bad example for me. But now that I was smoking he began again. My mother didn't appreciate having her house smell like smoke and issued an order – you will only smoke outside.

After supper that first evening the chief petty officers announced that we would be free to go on liberty, but were to be back on base by 2300 hours. I did some quick arithmetic in my head to translate that to mean 11:00 pm. Several of us headed to downtown Davenport. One fellow said something about taking a ferry ride. He led us to the waterfront. Here was a large ornate stern wheel steam ferryboat that looked like a showboat from the last century. It made regular runs across the Mississippi ferrying people between Davenport, Iowa, and Rock Island, Illinois.

Now this was something different and it looked like fun. We paid our five-cent fare and went aboard. Chairs and benches covered the lower deck. The upper deck was a dance floor surrounded by chairs and small tables. At one end a raised platform provided space for a band. He heard that a live band was aboard every Saturday night. Now a jukebox played Frankie Carle's "Boogie Woogie." It became one of my favorites.

We got off in Rock Island and strolled past the two or three taverns, liquor stores, and the two cafes in the downtown area. It seemed to me that this area had seen better days. Perhaps the more vital part of town had moved elsewhere. After looking around we boarded the ferryboat the next time it tied up and spent the rest of the evening riding back and forth, listening to the jukebox, and watching the river roll by. For now this was as close as we would come to going to sea.

We Begin To Look Like Sailors

Two weeks passed before the railroad located the boxcar carrying our shoes and uniforms sitting on a siding in Peoria, Illinois. A couple of days later our clothing arrived on campus. What a glorious day it was when the supply staff issued us whites, blue dress, and blue everyday uniforms. We also got underwear, sox, sweater, dress cap, watch cap, dungarees, chambray shirt, belt, neckerchief, and pea coat. And last of all we each got two pair of shoes – a pair of dress and a pair of work shoes. I felt like a wealthy man with all these clothes and two pair of new shoes on top of it all. It felt good to heave my old worn out civilian shoes into the trashcan.

Since it was summer the uniform of the day was whites. There was only one problem with my whites – the pant legs were too long. I got pants with the shortest inseam they had, but still I had to roll up the bottom of the legs up to keep them from dragging on the ground. A sailor with rolled up pant legs looks decidedly unmilitary. Because there was no tailor on the base I thought there was only one thing to do. I mailed my pants home to Mom for alterations. Fortunately I had another pair to wear until the shortened pair returned. They, too, were long, but I'd send them home to be shortened when my first pair returned.

The Navy Goes To The Ball

Now we had our uniforms. Captain Blackburn posted a notice announcing the Masonic Lodge was hosting a dance the following Saturday night. This dance was to honor the St. Ambrose sailors and to welcome them to Davenport. It was exciting news since it would provide an interesting diversion as well as a chance to meet girls. But my altered pants had not yet returned. How could I go with my pant legs rolled up? I looked like a comedian trying to mimic a sailor. But the urge to socialize was stronger than my embarrassment so I went.

The Masons showed they knew how to decorate for a party. There were flowers, balloons, and ribbons everywhere. Tables of punch and food lined one wall. A live band played the popular songs of the day. And all of the girls wore evening gowns. They looked like beauty queen contestants waiting for the evening gown competition to begin. It was breath taking.

I busied myself at the snack table and the fruit punch bowl. I wanted as few people as possible to see my misfit uniform. Further I really didn't want to dance since our church taught that dancing was immoral. I had danced twice without my parent's approval; once at our high school Sadie Hawkins Day dance and once at an after school dance. Someone had shown me a basic ballroom step, but I didn't dance it well. If the dance required more than the simple box step I was way over my head.

Soon I saw one of the beauty queens coming my way. She looked straight at me. I wanted to run or maybe crawl under the table, but she had zeroed in on me and maintained eye contact. She stopped next to me, smiled, and told me her name. I told her mine. She asked where I was from and I told her. Then as I feared she would she asked me to dance. Before I could answer she took my hand and led me to the dance floor. Thank goodness the band was playing something that worked with the box step. I managed to finish that dance without stepping on her feet or tripping over my rolled up pant legs. We sat at a table and talked for a while. Before the evening was over we'd danced a couple more times. Afterward as I walked back to the base I decided that despite my sloppy uniform I had enjoyed myself.

Classes Begin

The Navy and the college worked out the course schedules and classes began. The courses offered were similar to most liberal arts colleges except for a required course each day called "Naval Theory." Lt. Donahoe, our Executive Officer, taught us how the Navy was organized, the types of ships, and naval warfare strategy. The priests were the school's regular faculty and taught all the other courses except a civilian woman taught advanced algebra and trig.

I took all of the literature courses offered since I still planned to become a journalist after the war. The college did not offer journalism courses, but several of us decided the base needed a newspaper. The Captain approved and we set about the work of putting a newspaper together called "The Sea Breeze." It came out once a week and contained articles about members of the ship's company, some of the instructors, and some of our fellow students. There were announcements of events and even some attempt at humor.

It was enjoyable to be doing academic work again. Classes went smoothly and my grades put me on the Dean's List each semester. This had tangible benefits. The Captain decided anyone making that list would be entitled to unrestricted liberty over weekends. Usually travel during weekends was limited to no more than twenty-five miles from the base. Unrestricted liberty meant I could go any distance from the base as long as I was back by 2300 hours on Sunday evening. While it was satisfying to have such freedom I don't recall ever using it.

Buglers, Report For Duty

The Captain posted a notice asking for buglers. I had been a bugler in Cubs. In Boy Scouts I earned a bugling merit badge. That meant I had to learn all the standard bugle calls. So I tried out and became one of six buglers for the base. The supply officer issued Navy bugles and assigned duty on a rotating basis. That meant the same bugler would not have to blow Reveille every morning nor play taps every night. Each morning the flag raising ceremony required a bugler to play Colors as the color guard hoisted the flag. Each evening he played Retreat when it came down. Soupy was blown at mealtimes and First Call when all hands were required to fall in outside.

Bugling was good duty. I enjoyed everything about it except playing Reveille. I knew how to play it and I didn't mind getting up early when the duty watch woke me. It was just that my lips didn't function properly until midmorning. I tried exercising them, slapping them, and even drinking a cup of hot coffee, but nothing woke them up any earlier. So every time I played Reveille I made enough frightful noise to wake everyone, but my notes were a disgrace to Navy buglers everywhere. I envied Karl Killinger a fellow bugler. His lips woke up with the rest of his body and were ready to perform. He did a delightful job waking us up by playing "The World Is Waiting for the Sunrise" on his trumpet before blowing the strident notes of Reveille. His song gently nudged us to wakefulness first and then the insistent notes of Reveille got our feet out onto the deck.

Karl was an accomplished musician. After the war he continued band work and I believe he eventually worked with the Ringling Bros., Barnum and Bailey circus band. It was Karl who suggested that it might be appropriate to have a drum and bugle corps. We had a corps of buglers so efforts began to recruit drummers. Soon a group formed and after a few practice sessions the Captain asked us to lead the entire battalion on its Saturday morning march through the streets of northwest Davenport.

The Captain viewed our Saturday morning marches as part of our basic training, but he also hoped to impress the civilian onlookers and thereby assist the Navy's recruitment efforts. On our first outing we looked and sounded awful. I fear that our drum and bugle corps did not inspire anyone nor increase the number of recruits from the area. We knew only one tune, the trio from Susa's "Semper Fidelis," and we played it badly. As we marched our lines were ragged and probably half of us were out of step because we concentrated on playing. I would not have been surprised if our shipmates had refused to march with us. But after several weeks we became a unit that could march and play at the same time.

Then Karl Killinger suggested we should try to organize a band. Many of us asked for our instruments from home and practice began. The college offered its music library for our use. It contained many good Susa and Karl King marches. It was at this time that our own Karl Killinger composed the St. Ambrose Navy fight song, but I don't recall that we often played it. Once again we led the entire battalion on its Saturday morning marches through the streets of Davenport.

Saturday Morning Inspection

While the battalion was on the streets marching the chief petty officers and the ship's doctor inspected our rooms and belongings. Then when we returned from the streets we marched onto the central green of the campus and stood assembled for personal inspection and review. The Captain, Executive Officer, and the chief petty officers strode by each unit carefully checking the uniform and grooming of each man. A soiled or rumpled uniform, unshined shoes, long hair, or the lack of a shave could jeopardize ones chance for liberty. Finally at a given command the band began playing and marched in review before the ship's commanding officers assembled on the steps of the Administration Building. Each platoon in turn followed in review and returned to their spots. The band played the entire time. Each Saturday I was thrilled to see everyone so impeccably dressed and marching with such precision. Beside the review by our commanding officers, scores of townspeople showed up each Saturday to review "their" Navy. Also dozens of parents and relatives were on hand to see their special sailor. After the review the Captain dismissed everyone to go on liberty. Those who had not passed inspection stayed behind until they corrected their problems.

The Band Learns Pomp and Circumstance

St. Ambrose was an all boys' school in its pre-war life. Because of the draft most of their students now were in the military. Only a dozen or so civilian students remained. These men were studying for the priesthood and were exempt from the draft. The addition of 300 sailors on campus insured that St. Ambrose remained an all boys' school. But the church had not forgotten the Catholic women of the area. Marycrest a college for women was located about two miles away.

One spring Marycrest requested that our band play for their graduation ceremony in June. Karl Killinger handed out new music including the traditional graduation march "Pomp and Circumstance." We practiced this music and felt that we were ready. On the Sunday afternoon of the ceremony we marched to Marycrest and took our places on the central green. A raised platform at one end of the area held a podium and seats for the dignitaries. Rows of chairs for the graduates, their relatives, and friends lined the grass in front of the platform. The band had seats to the side.

We played a number or two and then began "Pomp and Circumstance." A line of girls in robes and mortarboards processed in. It was not a large class so we didn't repeat the music endlessly as is sometimes necessary. The nun in charge of the college spoke, as did several others. When it was time to award the diplomas two teenage boys placed a throne-like chair near the front edge of the platform. A rotund man wearing clerical vestments walked to the chair and sat down. I assumed he was the bishop or perhaps the archbishop. As each girl received her diploma she advanced to the throne, knelt, and kissed the ring he wore. The medieval pageantry of this ceremony enthralled me.

Afterward one of the nuns from the college invited the band to have fruit punch and cookies in the reception hall. This gave us a chance to meet some of the Marycrest students who served them. I noticed every time one of us approached a girl for conversation one or another of the nuns walked up and stood close by. This drastically inhibited our conversations. Finally this intrusive chaperoning became intolerable and we went outside, probably to the relief of the nuns. Before long we marched back to base.

We Buy Questionable Wheels

Don Tew and I graduated from high school together, went to Drake together, and now we were roommates in the Navy. Often we went on liberty together and traveled to Des Moines together on Christmas and semester breaks.

Over one break we decided to rent a car for the trip. Two shipmates also going to Des Moines rode with us to share expenses. Don and I took turns driving. When I began my turn I remembered the government had imposed a speed limit of thirty-five mph to conserve tires and gasoline. Dutifully I tried not to exceed that limit, but it seemed so slow! At thirty-five we'd never get home. I found myself gradually pushing the pedal harder and harder. After several miles we were moving at the brisk speed of sixty mph. The four of us were anxious to get home so it seemed a more appropriate speed and nobody complained. After a few more miles it seemed we were making incredible time. I glanced at the speedometer and saw ninety-six mph. That was a surprise. I thought about our car's questionable recap tires and backed off. We went the rest of the way to Des Moines at a much safer speed, but still above the thirty-five mph limit.

Don and I decided renting a car was nice, but how much more convenient it would be to have our own car. One of the sailors at the base said he had a 1939 Ford V-8 coupe with rumble seat for sale. He was from Rock Island, Illinois, so one day we went across the river and looked at it. It looked snappy. We drove it around town for a while and it seemed to run well. We decided it would be good transportation. Christmas break was coming. We said we'd give him $20.00 as a down payment so we could use it to get home and back. His total asking price was $125.00. We promised to pay the balance when we returned from break.

Now we had our own wheels. Two passengers signed up for the trip with the understanding they would ride home in the rumble seat. The day we left Davenport was bitterly cold. Our rumble seat passengers wrapped themselves in several blankets and hunkered down. We had gone only as far as Durant when the engine began knocking. I pulled into a station and checked the oil. It was low so I bought a couple of quarts. Our passengers were a little cold, but still seemed alive so we went on.

As we rolled into Brooklyn the engine was again making noises. This time I pulled into a station and asked if we could have enough of their used oil to fill us up. Our passengers were thoroughly chilled and waited inside the station to thaw out. For the next several miles they rode up front with Don and me.

Several miles later the engine began clanking again. We filled the crankcase with used oil at a service station. The owner found a five-gallon can that he filled with used oil for us to take along. We hit the road again and this time our passengers were back in the rumble seat.

After numerous stops to refill the crankcase we reached Des Moines. We had to help our half-frozen rumble seat passengers out of the car. We estimated that our car used thirty quarts of oil on the trip. When we tried the car out we drove it in town. Our speed was much slower than on the highway and the knocking hadn't shown up. But as soon as we hit highway speeds it knocked and began losing oil. I believe the rear oil seal and one or more of the bearings were bad.

Don and I had the car, such as it was, to use for the week we were home. We divided its time between us. One night I was driving it home and noticed it was low on gas. I was near the three gas stations at the Forty-second and University intersection. But they weren't open. "There must be a little gas left in the hose at each pump," I thought. I drove into the first station, uncapped the car's gas tank, and lifted the gas hose from the first pump to let it drain into the tank. I smiled when I heard gas trickling into the tank. I drained each hose. While draining hoses at the third station a police squad car roared in, fixed me in its spotlight, and two officers jumped out. "Don't move," they commanded. Then, "What in the world do you think you're doing, sailor?"

I told them and they hesitated for a moment then one of them said, "Well, all right, finish up. And we'll stay right here 'til you leave." He added, "The neighbors phoned you in. They thought you might be up to no good."

I got my gas and thanked the officers. As I drove away I quietly fumed that Don had left the tank so nearly empty.

At the end of our leave we left for Davenport. Our two passengers were glad that the temperature was decidedly warmer. Again we had to keep pouring oil into the car, but near Ledora a new problem developed. The radiator began steaming. We found the problem was a crack in the metal housing where the hose attached to the block. It was leaking coolant. We stopped and pulled tar from a seam in the highway. With a cigarette lighter we melted the tar into the crack. This worked for several miles, but then we had to repeat the repair.

Finally we limped into Davenport trailing oil and spouting steam. The next day we were still upset with our misadventure and cornered the owner.

"We sure don't want your car. You can have it back," we told him. "It's nothing but trouble and needs some serious repairs." I believe he knew it had problems and hoped to dump them on us.

"You can keep our $20 down payment. That ought to be payment enough for the use of the car," we said. He agreed and got his car back. In the end it all balanced out since Don and I had charged our two passengers $10 each for the trip.

Rum Runners
For a few weeks Don Tew had his parents' Hudson at school. It was convenient to have transportation available whenever you needed it. Some of our classmates thought so too and persuaded Don to make a run to Rock Island for liquor. In Iowa the only place you could buy a bottle of liquor was at a state operated liquor store. You had to be 21 years old to get a liquor book that permitted you to buy. All of us were only 18 or 19 years old. But Rock Island was different. There the liquor stores were private businesses and they weren't fussy about the age of their customers.

If he was going to make a whiskey run to Rock Island Don figured that he might as well make it worthwhile so he took orders from anyone on our deck who wanted to buy liquor. Then Don and I and two other sailors left for Rock Island. We bought a dozen or more bottles and stowed them under the front seat.

On our return to Davenport over the government bridge we wondered why traffic stopped then inched forward. Then we saw a police roadblock. They stopped each car and searched it. We assumed they were looking for people bringing liquor into Iowa illegally. We felt doomed. They'd find our liquor. We were all underage. How would we explain that to our parents and to the Captain? Surely they will arrest us. And what about the car? The police will impound it. How could Don explain that to his parents? There was no way to turn around and get out of line. So gradually we inched forward getting more nervous all the time. Finally it was our turn. An officer walked up, shined his flashlight in our faces, looked inside the car, and said, "Ok, sailors, go on." We asked why the roadblock and he said, "Some prisoners broke out of the Rock Island jail and we think they may have commandeered a ride." We were glad that we didn't look like escaped prisoners.

Chapter 10

THE IVY LEAGUE NAVY

I Leave St. Ambrose

When I enlisted the doctor found my eyesight was not good enough to be a line officer, but was satisfactory for the Supply Corps. Now after four semesters at St. Ambrose I moved on to a midshipman's school. My papers ordered me to report to the Naval Station at Lido Beach, Long Island, New York.

This was a long trip for a sheltered Iowa boy to make and I was the only one from St. Ambrose sent to Lido Beach. The clerk gave me a packet of train tickets to take me from Davenport, Iowa, to Chicago, Illinois, on the Rock Island Railroad. There I was to transfer to a Pennsylvania Railroad sleeper to carry me overnight to New York City. From Grand Central Station in New York I was to catch a Long Island Railroad train out to Lido Beach.

I looked forward to this trip because I would experience several new and exciting things: the hustle-bustle of Chicago's LaSalle Street Station, eating supper and breakfast in a railroad dining car, climbing into an upper berth on a Pullman car to try to sleep, and the next morning arriving in cavernous Grand Central Station.

I walked into the crowded waiting room of Grand Central Station. In the hour before my train left for Lido Beach I decided to stroll out onto the "sidewalks of New York." My first thoughts were, "New York City – I can't believe I'm really here! Look at those buildings. They're all so tall. And the people – there's so many of them. Where are they all going so fast?"

For a block or two I became part of that scurrying crowd. I drank it all in as the crowd swept me along with them. Finally I stopped, turned around, and worked my way back to the station.

"I could get lost out here if I go any further. Then I'd miss my train and who knows what the Navy would do to me then." I did the safe thing. I found the gate where my train was to be loaded and stayed close by to wait for it.

Lido Beach In The Off Season

At the depot I noticed a Navy bus parked nearby. The driver said he was available to take me to the base. Lido Beach had several fine hotels and was a summer vacation destination for people from all over the east coast. Now in the off-season they didn't look busy. As we approached each one I hoped it would be my destination, but the driver kept going. Finally we came to a collection of weather beaten wooden buildings built just beyond high tide on the beach. The bus stopped here. This uninviting jumble of wooden barracks, mess hall, recreation hall, and supply buildings was my destination.

The Navy trained gunners at this base, but for the next week it would also be a testing and screening center for the Supply Corps. It was November. It was cold, damp, cloudy, windy, and thoroughly dreary. The base seemed to be nothing but blowing sand and squawking seagulls. I had hoped for something better

Several hundred of us from V-12 Supply Corps training programs around the country were ordered here for testing and exhaustive interviews with naval and school administrators. They would assign us either the midshipman school at Harvard Graduate School of Business Administration in Boston or the Supply Corps School at Perth Amboy, New Jersey.

One of my first nights at the base loud gunfire close by suddenly awakened me. Still half asleep I sprang from my bunk thinking we were under attack. I looked out and saw it was merely the gunner trainees firing the antiaircraft guns lining the beach. They fired at a canvas sleeve towed behind an airplane. I went back to bed, but it was a long time before the shooting stopped. Night practice occurred every other night and it seemed to me it always started just after I'd drifted off to sleep. I never got used to the noise of gunnery practice during my brief time there.

By the end of the week the tests and interviews were finished. Harvard and Navy administrators selected the top 126 of us to go to Harvard. We would take the regular curriculum in the graduate school and after two years have our masters in business administration. The Supply Corps would assign us duty at a base or a ship as the only Supply Officer. We would be responsible for everything including payroll. The remainder of the men were sent to Perth Amboy Naval base where they would receive six months of training, commissioned, and then assigned a ship or base where they were one of several supply officers.

Midshipman life begins

I felt fortunate the morning we left Lido Beach for the train ride up to Boston. Fortunate to be leaving desolate wind swept Lido Beach and fortunate to be going to Harvard. The trip up the coast was exciting for an inlander like me. Periodically I saw the ocean and some times sand dunes. The train rolled through Stanford, Bridgeport, New Haven, and at lunchtime we were in New London. This is the home of the Navy's submarine base. As I sat in the dining car eating I saw a submarine cruising down the river on its way to sea. It looked much smaller than I'd expected.

It was late afternoon when the train arrived at Boston's Back Bay Station. A cold rain made the streets glimmer. Lights of cars reflected brightly off it. In this late afternoon gloom the city looked dark, old, and forbidding.

Busses waited to take us to the school. Our dormitories on campus were brick with cut limestone trim. After my austere dorm room at St. Ambrose my room in Mellon Hall seemed elegant. It had a lot of space even with three study desks and overstuffed chairs. The final luxurious touch was the ornate working fireplace. A doorway opened to a smaller room with three beds. I met my two roommates twins from California. They seemed decent enough although back in high school their condescending attitudes would have labeled them as snobs.

The Navy quickly pushed us into a daily routine. We were up at 6:00am and put on sweatshirt and pants for the three block run to the gym. After twenty minutes of calisthenics we jogged back to the dorm for a shower, shave, and then breakfast in the dining hall. A civilian company prepared and served the food at Harvard. It was tastier than at Lido Beach and the atmosphere more enjoyable, too. After breakfast we went off to classes until 4:00 in the afternoon. After that it was study time until 11:00pm or 12:00pm and sometimes later.

The business school used the Case Method as its teaching approach. Someone said Harvard developed this approach and other universities adopted it later. In this approach each student receives a packet containing pertinent information about a company. The information is so detailed that you feel you know everything there is to know about its management, its financial status, its employees, and the community where it's located. The students then must answer questions about the company's further growth, marketing strategies, financial planning, or personnel policies. Using the information at hand the student must decide how to advise the company on these issues and describe his reasoning.

I recall one case that described a shoe manufacturing company that made men's work shoes for almost one hundred years. The manufacturing process for making these shoes, the factory layout, the sources of its raw material, its equipment, the workers' skills, financial structure, marketing approach, sales over the last five years, assets and liabilities was given. We were told this company's management was considering expanding its line of shoes to include men's dress shoes and/or women' shoes. Information was given us listing the kinds of additional equipment needed, number and skills of employees required, amount of factory and warehouse space needed, and changes in marketing required for any expansion. We were to decide: Is this a good (profitable) idea? How would you advise the company and how did you reach your conclusion?

I thought that focusing our classroom discussions on practical questions was an advantage over traditional lectures. Even though you were trying to answer specific questions you still had to deal with accounting, marketing, personnel, inventory control, and public relations issues in order to reach a solution.

But while the method appealed to me I found the technical information related to financing and funding daunting. I simply did not have the background to understand most of the information given us nor to appreciate its significance and interdependence. I had taken the only business related course offered at St. Ambrose – beginning bookkeeping. I had a lot of catching up to do. I asked questions in class even though many times they were stupid questions. But the more I worked the more confused I became. Trying to learn these business basics on the run while trying to do the complicated work currently assigned was a stressful battle.

Historic Boston and More

But there were diversions. After all I was in Boston and I had liberty every weekend. I frequently walked from Soldier Field where the business school is located across the Charles River footbridge to Harvard's main campus in Cambridge. The buildings were old and built in a style rarely seen in the Middle West. And none of the streets ran straight. It was as though they originally were cow paths and later were cobbled then paved as the community grew. I often caught the subway to downtown Boston and became a tourist visiting Old North Church, Bunker Hill, and other historic sites.

The Saturday afternoon before Thanksgiving I was downtown when two girls about my age stopped me and asked, "Excuse us. Are you from out of town?" I told them I was. "Do you have any plans for Thanksgiving?" When I told them I didn't they invited me to the home of one of the girls for Thanksgiving dinner. They told me how to get there and suggested what time I should arrive. I appreciated their invitation, but I was surprised. I assumed people in big cities, especially big eastern cities, were not friendly. Their invitation was unexpected.

On Thanksgiving I found the apartment and met the girls again as well as the mother of one of them. They were very gracious hosts and the meal was very well prepared. Of course the mother made the traditional turkey, but since I have never liked chicken or turkey it was difficult for me to enjoy the meal. I took a token piece of turkey, however, and managed to eat it.

This was not the only act of friendliness I experienced while in Boston. At Christmas time a family invited me to their suburban home for Christmas dinner. This time I did not have to find my way on the subway and bus. My host and her father picked me up at the dorm in their Buick. The father was a banker and apparently had a comfortable income. His wife did not have a career outside the home, but was active in the Republican Party. I met their daughter some weeks earlier at a dance held by the Republican Party ladies in a grand mansion in the Back Bay area of Boston. It was their daughter who invited me for Christmas. The dinner was superb, but again it included turkey. And once more I managed to eat a token piece.

It was a picture postcard snowy New England Christmas day and the hosts were friendly people, but I was lonely. This was my first Christmas away from home. Fortunately it was my only Christmas away from home.

Old Ironsides

On liberty with a classmate I went to the naval shipyard in Boston. The gate guard saluted and admitted us without question. We went specifically to see "Old Ironsides." This illustrious wooden sailing ship is the oldest ship still commissioned in the Navy. We walked up the gangplank and at the top gave a snappy salute to the quarterdeck (where the flag is flown) and to the watch commander. He said we were free to look everywhere we cared to.

A wooden roof covered the main deck to shield it from the weather. Water, sewer, electric, and phone lines ran from the dock to the ship. Otherwise there didn't appear to be many changes. I was particularly interested in the gun deck. It was impossible to stand completely upright. Then I realized that 18th Century sailors must have been shorter than today's sailors. The deck was red to disguise any blood drawn during battle. After a leisurely tour of the ship we walked to the gangplank to return to the quay. From atop the gangplank we saw many other ships in the yard.

I Go To Sea – Almost

A new destroyer-escort caught our attention. It was the type of ship we both wanted to serve aboard when we went to sea. Everything about that ship shouted, "Speed! Efficiency! Fire Power!" We walked to her mooring and up the gangplank saluting the quarterdeck and the watch commander as we went aboard.

"Will it be ok if we look around, sir?" we asked the watch command.

"Sure, make yourselves at home," he said. This was a new ship and the crew was getting her ready for a shake down cruise. "Just don't get in our way."

We were like a couple of kids in a toy store as we admired every new piece of equipment we saw. The engines were powerful looking monsters. Now they were silent although we heard the low rumble of an engine somewhere. Perhaps it was the generator for the ship's electrical system. The radio room smelled of new wire and warm electronic components. Racks of equipment impressed me and I ached to get my hands on those dials and buttons. The bridge, too, had dials, gauges, switches, and levers of all kinds. The ship itself smelled of fresh paint.

Everything above the waterline was a blue, gray, and white camouflage pattern for duty in the north Atlantic. Indeed this ship looked ready for whatever the north Atlantic and the Germans could throw at her.

We climbed below again to check out the crew's quarters, the galley, mess, and ammunition lockers. We wandered through the ship for over an hour then decided we'd seen everything and went topside. As we came on deck the ship was riding at a slightly different angle to the dock. The stern line no longer held the ship to the quay. The space between the ship and quay was widening. We looked up and saw the gangplank lifted high in the air by a crane on shore. The engines had come to life imparting a different sound, vibration, and feel to the ship.

It seemed to us the ship was leaving the yard to begin its shake down cruise. Apparently they had forgotten we were aboard or perhaps they thought they could use two additional hands. Either way we were going to sea! While that would be a great adventure for us we didn't think that our commander at school would share our excitement. In a panic we looked for the best way to jump ship. The forward gangplank was still in place. We dashed for it and got back onto the dock safely. We both hoped to go to sea, but just not today.

My Ivy League Days End

The first semester was almost over. The Skipper sent us to the Harvard Coop where we could order our officer uniforms. At the end of the semester we would be commissioned ensigns and then continue our study at Harvard.

Shortly after I had my measurements taken and the uniforms ordered the Skipper requested I come to his office. He asked about my academic work. He said the reports he'd seen did not look good. I told him how I was struggling since I lacked the background course work for graduate school. He understood, but said he must drop me from the program. This was a hard blow for me. I simply was not accustomed to failing. Yet I realized that for the past several weeks I had been struggling, but was falling further behind. The entire semester had been a long, stressful, tormented nightmare.

The Skipper apparently knew I felt like a complete failure. He took great pains to cheer me up. “I know that right now it must seem huge, but this is not the end of the world for you.” He continued, “Under the circumstances you made an admirable effort. You should not be ashamed of the work you have done.” He stood up and stretched out his hand to shake my hand. “You gave it a good try and I suspect you feel like a burden has been lifted.” He was right I had given it my best and I felt relieved I would not have to continue.

I was decommissioned as a midshipman and sent home as a seaman first class. I was on a thirty-day leave with orders to report to the Great Lakes Naval Training Center when the leave was over.

Chapter 11

THE DETROIT NAVY

And Now To Boot Camp

My parents were proud when the Navy sent me to Harvard. When I washed out I felt I let them down. Now a thirty-day leave at home gave me a chance to recharge after the prolonged stresses of that experience. I was bitterly disappointed, but felt certain I would get a worthwhile assignment when I returned from leave. But Mom was not convinced. She worried that my only future in the Navy was with the Pacific fleet. She thought that would surely put me in harm's way and it troubled her.

Mom insisted that I find a safe assignment. She tried to convince our pastor to use his influence to get me a chaplain assistant's assignment. It's probably natural for a mother to try to protect her offspring, but it embarrassed me. Besides, what made her believe that a chaplain assistant's post would be danger free? I did not want the pastor or anyone else to pull strings to get me a safe assignment in the Navy. I believe our pastor understood what Mom was trying to do. He also understood my feelings so nothing ever came of it. At the end of thirty days I left for Great Lakes.

For most sailors boot camp is their first assignment in the Navy. I had been in the Navy over two years yet had not gone through boot training. At Great Lakes I was part of a group of several hundred who had been in Navy V-12 or midshipman programs and now we began boot training. It was not the rough, rock 'em, sock 'em, chew 'em up approach typically dished out by the Chief Petty Officer in charge. Our Chief treated us like intelligent human beings. We weren't required to wear the "boots" that usually distinguish a boot camp trainee. Our days were comfortably filled with aircraft identification drill, antiaircraft gunnery practice, swimming, and life saving work. One day an old Chief Petty Officer gave us a class in knot tying.

I wondered how useful knot-tying skills were in the modern Navy unless we served aboard "Old Ironsides." There was plenty of free time for softball games. This was country club living compared with the usual boot camp training. We finished our training in six weeks.

Off To School Again

We were tested and interviewed to determine our next duty assignment. During this time I heard about Specialist Q, but didn't know much more than they worked in naval intelligence. I assumed they might be coding, decoding, scrutinizing reconnaissance photos, and perhaps even observing enemy ship movements first hand. It sounded like exciting work and I wanted such an assignment. My tests showed I had the intelligence and other qualifications they were looking for. When I reported for my last interview I requested assignment to Specialist Q training. "Nope. Sorry, but right now there's a critical need for radio technicians," the officer said. "You're going to Radio Tech School."

The next day several of us became students at the Navy's Pre-Radio School located in the Garfield Park area of Chicago, Illinois. The school was in the Hugh Manley High School building. Here we would learn electrical theory, shop work, and math before moving on to Radio Tech School at Dearborn, Michigan.

The Navy took over the school for our housing, shops, and classrooms. We slept in the gym on steel bunks stacked three high. Now a stack of three bunks by itself is dangerously top heavy, however, bolting four groups of three-high bunks together to make a block of twelve added stability. Even though the bunks were stable, every time someone rolled over everyone in the block felt it. In time we got used to it.

I was glad for the chance to learn electrical theory. I enjoyed the shop work with metal fabrication, circuit soldering, following a schematic, and doing experiments using an oscilloscope. Class work was not difficult and I looked forward to the time when we'd actually work on some of the Navy's radio equipment.

We had liberty every weekend and on one of my journeys downtown I toured the Chicago Art Institute. This was my first visit to any art museum. I was awed to see in real life some of the paintings and sculpture that I had only seen pictured in books.

I returned to the Art Institute many times while stationed in Chicago. On one of my trips I strolled into a semi dark room. Lighted windows at eye level lined its walls. Behind each window I saw a miniature room replicating a specific historical room or a room typical of a specific architectural period. The furniture, the accessories, and the room itself were only one-twelfth the size of their full size counterparts. How could anyone build such small and delicate pieces? This was my introduction to miniatures and the famous Thorne Rooms. I did not know then that many years later I would still be fascinated with miniatures or that part of my living would come from selling the miniatures I would build.

Back To Great Lakes

I had many ear infections when I was a child, but eventually "out grew" them. Now I was having ear trouble again. The school doctor prescribed sulfa drugs to treat the infection and the ear aches gradually improved, but now I broke out in a rash from head to foot. Even the bottoms of my feet were covered. The itching was torture. The doctor said he had done all he could and called two corpsmen to haul me to the Great Lakes Naval Hospital in an ambulance.

The dermatology ward physician felt certain I was having an allergic reaction to the sulfa drugs. He prescribed medication. The nurses filled a bathtub with warm water and cornstarch where I soaked for an hour or so. The cornstarch soak helped and I was able to get a night of restful sleep. After taking the medication and relaxing in corn starch water a couple times a day for two or three days I felt much better and the doctor released me back to Hugh Manley. Our class soon finished pre-radio and the Navy shipped us to the Radio Tech School at Dearborn, Michigan.

The Ford River Rouge Plant

The Ford River Rouge auto plant was the largest manufacturing plant in the world. Someone said that more then 100,000 people worked in its complex of buildings. I could see several large buildings with covered conveyor systems linking them together. A bank of eight tall smoke stacks grew out of one complex of brick buildings. I assumed this was the foundry and power plant. Each stack seemed to spew a different color smoke and all of it smelled badly.

A scrap metal yard sprawled along one side of the plant. Train cars loaded with scrap iron rolled in. An electromagnetic crane unloaded the cars and dropped the metal over the top of one or another of the many mountains of scrap. Metal crashed and tumbled down the sides eventually coming to rest in the jumble. Ordinary scrap was noisy, but old railroad car wheels dropped onto the piles clanged like cracked bells all the way down to their final resting places.

Across the street from the plant a rendering works was busy day and night. When the wind blew from that direction the stench could make you gag and your eyes water. It thoroughly destroyed appetites.

The Rouge River ship canal ran on the other side where the plant's ore unloading facilities were located. Long ore boats came across the Great Lakes from Minnesota and unloaded here. Of course the unloading machinery and the ship's horns added to the general noise level, but the worst part of the canal was the mosquitoes. The marshy ground surrounding the canal seemed to breed an extremely virulent variety.

Finally there were the buzz bomb motors. The Ford Motor Company had a contract to build jet engines for possible use on buzz bombs similar to the infamous bombs of the London blitz. Each engine received a stationary test run. The tests went on day and night in an area next to the scrap metal yard. The test began with a deep boom that shook our building then the engine roared to life and droned away for an hour or more. After a period of wonderful quiet the next motor thundered to life.

And where was the Navy's Radio Tech school located? In was in the middle of all of this. The Navy built temporary wooden barracks, mess, and classroom buildings here apparently without benefit of any rational thought. But despite the noisy, odorous distractions with their possible threat to health we began classes. The class work was interesting and not difficult. The instructors were competent and the students seemed congenial.

Liberty In Detroit
Our noisy, smelly living conditions made us long for the weekends. It gave us a chance to get away and breathe fresh air. I often went to the downtown USO. All of their food was good, but their egg salad sandwiches were my favorite. The USO also handed out passes for free hotel rooms. By staying downtown Saturday night I didn't have to return to the base until Sunday evening.

One Saturday the USO had an offer from a yatchman at the Detroit Yatch Club. He offered a sailor the chance to go sailing with him on his ketch. I snatched that offer and went out to the Yatch Club on Belle Isle in the Detroit River. I'd never seen such a collection of large well-polished sailboats in my life. The middle-aged owner of the ketch greeted me warmly and welcomed me aboard. His boat's hull, masts, bowsprit, and booms all were made of wood. Bunks, a head, and a galley were below decks. It was a trim looking craft twenty-six feet long.

I helped him stow some food and drinks then we cast off the mooring lines. He started the inboard engine to ease out of the slip and into the river. He headed up river toward Lake St. Claire. As we neared the lake the river widened. We passed Peche Isle and the lake began. He turned the engine off and I helped him run up the jib. With the jib up we gained enough speed to have steerageway. Next we ran up the mizzen sail. Finally we set the main sail and he trimmed them all. With the moderate breeze and all the canvas out the boat gained speed. It moved smoothly through a slight chop stirring up foam that rolled from the bow along the sides. It was relaxing to glide smoothly without engine noise or fumes. The only sound was the gentle hum of the wind as it sang through the stays, halyards, and lines. Occasionally we heard a splash as the bow broke through a larger wave.

As we got further out into the lake I couldn't see the far shore, but as I looked back I saw the Detroit skyline receding. Finally the tall smoke stack at the Edison generating plant was all that remained of the skyline. On our return it would be a landmark to guide us toward Detroit.

Soon the owner asked if I would like to steer the boat while he went below to fix lunch. I eagerly accepted and sat down at the tiller. I was having the time of my life. The sun, the steady breeze, the gently motion of the boat, the pressure against the tiller, and the hum of the wind all contributed to my enjoyment. I was a sailor who had finally gone to sea even though it was fresh water.

After a while I noticed a large ore boat coming up on our stern. We appeared to be on the same heading. The ore boat being faster than the ketch was rapidly overtaking us. Before long he was so close I began to worry, but then I knew the rules of the road said that vessels under sail have the right of way over powerboats. Also the overtaking vessel is the burdened vessel meaning that it must steer to avoid a collision. Just then the owner came on deck. He looked horrified when he saw the ore boat about to run us down. He quickly grabbed the tiller and steered us to one side as the ore boat steamed by. I explained that I thought sailboats had the right of way. "Not on this lake they don't!" he replied. "Lake St. Claire is shallow so a twenty-six foot channel was dredged to give these boats access. We were in their channel and they would rather hit us than move out of it and run aground." I later learned that the average depth of Lake St. Claire is ten feet and its greatest depth is only twenty-five feet.

The rest of the day sailed along without further near catastrophes. Eventually we were so far out into the lake that I don't believe I could see land in any direction. Later in the afternoon we headed back and watched the Edison smoke stack grow taller as it guided us to Detroit. It was a wonderful day for me. I decided I would accept any and all offers the USO might have for sailing.

The next weekend my host had not offered a sailboat ride. However, there was an offer from someone in the Crescent Yatch Club. That club was up toward Grosse Pointe Farms. This time the host was a younger man. His boat was every bit as nice as the one the week before with the usual bunks, head, and galley; however, the weather was not as nice as the previous week. It was cloudy, cooler, and windier. Rain was a possibility later.

With everything safely aboard he started the inboard engine and we left the anchorage. As we moved into the lake the sky turned darker and the wind freshened. He steered cautiously as we met larger waves. The bow pitched downward completely losing itself under the oncoming wave. Then it rose as the wave rolled under us. A large part of the wave came racing along the deck toward the two of us in the cockpit.

We worked our way forward intending to run up a small jib, but after three or four more large waves went surging along the deck my host shook his head and motioned me to follow him back to the cockpit. "I don't know about you, but I think we'd better not go any further today," he said. That was fine with me. I'd seen movies of ships at sea breaking through large waves sending foaming water rushing back over the deck and always wondered what it would be like. I now had a small taste of it. It is exciting, but it's not the way you'd want to spend an afternoon when on a pleasure cruise.

We turned around and shortly were in comparatively quiet waters. We breathed a sigh of relief as we tied up at his slip. He said he wasn't experienced in sailing with waves so high and was glad to be safely back at anchor. We tidied up the boat and tried to dry out. He had been trying to learn about navigation at sea and asked me to explain a few things to him. When he got out the book he'd been studying I felt I was on familiar ground. It was Mixter, *The Primer of Navigation.* This was the text we used for our navigation course at St. Ambrose. The rest of the afternoon we discussed navigation as we poured over the charts he had of Lake St. Claire and some of the great lakes.

For the next few weeks I went sailing almost every weekend, but the last trip was the most memorable. This time I sailed on a forty-foot schooner. The vessel looked like a well-preserved relic from the early 1900's. Over the years its owner maintained it so it still looked sparkling new. The owner invited ten of us sailors to join him, his wife, and several of their friends. We helped bring bags and boxes of food and drink aboard. He pointedly told us we could have all the beer we wanted, but the hard stuff was for his other guests. Perhaps he'd seen how some sailors act after drinking whiskey.

With the schooner's ancient engine popping we edged out of the slip at the Detroit Yatch Club and into the Detroit River. We moved up the river toward the lake and under his direction began hoisting the sails. The river widened out into the lake, he shut off the engine, and suddenly it was quiet. As the sails filled and were trimmed you could feel the ship lurch forward quickly and pick up speed. A more relaxing high-pitched sound of wind through the lines and the gurgle of the bow wave replaced the popping engine noise. The breeze was steady and strong that day sending the boat's lee rail down into the water. It kicked up foam that went surging along the deck toward the stern.

Now with the sails up and trimmed we sailors had nothing to do but sit on deck with our backs to the side of the cabin and bask in the sunshine. Many of the other boats on the lake that day sailed over to take a close look at the wonderful schooner. One fellow came out in a large inboard runabout. He shot dozens of pictures while his partner guided the boat toward us from every angle. Several times he raced under our bowsprit snapping pictures all the time. I didn't blame them. This immaculate wooden schooner under full sail and canted over with its lee rail awash was indeed a thrilling sight to behold. Eventually the day ended and I had to leave the clean fresh air of Lake St. Claire for the foul air of the base.

Oh, To Be Back In Pennsylvania

A shipmate about my age from Pennsylvania and I went on liberty in downtown Detroit several times. He was a good conversationalist, humorous, and a thoroughly likable guy. However, more than anything else he wanted out of the Navy. Night and day he thought about it and talked about it. He felt it had been a mistake to enlist. He had a civilian job that exempted him from military service, but one night during an argument his girl friend accused him of being a draft dodger. He got angry and to show her he enlisted. By now his anger had cooled and he wanted out.

Almost every other day he reported to sickbay to describe symptoms that he hoped were serious enough to get him discharged. It hadn't worked. Then he thought of a scheme that he just knew would do it. The next time we went on liberty to downtown Detroit we'd stand on a corner in Cadillac Square and he'd suddenly fall to the pavement. I was supposed to run for help. He assumed he'd be loaded into an ambulance and taken to a hospital. Doctors would have tests run. Of course they would find nothing. Yet he thought there might be enough unanswered questions that the doctors would recommend a medical discharge.

Not long after that we both were in Cadillac Square, but neither of us was thinking about his fainting scheme. Along with thousands of other people we were celebrating V-J day! We were at school when the word came that the Japanese had surrendered.

The instructors dismissed classes and many of us left for downtown. Later some of our friends told us that shortly after we left the base the Skipper decreed that no one could leave. After facing a near mutiny he changed his mind and everyone, including the Skipper, left for downtown Detroit.

I was never in a wilder, happier, more cohesive group of people as I was that evening and night. Nor do I expect to be a part of such a marvelous celebration ever again. Everyone was smiling, laughing, cheering, and talking excitedly. People hugged and kissed each other. Tavern owners, shopkeepers, and ordinary civilians handed out beer and wine. Impromptu singing and dancing broke out here and there. Many of the Chinese residents of Detroit shot off fireworks.

There was no destruction of property as often happens during some of today's exuberant celebrations following a sports victory. We were celebrating a far greater more important victory. I believe that no one even considered property destruction an appropriate way to celebrate a victory of such grand proportions.

The Schemer Schemes Once Too Often

After V-J day the need for additional radio technicians ended and our school began to shut down. The Skipper transferred us in small groups to other facilities for reassignment. The Navy devised a point system for discharging its sailors. As I recall the system you received one point for each month of active duty plus another point for each month spent in duty overseas. Most of us in the Radio Tech School had few points. We would not be eligible for discharge any time soon. It seemed clear that most of us would likely be sent to the Pacific fleet to relieve those sailors who'd been out there a long time and had enough points for discharge.

My reluctant shipmate from Pennsylvania was not happy with this prospect. He wanted to be out of the Navy right away. So he devised another scheme. He called his girlfriend and asked her to send him a telegram saying that his mother was critically ill and that he should come home as soon as possible. She sent the telegram and with it he was able to get an emergency leave.

The Executive Officer posted the first draft of students sent for reassignment on the same day my shipmate left for home. His name was on the list and so was mine, but since he was on leave he didn't make this draft. Our group went to the Great Lakes Naval Training Station. Two weeks later my friend returned from leave just in time to be included in the next draft. This time the group went to the San Diego Naval Base. Apparently the Radio Tech School alternately sent transferees to Great Lakes and to San Diego. I heard about all of this several weeks later in a letter from my friend written at his new hot steamy base in the Philippines. Obviously his scheming backfired.

Chapter 12

THE GREAT LAKES NAVY

A day or two after I arrived at the Great Lakes reassignment unit the petty officer in charge ordered fifty of us to the processing room. When my name came up I went to the table where a bored officer sat scanning my service record. He looked up asked just one question, "What size ship do you want?"

"A small ship sir, the smaller the better."

That was the extent of my screening. As I prepared to leave he said, "I see you've had some college." Then he said, "How fast do you type?"

"Around 50 words per minute."

He grunted, filled out a form, and handed it to me. "Here, I've got a job for you on the base. Report to Main Side."

At Great Lakes, Main Side referred to the older part of the base. It was the part that existed before the war began and all the new temporary structures were hastily built to accommodate our expanding Navy. In a way Main Side was synonymous with Old Navy spit and polish.

I found the building and talked with the officer in charge. His unit screened sailors when they returned from the fleet. Typically the Navy brought men to the West Coast and gave them a thirty-day leave at home. At the end of their leave those who lived in the Middle West reported to Great Lakes. In the meantime their service records came to Great Lakes for processing. The unit consisted of an officer in charge, two Wave yeomen, two male yeomen, and myself. I moved into a barracks closer to Main Side and began work the next morning.

Permanent Ship's Company

Now after three full years in the Navy I had an assignment that was not a formal training program. For the next nine months I was part of the ship's company personnel division at Great Lakes. The work was much like a civilian job from 0800 to 1700 hours five days a week. When not at work I was free to leave the base or I could use any of the recreational facilities on the base.

The Main Side library had many books of adventures at sea. I discovered and read Joshua Slocum's *Sailing Alone Around The World.* Another memorable book was *Stars to the Windward.*

Main Side held worship services in its huge auditorium every Sunday morning. It was here that I first heard "The Sailor's Hymn" and sang it with a congregation of several hundred, mostly male, voices. It was such a moving experience I felt goose bumps of excitement tingle my spine. That hymn is one of my favorites. Even now when I hear it or sing it I get goose bumps and a lump in my throat.

I often played softball. These games just happened when several of us gathered at the ball diamond at the same time. On weekends most everyone in our barracks went to Chicago or Milwaukee on liberty. Great Lakes is almost equal distance from each. Getting to either place was convenient because the North Shore Railroad ran past the gate. During these weekends I frequently went back to the Chicago Art Institute. For me the main attraction was the Thorne miniature rooms, but I enjoyed the paintings and sculpture as well. Often two or three of us from the base made liberty together in Chicago and went to the large dance halls. At best those evenings were an empty diversion until the Navy discharged me back home to my real life.

My Family Comes To Visit

Once when I was home on leave my folks offered to let me drive their 1936 Plymouth back to Great Lakes. While I had it Grandma Bowlsby rode the train to Chicago to visit me. She arrived on Saturday morning and I met the train, got rooms for each of us for that night, and then we toured the city in the Plymouth. At lunchtime I stopped at one of the USO's and asked for two box lunches. I told them that my buddy and I were passing through and wanted lunch. Grandma and I ate our USO lunches in Grant Park. She said this was her first time in a large city. "How do you keep from getting lost," she asked.

Another time Mom and Pat came for the weekend. We didn't eat USO box lunches, but we did go sightseeing. Then on Sunday morning we drove up to Skokie, Illinois, for morning service at the church where Harold Scholes was pastor. We knew Harold when he was the youth pastor at First Federated Church in Des Moines. We were late and Harold was already into his sermon when we walked in and sat down. He looked surprised when he saw us and stopped preaching in mid-sentence to welcome us. He explained to his congregation that we were old friends from First Federated. After church we had lunch and a long visit with him.

One weekend Dad came to Chicago. Again I drove us around to some of the usual sites. I was grateful to have some time alone with Dad. I remember sitting in Grant Park and discussing everything under the sun. He had been in the Army during World War I and as we chatted that day it seemed as though we shared the bond of two military buddies.

Instead of leaving for Des Moines Sunday evening he took the El train down to his brother Art's apartment for a week's visit. Art was in poor health and Dad thought this might be the last chance he'd get to visit him. The following weekend Dad and I got together again before he left for home.

It was good Dad went to visit Art and Josie when he did because it seemed only a few weeks later Art died. I still had the car at Great Lakes and drove down to Chicago for the funeral on a Saturday. I didn't make good time and was unsure where the funeral home was. Then at a busy intersection I saw the funeral car returning from the cemetery with Dad, Josie, Aunt Bertha, and Uncle Ernest. I swung around and followed them.

Even though Aunt Josie had just buried her husband she did not allow grief to keep her from being a good host. She prepared a fine meal for us, arranged places for each of us to sleep, and seemed anxious to comfort us about any sadness we felt because of Uncle Art's death. Everyone spent the night and the next day I returned to the base.

I Discover Milwaukee

One weekend I decided to go to Milwaukee on liberty. I wanted a change from Chicago. Junior Rand, Clarence Cassidy, and I drove there in the Plymouth. Junior was from Eagle River, Wisconsin, and had been in Milwaukee before. Clarence was from Cincinnati, Ohio, and this was his first visit. We looked along the shore, drove around town, and toured through the downtown area. We ate supper at a large restaurant serving German food. It was excellent, but I felt stuffed like after a Thanksgiving dinner at home.

That night we looked for a place to stay. The USO didn't have discount coupons for hotel rooms and we didn't want to pay full price. We decided to sleep in the car. I drove to the edge of town and turned onto a dirt lane that looked as though no one used it. It was dark and quiet after I switched off the motor and headlights. It took a little time for everyone to get reasonably comfortable in the tight confines of a 1936 Plymouth two door, but eventually we all fell asleep.

I don't know how long we'd slept before the whistle of a steam locomotive began to nudge me awake. It was getting louder and more insistent. Then a bright light shone into the car. Now I was wide-awake. The locomotive's headlight fixed us squarely and its whistle was loud and urgent. "Did I park on a railroad crossing?" I asked myself. I didn't see any train tracks when we stopped. But there it was a train was heading straight for us!

By now we all were wide-awake. I tried to start the engine, but in my haste I flooded it. We decided we should get out of the car.

Three panic-stricken sailors trying to leave a two-door car at the same time quickly became a tangled jumble of arms and legs. We kept an eye on the approaching train as we scrambled to get out. Then suddenly like a miracle the headlight began to swing to one side. Only fifty yards away the train had reached a curve in the tracks. It was not going to hit us! We had not parked on the crossing. The tracks crossed the lane several hundred yards further on.

We settled back into our seats, but with the adrenaline flowing it was a long time before any of us went to sleep.

Erma's Friendly Family Tavern

Another weekend I dropped off a shipmate at his friend's house in northwest Milwaukee and then headed back downtown. While stopped at a traffic light a middle aged-civilian waiting for a bus walked out to the car and asked if I would give him a lift. I agreed and we engaged in small talk until we got close to downtown. "Just drop me up ahead there by the tavern," he said. As he got out he said, "Come on in. Let me buy you a drink."

Everyone in the room seemed to know my passenger and greeted him warmly. The bar ran down one side of the room. Tables and chairs spread out over the rest of the room. A lively polka played on the Wurlitzer jukebox. People sat on most of the bar stools and at many of the tables. He introduced me to everyone in the room and then we sat down at the bar in Erma's Family Tavern. He bought me a beer. "In payment for giving me a lift," he said.

Erma stood behind the bar drawing beer, pouring shots, and chatting with everyone. She was a large affable woman who spoke with a Polish accent. She presided over her bar room with motherly compassion. Often this included a motherly rebuke when someone got out of line. She welcomed me. "Sailors don't usually come here. I guess that's because we don't have any single girls." She added, "Anyway I'm glad to have you."

A tavern like Erma's was a new experience for me. Most of the taverns I'd seen were noisy and rowdy. Erma's seemed more like a social club where husbands and wives from the neighborhood came for an evening of conversation with friends. They had a few drinks, perhaps danced a polka or two, discussed everything under the sun, and played cards. The emphasis was on socializing not on drinking. I spent the evening at Erma's and then drove downtown where several of us had a room for the night.

I often stopped at Erma's over the remaining months I was in service. Junior Rand and I got acquainted with most of the regulars and enjoyed the friendly atmosphere there. Back at the base several of our shipmates heard us talk so much about Erma's they asked to come along on our next trip.

Most of the Saturday night regulars were there when Junior and I arrived with three of our shipmates. Everyone welcomed us. Our friends from the base began to pour down drinks like they must have done at singles bars downtown. They eyed the wives in the tavern and soon were asking them to dance. Even assuming the wife wanted to dance with you it was proper at Erma's to ask her husband's permission. Our friends disregarded such convention and aggressively pursued the wives as though they were pursuing single women in a rowdy downtown bar.

From behind the bar Erma gave me an assortment of nasty looks. All of them said unmistakably, "Get these louts out of here. NOW!" Junior and I understood and took our friends in tow. We said, "Come on. Let's go down the street. We know a place with lots of women and a floor show as well."

That sounded more exciting than Erma's and they walked with us to the other place where indeed there were many single women and a floorshow. Junior and I left them and went back to Erma's. We apologized to Erma and promised that we wouldn't bring any more guys like that to her bar. And we kept that promise. If we hadn't I truly believe Erma would have heaved us both out onto the street single-handedly.

Sailors Return From The Fleet

Our work at the base was not difficult yet there was enough challenge to keep it interesting. Many sailors came back from the fleet with enough points to warrant discharge We brought their service records up to date, formed up drafts of men, and shipped them to discharge centers. We sent some to the discharge center in another part of the Great Lakes base and others to the discharge center at Wold Chamberlain Field in Minneapolis.

Only six of us were in the unit when it started. We worked in the personnel office on Main Side. Now the unit had grown to about thirty people and occupied a former barracks in one of the new areas of the base. Our original unit secured a Chevrolet panel delivery truck for hauling service records and supplies. As the unit grew the truck somehow disappeared from the unit's inventory of equipment. The commander reassigned our unit's first officer in charge and his replacement knew nothing about "our" truck. A few of us from the original staff used the truck both on and off the base whenever we wanted transportation. When it needed gas, a wash job, or servicing, the motor pool took care of it. We were delighted to have the truck as a fringe benefit.

Midnight Snack Special Delivery

Cassidy and I returned from liberty one night and were hungry. No mess halls served food in the middle of the night although a few cooks and bakers were on duty preparing for breakfast. We devised a plan. I phoned the unit's mess hall. "I am Captain Perkins. I've just brought in a draft of twenty men from the West Coast," I told the chief cook. "They haven't eaten in a while. I'll need sandwiches and milk to feed them. I'm sending two men down in ten minutes to pick up the food."

Cassidy and I waited a few minutes and then we went to the mess hall not sure whether they believed my story. They might have figured out it was a hoax and we'd be greeted by the Shore Patrol rather than sandwiches and milk. When we didn't see a Shore

Patrol jeep parked in front of the mess hall we went in to get our food.

"We're here to pick up the food Captain Perkins ordered," Cassidy announced. They had it boxed up and ready to go. It was almost more than the two of us could carry, but we got back to the barracks and sat it on a table in the day room. Many other shipmates were awake or coming in so the entire barracks had a late night banquet of sandwiches and milk courtesy of Cassidy and Perkins.

My Duty Tour Winds Down

In the spring of 1946 I had enough points to be eligible for discharge. So this time I became a member of a draft sent to the discharge center at Wold Chamberlain Field in Minneapolis, Minnesota. I don't know how many of us there were, but as I recall we filled four or five train coach cars. The train left Great Lakes after supper and bounced and swayed along all night on our trip to Minneapolis. The bouncing and my excitement over getting out of service made it hard to sleep. We arrived in Minneapolis the next morning and Navy buses took us to the base for breakfast.

Getting discharged from service is much like enlisting in service. There is paper work, a physical examination, and even testing. This happened over about two days.

On the evening of the first day we heard there was a tavern on the base. I found it in a large mess hall. The brilliant white walls and the large fluorescent lights made the room brighter than it needed to be. Seating was at mess tables with attached stools that swung under the tables when not in use. The Navy bartenders poured beer into small plastic cups once every thirty minutes. When it was dispensing time you had to line up, walk past the beer table, pick up a plastic cup, and then pay for it at the cashier's station. If you came in between dispensing times you had to wait. Never had beer been dispensed in a more clinical atmosphere. There was none of the camaraderie usually associated with having a couple of beers with friends.

I picked up a cup and sat down at a table to talk with some of the other guys. No one seemed to enjoy the conversation or the beer. I finished my cup and left.

A day or two later I had been processed through the discharge center and was very close to being a civilian. The last stop in the process routed me to a room where one of the several women working there took my uniform blouse and sewed on a "ruptured duck" just above the pocket. This patch signified that I was a discharged veteran. I put my blouse back on and the clerk gave me a train ticket to Des Moines on the Rock Island Rocket. A bus took several of us downtown to the station and we left that evening for home

.

A Civilian Again

It was a great feeling to get on that train. As it pulled out of town it felt like my Navy days were truly ending. Not only was I moving away from Minneapolis, but I was also moving away from the Navy. This chapter of my life was closing.

I believe that each one of us felt some of these same emotions. It was a happy time and the civilian passengers on the train seemed to sense our joy and wanted to celebrate with us. Several of them passed us little bottles of whiskey. There was a lot of talking and laughing so that the time raced by. Finally the conductor walked through the car announcing, "Next stop Des Moines."

Coming home from service to stay was something I'd looked forward to for a long time. Many times I'd thought about how it would feel to walk down the steps and off the train onto the station platform – to be home for good. Evidently I had gathered my sea bag and walked down those steps off the train onto the platform. The sad part is I don't remember doing that. After hearing the conductor announce, "Des Moines," the next thing I remember I was sitting in the waiting room at the Rock Island depot. My sea bag lay on the floor at my feet. It was 4:00 o'clock in the morning and I was in Des Moines.

I don't believe I'd been there long, but now I thought I should phone home. I hadn't been able to tell my folks exactly when I'd be getting in. They were anxious to see me and might not be too upset at receiving a call at 4:00 in the morning. I phoned and a little later when they walked into the depot I choked up with emotion. I shook my dad's hand and said, "Finally this is it!" He hugged me and so did my mother. I believe they were probably as teary-eyed as I was. The first thing my folks did when we got home was brew up a pot of coffee. They could tell I'd been celebrating. But drinking or not they were glad to have me back home safely.

Chapter 13

COLLEGE UNDERGRAD DAYS

Transition To Civilian Life

I was out of the Navy. I was home. And I was living in the same room I'd left three years earlier. I'd been looking forward to being back home for a long time, but now it didn't seem so grand after all. When I was in the Navy there was a sense of purpose in my life. There were things I had to do and what I did fit neatly into the grand scheme of things, but now there was nothing that I had to do nor was there any place that I had to be. I could get up in the morning when I felt like it. I could go to bed at night when I wanted to. In the hours between getting up and going to bed no body expected me to do anything. I didn't miss Navy regimentation, but I did miss having something useful to do. I was at loose ends.

After being bone-idle for two weeks I began making plans. I'd heard that financial aid was available to vets until they found employment. A returning vet could draw twenty dollars a week for a maximum of 52 weeks. I signed up at the Employment Office and became a member of the "52/20 Club." I also filled out a form seeking a job.

Not long afterward the employment office referred me for a lens grinder job at the American Optical Company in the Des Moines Building. The job required that I take lens blanks for eyeglasses and select the proper pattern so they could be ground to the correct shape to fit the frames the customer had selected. Then I fit the glass lens blanks into the automatic grinder and started it grinding. At first it was challenging since everything was new to me, but I could see it would quickly get monotonous. But then I did not plan to work there forever. The end came sooner than I thought. I got a bad cold and called in sick for a couple of days. They said I didn't need to come back at all.

Back To Drake

About this time I applied for readmission to Drake so I could complete my undergraduate degree. I was a journalism major when I first enrolled then declared a business major when it became clear that I'd be in the supply corps in the Navy. Now I felt strongly that I should major in psychology with the ultimate goal of doing clinical work. In the fall of 1946 I returned to Drake and began work as a psych major. Because of my credits transferred from St. Ambrose I was now a junior.

Working On The Railroad

When I was in college Mr. McLain, one of our family friends, asked if I'd like a summer job working on the railroad. He was in charge of the mail and baggage handling at the Union depot and needed someone to fill in for vacationing baggage men. Like most college students I needed to work during the summer and said, "Sure."

As baggage and mail handler I pulled those four wheel baggage carts, that used to be so prominent at train depots, up to the baggage and mail cars while the train was stopped at the depot. I'd load on the mail sacks and passenger baggage and take off baggage and mail destined for Des Moines. In the 1940's six railroads ran passenger trains in and out of town.

I pushed and pulled loaded baggage carts and tossed mail sacks. That was heavy work, but it got worse on days when an over the road trailer from Meredith Publishing Company pulled into our sorting area with a load of magazines. The publisher had sorted the magazines by town and stuffed them into mail sacks. All we had to know was which rail line served which town. Then we put the sacks onto the correct carts. Not only were there many mail sacks to handle, but they were heavy. No sack was supposed to weigh more than ninety pounds, but many did.

While a baggage man took vacation all the other men based on their seniority could bid to fill his job while he was gone. I got the shift left over. It always seemed to be the midnight to 8:30am shift. Working the night shift made me realize that nights are for sleeping not working.

Although I never adjusted to sleeping in the daytime I found it was still possible to catch some sleep at night. I marveled how my supervisor wasted no energy when he loaded or unloaded a cart. He also conserved energy in another way. He slept. As soon as we worked the last train of the night he stretched out on one of the shelves in the rear of the baggage room and went to sleep. I selected a shelf, too, and found that I could catch almost two hours of sleep until the next train arrived early in the morning.

I enjoyed the job. It helped build muscles, most of the time I was out doors, and the pay was excellent. Between trains I had an opportunity to observe railroad men.

I particularly remember one man. Seth had been a steam locomotive engineer for the Milwaukee Railroad. He was now retired and lived by himself across the street from the depot at the old Milner Hotel. Every morning at precisely 7:30 Seth walked slowly over and sat down on one of the benches on the platform. Dressed in freshly laundered bib overalls, blue chambray work shirt, stout work shoes, and denim overall jacket, he looked as though he was reporting for work. White hair showed from under the edge of his denim shop cap and a gold chain dangled from the railroad pocket watch in his bib overalls.

Shortly after Seth arrived each morning Milwaukee train number 33 backed into the station to load passengers, baggage, and mail. It came in from the rail yards west of the depot. First came one or two coach cars, then the baggage car, the tender, and finally the engine hissed and snorted into the station. I loaded the mail and baggage and then had time to watch the retired engineer.

Seth had made this run for many years. When he heard the train coming from the yard his face brightened and he stood up to greet it. As the engine eased to a stop he walked out and strolled around it giving it a thorough loving inspection. Then he looked up and talked with the current engineer and fireman in the cab. Soon he was up with them checking everything over just as he must have done hundreds of times during his career. Finally he checked his watch and reluctantly climbed down from the cab. He stood close to the engine's huge drive wheels. From somewhere down the platform the conductor cried, "All 'board!" The engineer turned a valve that started fine trickles of sand flowing onto the rails in front of each drive wheel to improve traction. Then he cracked the throttle. There was a hiss of steam followed by a series of rapid thunderous puffs up the stack. The wheels spun, then caught, and run number 33 was on its way to Spirit Lake.

Seth stood alone watching until the train was out of sight. And he remained on the platform listening intensely as his engine's distinctive whistle sounded at each crossing on its way out of town. Although he was standing on the station platform I felt that in spirit he was once more in the cab firmly gripping the throttle and pulling the whistle lanyard at each familiar crossing. He stood on the platform deep in reverie until he no longer heard the whistle then slowly crossed back to the Milner Hotel.

For several weeks Seth arrived at precisely the same time each morning, but then I didn't see him for several days. I asked some of the other men if they knew why he no longer came. They said, "Haven't you heard? Seth died in his sleep last Tuesday." I was surprised since he hadn't seemed old or infirm to me. But perhaps death had come more quickly for Seth since retirement had already taken his one absorbing love – the railroad and run number 33.

Those Greeks On Campus

Fraternity and sorority activities always seemed a big part of the social scene at Drake. During rush week I visited the Sigma Alpha Epsilon fraternity house for a couple of social events. I wasn't sure that this fraternity or any fraternity was worth my effort and money. One evening I was at the fraternity house for socializing when an alumnus came in acting like a drill sergeant.

He ordered people around, criticized their grooming and clothing, and told them their academic performances last semester were unacceptable. After three years of military discipline in the Navy I had no desire to continue it in civilian life. The alumni's performance made it easy for me to decide that I wanted no part of this fraternity. If all fraternities were like this I was not interested.

Not long after that, however, my old high school friend Carter Hatch asked me to accompany him to a meeting of the Chi Delta fraternity. This was a local fraternity not affiliated with any national group. The chapter at Drake was the one and only one. It developed its own policies and wrote its own rules. I liked that. From my earlier days at Drake I remembered the Chi Delts attracted the athletes and the members always seemed to be having loads of fun.

Carter, Bill Benskin, and I joined Chi Delta and began to participate in its activities. Everyone was looking for a house and found one for rent on Cottage Grove. It did not look impressive like most of the other Greek houses on campus nor did it have drapes, rugs, or furniture. But it became a comfortable home for some of our out of town members and a social place for the rest of us. Later Jack Runyon one of our classmates from Roosevelt joined. By then the house had acquired a greyhound dog as a mascot. For some reason Jack became its chief caretaker. It was a common sight to see them together on campus. The dog probably attended many of Jack's classes. You could always identify the Chi Delts on campus. They wore Kelly green warm up jackets and often had a greyhound with them.

During my senior year the university administration began exerting pressure on us to affiliate with one or another of the national fraternities. They felt it would look better if their recruiting brochures could report that all of their fraternities were national. Representatives from several national fraternities visited us and made their sales pitches. I did not want to affiliate with any national fraternity. I wanted us to remain independent, but the majority voted to become a chapter of Sigma Phi Epsilon. Officially we became Sig Eps, but some of us always remained Chi Delts at heart.

The Eye Camera

Dr. B., head of the psych department, had pioneered some research to discover how people viewed printed and graphic material. To do this he invented a camera that photographed the reflection from a light source as it bounced off a subject's eyeball while looking at the target material. He recorded these reflections on 35 mm movie film. From that he mapped where the subject looked, how long he or she looked at an area, and in what sequence. Most of the studies using the eye camera dealt with advertising copy in an effort to show how effective the copy might be in capturing and holding a subject's attention.

As a part of my course work Dr. B. asked if I would like to run some research on new packaging cartons the F. W. Fitch Shampoo Company was considering. The Fitch Company had been in business in Des Moines for many years. They sold their Fitch Shampoo nation wide. The Company gave us the four new carton designs they were considering. Our job was to determine which carton caught a potential customer's eye and held it longest.

We set up the cartons and the eye camera in the basement of the Cowles Library on campus. As I'd done with other projects I went upstairs to the library and asked students if they'd be willing to take about five minutes to participate in a research project. Then I took them downstairs, positioned them in the machine, and recorded how they looked at the cartons for a specified length of time. The machine recorded about 200 students. The interpretation of the results was time consuming, but one carton definitely had an edge over the others. Dr. B. did the statistical analysis of the data and it was clear we had a winner. He wrote the report and sent it to the company. Several months passed and the Fitch study was no longer in the forefront of my mind when one day I was in a store and there it was. Fitch

Shampoo was in its new carton and it was the one we'd recommended. It was satisfying to see tangible results from a research project.

Scandal At Drake

Almost everyone on campus knew that one of our professors often tried to escalate his teacher/student relationship with female students to a more intimate level. No one had observed any gross impropriety yet coeds knew they should be wary around him.

I noticed one of my female classmates frequently walked with this professor to his office after his lecture. Several times when I went to his office to discuss one or another of the class assignments she was there. Once or twice I thought I saw lipstick smeared on the professor's lips.

I wondered whether his fascination with female students now had progressed beyond simply ogling and making suggestive remarks. One day I knocked on his office door, heard him say, "Come in," and was shocked to see him zipping up his pants and tucking in his shirt. The coed was beside him on his side of the desk and was straightening her clothes. This time there was no doubt. That was definitely lipstick on our professor's lips and cheeks. Why had he told me to come in? "I'll come back later," I suggested and left.

The next day I discussed this with two of my student friends. Although they had not observed anything quite as specific as I had they felt our professor was not behaving, as he should with female students. The campus rumors about his inappropriate behavior reflected badly on the entire university. We decided to discuss our concerns with the Dean of the Liberal Arts College.

I believe the Dean knew our professor forced his attention on female students, but he lacked specific information about any actual episode. I did not feel good reporting what I had observed. Yet I felt that what our professor did was wrong. This intelligent gifted teacher was not acting as a leader, but was behaving like a lecherous old man.

"That's exactly the kind of incident I've been worried about," the Dean said. "Tell you what – I'll have him in here tomorrow afternoon and confront him about this. Will you three be kind enough to come over and stand by in case you're needed?"

The next afternoon we waited in an adjoining office while the Dean talked with the professor. We nervously discussed what might be happening next door and hoped we would not be needed. After an hour the Dean came in and told us he'd asked for the professor's resignation. The professor gave it and would leave Drake immediately. The Dean thanked us for our help. I felt badly for the professor, but believed it was best for Drake.

Finally Graduation

I had been out of the Navy for two years when I finished my BA at Drake and graduated the last day of May 1948. It was traditional for the faculty and graduating students to assemble in front of Old Main dressed in their gowns and mortarboards. A four-person color guard carrying the American and the Drake University flags lead the procession. The Dean asked me to represent the College of Liberal Arts in the color guard for this academic procession. The University president, the faculty, and then the graduating seniors followed the color guard.

The procession moved across campus, crossed University Avenue, and moved into the Christian Church auditorium. Several people gave speeches, but I don't remember who they were or what they said. After the speeches we received our diplomas. My parents and my sister were there and as I accepted my diploma I felt more pride than I'd expected to. In fact I felt a lump in my throat and tears in my eyes. The following day I was to leave Des Moines for the next phase of my education – this time at a mental hospital.

Chapter 14

A SUMMER IN A MENTAL HOSPITAL

Early in my senior year at Drake I applied for a summer job at a Mental Health Institute. I wanted exposure to the type of work I planned to go into. I also applied to Tulane University to do my graduate work in clinical psychology beginning in the fall. Dr. Graves, Director of the State Board of Control, said I could begin work at the Independence, Iowa, Mental Health Institute as soon as school was out.

The day after graduation from Drake University I drove to Independence in the 1936 Plymouth my folks gave me as a graduation present. As I approached from the west on highway 20 the Institute seemed to rise from among the trees. Its gray stonewalls topped by a mansard roof reminded me of a mansion from a gothic horror story. The central part of the building was taller than the rest and according to the sign in front it housed the administrative offices.

I asked the receptionist to see Dr. Stewart the Superintendent. She looked surprised and said, "I'm sorry, but Dr. Stewart died a few weeks ago."

I told her that I was supposed to begin work there. "Is there someone else I could see?" I asked.

She sent me to Mr. MacArthur the male ward attendant supervisor. He wrote down pertinent employment information and explained that I was to work as an attendant on wards that were short handed. Also I was to fill vacancies when an attendant went on vacation. The hours were from 6:00 am until 6:00 pm six days a week. The MHI would provide room, board, and laundry at no cost. I believe the salary was around $80.00 per month. He gave me a set of keys and called one of the attendants to take me to my room.

We rode a rickety elevator to the top floor of the central building and walked into an abandoned ward. It housed patients until recently when the administrators realized it would be difficult for them to get out in case of a fire. I was to live in a room on the ward with eight other summer employees. The administrators assumed that staff would have a better chance in a fire than would patients.

I Debut At Grove Hall

After lunch an attendant from Grove Hall took me to the Hall with him. It seemed that each new attendant began work at Grove Hall. After seeing the place I think I knew why. If you survived the smell, the noise, and the outlandish behavior of the patients you could survive anywhere at the Institute. Duty at Grove Hall was a type of initiation.

The Hall was a two-story brick building behind the administration building. It housed bedfast patients on the top floor and ambulatory patients on the ground floor. Someone committed to a mental health institute in the 1940's might spend the rest of their life there. The Institute was like a self-contained feudal community. It had its own dairy and raised its own vegetables and fruits. It had a TB sanatorium and its own nursing home – Grove Hall.

I was to work with the bedfast patients on the second floor. One large room held perhaps fifty hospital beds. Most patients wore only a hospital gown or no clothes at all. Many had their wrists and ankles restrained so they wouldn't thrash about get out of bed and hurt themselves. The smell of urine was strong because many were incontinent. We had to help others to the bathroom.

I spent my time changing bed linens, washing patients, putting on clean robes, and feeding them. A few of the ambulatory patients from downstairs helped with the work, but were not to touch another patient. Mostly they mopped floors, carried away the dirty sheets, brought up clean linen, and scrubbed the toilets.

I remember one patient who could sit in his bed and feed himself, but he always managed to keep a small crust of bread after each meal. It must have served some ritualistic need for him. He'd roll it into dough and then spend several hours massaging his body with it.

Bart, another patient, was elderly and had worked as a teamster. He scooted down in bed until his feet touched the footboard. Then he took up imaginary reins and began to holler at his team. "Ho! Jack! Giddup Prince! Hey, hey, go! We go to the depot. Come on! Go, go! Giddup, giddup." All the while he bounced in his bed jerking on the reins and pushing his feet against the footboard. He seemed to have a regular route hitting the depot, the lumberyard, the grain elevator, and several places I couldn't understand. He was very suggestible. If I'd say, "Hey Bart, there's a pickup for you over at the elevator," he'd start talking about the elevator and driving his horses over there.

Fire Drill

One day Dr. Graves, director of the Board of Control, visited Grove Hall to inspect the patients and their accommodations. He asked many questions about their condition and care. And he wanted to know, "In case of a fire, how would you get these patients out?"

Two or three of us working on the ward that day were summer workers and new to the job. We hadn't thought about evacuating patients in a fire. Finally one of the guys had an idea. He said, "How about taking the patient and his mattress right off the bed, putting the mattress and patient at the top of the stairs, and giving the mattress a shove down the stairs."

It sounded to me as though it might work. Dr. Graves said, "Well, let's give it a try."

We took a mattress from an empty bed and carried it to the stairs. We were wondering which patient we could use as a passenger when Dr. Graves said, “No, don’t put a patient on there.” And pointing to the attendant who’d made the suggestion he said, “You be the patient.”

Four of us put the mattress with its reluctant passenger at the top of the stairs and gave it a hefty shove. It started slowly then gained momentum. The passenger tried desperately to hold on but when the mattress swung sideways he fell off. He bounced down three or four more stairs without the mattress before coming to rest. He looked battered and bruised. It was apparent this would not be an efficient or safe way to evacuate patients. Although we discussed it for several minutes we never came up with a satisfactory solution. All of us fervently hoped Grove Hall would never catch fire.

Strawberry Picking Time

After working a few days at Grove Hall I was reassigned to Farmers’ Lodge. All these patients were ambulatory and while they were still considered psychotic they were thought to be stable and posed no particular risk to themselves or to others. Most of them worked on garden crews. As their attendant it was my job to accompany them to the fields and supervise their work there.

The strawberries were ripe so picking them was the big job of the moment. Each morning a tractor pulling a hay wagon stopped by the Lodge to take us to the berry patch some distance from the buildings. Almost all of these men had been farmers and were accustomed to working outdoors. They knew what to do and seemed to thoroughly enjoy doing it. However the work did not stop their hallucinations or their ritualized movements. John frequently stopped picking berries while he held a heated argument with an invisible antagonist. After a minute or so he’d return to berry picking.

Pete would plead, “Don’t! Please don’t hurt me! No, no, I didn’t mean to. Don’t hurt me!” After this brief outburst he’d resume picking berries. Almost every patient talked to himself or to unseen people. It was a noisy crew, but it was a productive crew. I picked berries, too, but tried not to be distracted from my main job, which was to bring back the same number of patients as I took out.

Charlie was one of my most productive workers even though he, too, talked nonstop. Almost every Sunday during the picking season one or another of the neighboring farmers phoned the Institute demanding, "Come and get Charlie out of my strawberries!" The crew didn't work on Sundays, but Charlie was such a dedicated worker he refused to take the day off. He went on picking berries wherever he could find them.

One day a supervisor asked me to go with him to bring back a patient who had walked away. Someone spotted the patient a mile or so from the Institute near the Illinois Central railroad tracks. We drove over, got out of the car, and walked down the railroad right of way. As we approached the railroad bridge over the Wapsipinicon River we spotted the patient on the other side of the tracks. We also saw that a train was approaching and hoped he wouldn't jump in front of it. By now the train was too close for us to cross the tracks safely and catch him. We waited while the long freight passed and were relieved to see him still standing where we first saw him. When we stepped across the tracks he started for the river. Without hesitating he rushed into the water as though he intended to walk to the other side. We waded after him and fortunately reached him before he got to deep water. We got him back to the Institute soaking wet, but otherwise safe.

The Infamous Locked Ward

Hospital rules required attendants to keep the doors locked on most wards. Even so they called only one ward "The Locked Ward." Security was especially tight there because it housed the most violent and escape-prone patients. Attendants never allowed them outside even for short walks or exercise. With its reputation I felt nervous when I reported there for duty.

Two of us worked the ward. The other attendant was an elderly man who had been at the Institute for many years. Most of the time he was napping, confused, or forgetful. Frequently patients had to remind him he'd forgotten to lock the door or that it was time to hand out medication. It was a revelation to me that these psychotic patients actually looked after their caregiver as much if not more than he looked after them.

Patients could not smoke on the ward, but twice a day could smoke in the basement of the building. At mid-morning and at mid-afternoon I lined up all the smokers and we walked down the enclosed stairs to the smoking room. I lit each man's cigarette because only attendants could carry matches or lighters. The room had no ventilation so the smoke quickly got so dense it was hard to see across it. Even without smoking a cigarette you probably could experience the same effect just by inhaling. After smoking frantically for the allotted thirty minutes everyone walked back upstairs to the ward.

One day I asked a patient to come with me to the day room. He didn't want to and loudly protested. As I stood waiting for him to come with me he suddenly lifted his bare foot high above the seat of a wooden captain's chair then stomped on it with such force the chair split apart. He picked up a large piece of the broken seat and rushed at me poised to strike. I stood ready to block his blow, but suddenly he stopped just three feet away and dropped his makeshift club. He walked docilely with me to the day room as I'd requested. That was the only time a patient threatened to harm me.

While I worked on this locked ward I learned how effective the Institute's grapevine is. When I came on the ward one morning at 6:00 am one of the patients asked if I'd heard that Bill S. had escaped during the night from his ward in another part of the building. I hadn't heard that and was surprised a patient on a locked ward already knew about it. Later at breakfast I checked and found that his information was correct. Many times that summer the grapevine was not only fast, but also was accurate.

Duty On The Infirmary Ward

After filling in on the Locked Ward for two weeks the supervisor next assigned me to the Infirmary Ward. I worked there for the rest of the summer. The Infirmary was a two-story brick building separate from the main building. The patient wards stretched out from either side of the central part of the building. One side was for women and the other for men. The center area held offices, kitchen, dining rooms, and several treatment rooms.

I worked with Mrs. MacArthur wife of the male attendant supervisor. She explained my responsibilities clearly and I felt she would be a pleasant person to work with. Our ward had been the postoperative ward when the Institute did surgery. Now most of our patients were in casts for broken arms or legs or they had other illnesses.

One of my patients was a black man about twenty who sustained a deep bruise to his thigh while playing softball with other patients. It became infected and a cavity opened up reaching down to the bone. The treatment ordered for him was medicated gauze packing. First thing every morning I used long tweezers to pull the old slimy gauze bandaging out of the cavity in his thigh. Next I cleaned the wound with an antiseptic. I slathered a fresh length of bandaging with a black medicated ointment and packed it solidly to the bottom of this cavity. Finally a protective gauze pad covered the wound. It was a foul smelling and repulsive job.

At first it took almost three feet of gauze to pack his wound. As the wound healed it required less and less. By the end of the summer it took only six to eight inches of gauze to fill the cavity. When I finished treating his wound each morning it was breakfast time. The first few days on this assignment I didn't have much appetite, but gradually I became accustomed to it and could eat a hearty breakfast.

A Textbook Example

Another memorable patient was Obed. My abnormal psych textbooks told about catatonic schizophrenia, but this was the first such case I'd seen. The textbooks said "waxy flexibility" was one of the classic symptoms. When you lifted one or both of Obed's arms over his head and let loose his arms would stay in that position almost indefinitely. Sudden violent outbursts were also a symptom described in the books.

Obed usually sat quietly on the ward not talking to anyone or moving around. But it wasn't many days before I saw this other symptom of his illness. One day he became enraged and suddenly rushed up out of his chair and ran straight across the room into the wall. He got up, hollered unintelligibly, and ran down the ward. A couple of us finally stopped him and put him in restraints. After several minutes he calmed down.

Obed was blind or had very poor vision in one eye. Before coming to the Institute he tried to cut out his eye with a razor blade. He said he was following Biblical instructions that admonish a person to cut out his eye and cast it away if it causes you to sin. He was not successful in cutting it out, but his attempt impaired his vision and left several scars around one eye.

Many days Obed refused to eat and stood rigidly in a corner. He would not walk with the rest of us down to the dining hall. On those days I led Obed then had to feed him. He did not talk nor give any indication he knew what was happening. That was why I was surprised after the summer was over to get a short note from him saying, "Do you remember taking me down to the dining room and feeding me?" He had been aware after all and seemed to be thankful for my concern and help.

Treatments Old And New

The Hydrotherapy Room looked like a large shower. It had white tile walls and several drains in the floor. Water pipes fitted with valves and gauges came from the floor in the center of the room. The pipes fed a nozzle aimed out into the room. From this control station an operator could direct a jet of water to any part of the room and onto a patient. The operator could change the volume of water spraying out, its temperature, and the spray pattern much like today's shower sprays.

Hydrotherapy had been a popular treatment for calming agitated patients, but had fallen out of favor. The Institute no longer used it. Today's whirlpool hot tubs might have a similar calming effect.

The Institute still practiced another of the old therapies for agitated patients. When a male patient anywhere in the Institute became agitated the staff brought him to our ward for ice therapy. We covered a bed with a rubber sheet. Over that we laid three or four woolen blankets. Finally another rubber sheet covered the top. We undressed the patient and held him on his back on the sheet with his arms down at his side. Usually it took four or five attendants to do that, but when he was on the bed we packed several buckets of crushed ice around him. We wrapped the rubber sheet and the woolen blankets around him so that in the end just the patient's head stuck out of his blanket cocoon.

The patient couldn't move, but usually remained vocally abusive. His loud stream of profanity moans and gibberish often continued for several hours. In the end the patient was exhausted enough to lie quietly. During the time he was in the icy cocoon we monitored his pulse and respiration rates closely. We kept some patients over night, but released others after four to five hours. It depended on how soon they calmed down. This probably was not an effective way to calm a patient, but it might have been good training for the Polar Bear Club.

Shock Therapy

The most frequently used therapy for depressed patients at the Institute in 1948 was electric convulsive shock therapy. This replaced insulin shock therapy that was harder to control and probably less effective. All shock treatments for male patients at the Institute took place on our ward. The patients came to the shock room and lay on their backs on a table with a padded top. The shock machine, a small black box about the size of a bread box, sat on a side table at the patient's head. Controls on the front of the machine allowed the doctor to adjust the amount of current that would flow and the duration of the shock. The current was minuscule and the time was in milliseconds. We fastened an adjustable band across the patient's forehead and around his head. The band held two metal electrodes about the size of silver dollars on each side of his head against his temples. We smeared the electrodes with a conductive jell and attached a wire to each one. The wires conducted the current from the machine.

The doctor gave the patients nothing to sedate them before their shock treatment. Most seemed extremely nervous while they waited their turns in a side room. With the patient on the table and hooked up to the shock machine four attendants stood at the sides. Two held the patient's arms and two held his legs to insure he did not fall off the table during his convulsions and that he did not sprain or break an arm or leg while flailing about.

Usually I was one of the attendants helping to restrain patients during shock. When everything was set the doctor said, "Ready" and pushed the button to trigger the shock. The patient immediately lost consciousness and went rigid from head to toe. After a few seconds grand mal seizure convulsions began. The seizure usually lasted about ten seconds then the patient slowly relaxed. We carried him to a bed where he rested for thirty minutes before returning to his own ward.

One day a newly hired attendant from Missouri was assisting with the therapy. He was holding one of the patient's legs. The doctor said, "Ready" and pushed the switch. The patient immediately lost consciousness and went rigid. The new attendant's face turned pale. He let go of the leg, jumped back from the table and shouted, "Mygawd doc, you done killed him!" By then the convulsions had started and the patient's free leg was threshing about. The doctor hollered, "Shutup and grab that leg!"

The range of medications available for patients in those days was limited. This was before most of the psychotropic drugs. There were some anti-convulsive medications available for patients with epilepsy and barbiturates were also available. A psychologist had recently joined the staff, but she had to devote most of her time to developing test information to help make a diagnosis. She did not have time for individual or group counseling. Her office was on the ward where I worked and since I hoped to do my graduate work in clinical psychology I tried to learn as much as possible from her about the testing patients.

Autopsy Up Close

In addition to the psychologist one of the physicians also made a special effort to explain things to me and often invited me to observe anything he thought might interest me. One day he asked me to sit in while he screened TB patients using a fluoroscope. I watched closely as he inspected their lungs on the screen. It was amazing to see beating hearts and breathing lungs. He pointed out the scarring done by the TB and compared it to previous screenings.

Another time he said he'd be doing an autopsy in the Institute's morgue. When I went to the morgue he was laying out a female patient who had died that morning. It was not clear what caused her death, but he wanted to find out. She had been an epileptic so he planned to do extensive biopsies of her brain.

He used a scalpel to cut across her forehead down to the bone and on around her head. With that done he began to pull her scalp away from her skull. It reminded me of someone peeling an orange. Now there was no skin or hair left above her eyebrows. He picked up a small electric saw and began cutting through the bone to remove the entire top of her head.

A doctor standing beside me who also was observing must have noticed that I was turning pale. "You planning to stay for this?" he asked.

I responded, "Yes, I hoped to, but now I believe I've changed my mind."

With that I turned and walked unsteadily outside to sit in the shade of a tree while the landscape slowly spun around me. After ten minutes or so I felt better, but I didn't go back. Instead I returned to the ward. Later the doctor who'd done the autopsy tried to assure me that feeling queasy is not uncommon even for medical students. He confided that he fainted dead away and fell to the floor at the first surgery he observed.

Some years later the Institute's morgue building became the Vocational Rehabilitation office when I worked as Chief of Mental Health Services for Voc Rehab. The supervisor of our Independence field office had his desk in the room where I witnessed the beginning of an autopsy. That gave me an odd feeling every time I called on him.

Patients Get Outside

Some of us college kids working at Independence for the summer noticed that the basketball hoop and volleyball court behind the Infirmary were never used. Mrs. MacArthur told me that ordinarily there wasn't enough staff available to take patients outside and supervise them. We asked the doctor in charge and received permission to take some of the patients outside. This was an exciting time for the patients since they rarely got outdoors. But I believe it was a stress-filled time for those of us who were to supervise them. "What if they decide to run away?" I thought and, "What if a patient gets hurt while playing volleyball or shooting hoops?" But we tried not to think about that as four or five of us took out about thirty patients for some sunshine, fresh air, exercise, and relaxation.

The transformation was amazing. Inside on the ward most of these people looked and acted like patients. They sat for hours at a time or walked listlessly up and down the hallway. They often conversed with the angry voices in their heads. Shortly after they got outside they seemed like normal human beings. They were attentive, conversed animatedly, and walked about purposefully. They even joked with one another as they played volleyball or basketball. When nobody tried to run away we all felt more comfortable and tried to find time to take the patients outside at least once a day.

Some of the college women working at the Institute for the summer asked to bring some of their patients outside at the same time as the men were outside. This request caused some of the regular staff to raise their eyebrows and warn, "The mingling of the sexes will create huge problems. You're just asking for trouble." But we did it and it seemed therapeutic for both the men and the women. Patients began looking forward to their outdoor recreational time and I like to think that maybe these short sessions outside helped their overall treatment.

My Folks Visit

My Mom, Dad, and sister came to Independence one weekend to visit me and to see what the Institution was like. On Saturday afternoon there was a softball game between some of the male patients and some of the male staff. We joined the small crowd of patients, staff, and visitors in the bleachers to watch the game. Neither team was skillful, but both teams were having fun and that was the main purpose of the game after all.

I noticed a patient sitting at the end of our row watched Pat, my sister, more than he watched the game. Every time I looked he had inched closer to her. When Pat finally became aware of his attention she was uncomfortable. Then when he was close enough to say "Hi," she became flustered. Ordinarily Pat was not a shy person, but since he was a mental patient she felt she might say the wrong thing and he'd go berserk. She didn't even trust herself to say, "Hi." We left the game shortly after that.

My mother and sister shared a room for the night at the nearby motel. We had an extra bed on our ward so I invited Dad to stay at the Institute with me. He accepted and at bedtime we went up to the ward. It was common to hear yelling and screaming from the nearby patient wards all hours of the day and night. I was used to this, but had forgotten how disturbing it had been the first few nights I lived there. It was frightening for my Dad. All night he worried that one or another of the angry sounding screamers might break out of their ward and come to do him bodily harm. The next morning my mother and sister looked refreshed after a good night's sleep, but Dad looked haggard. I believe they returned home with some idea what it's like in a mental institution.

Summer Ends With A Crash

In mid-September I began thinking about leaving the Institute. All except one of the other college students was gone. I could have stayed and worked as a permanent worker, but I thought I'd rather do other things. Tulane University turned down my application for their fall semester because it arrived after their deadline.

On September 20, 1948 I turned in my keys, said my goodbyes, and headed for Des Moines. It had been an exceptional summer loaded with fun as well as many new experiences. My time at the Institute confirmed for me that I wanted to go into clinical psychology.

It was raining when I turned onto the Marshalltown cut off, but visibility wasn't bad. After several miles I passed a car, but when I pulled back into my lane the outside wheels dropped off the pavement onto the soft shoulder. I lost control. The car flipped over going down the steep embankment throwing me out the driver's side door. I thought, "I've been thrown free." Just then that seemed a good thing, but when I came down my right heel hit the ground and flipped me back into the air. I spun around. Then as I flipped and spun across the ground several more times I remember thinking, "Will I ever stop bouncing?" When I did stop I was lying next to a fence.

I tried to stand up, but discovered my right ankle and my back both were extremely sore. Otherwise I detected no problems.

Several cars and a chartered bus had stopped. Two black men ran down the embankment. They hollered, "Are you all right?" They helped me up the embankment to the shoulder.

After a brief discussion they laid me down in the aisle on the bus. My ankle throbbed. I raised my head to look at it and saw it was twice its normal size. Surely it must be broken, I thought. As the bus headed toward Des Moines I asked one of the passengers, "What group is this?" They said they were Republicans heading to Des Moines for a rally. At least I was with the political party of my choice at that time.

At the junction a few miles down the road the bus stopped and a highway patrol officer came in. "How you feeling?" he asked. I told him, "Not too good."

He said he'd been back at my car and had taken all of my luggage, radio, and books out. They would be at the patrol headquarters when I wanted them. He'd also called for an ambulance. I thanked him.

The doctor in the Methodist Hospital emergency room smiled and said, "Well, first let's get your ear sewed back on. You may be around here for a while and I don't want to look at that dangling ear."

I didn't realize my ear was dangling. Apparently as I sailed out of the car my left ear caught on the door. She reattached it with a few well-placed stitches.

The x-rays of my ankle showed it was not broken, but was sprained. They bandaged it. The x-rays of my back didn't seem to show anything so they released me to go home.

The next morning the hospital phoned to say they had reviewed the x-rays of my back and wanted to take more. They thought there might be a problem. This time the x-rays clearly showed compression fractures of two of the lower vertebrae. Dr. F.

Eberly Thornton advised a full body cast. His assistants fitted me in a knitted woolen sleeve and suspended me face down between two tables. My shoulders and chin rested on the edge of one table while my thighs and knees rested on the edge of the second table. The doctor pushed down in the middle of my back to force it into a severe arch. They slopped plaster from my hips to my armpits to hold me in that position.

After what seemed like hours in this agonizing position the plaster began to set. They took me to a room and put me in bed with a couple of pillows under the small of my back. They assured me the plaster would be hard by morning. It was another miserable night. I hurt everywhere and the cast made it hard to breathe. When the plaster was dry an intern sawed out a hole the size of a dinner plate over my stomach to make breathing easier. The doctor sent me home feeling like a rigid, over weight, top-heavy monster – a monster that ached all over. It was hard to do anything but sit.

Chapter 15

INACTIVE INTERLUDE

Forced Inactivity

God always seems to allow some physical problem to occur to get my attention and force me to rethink the direction I am taking my life. Now I had a broken back and a heavily bandaged ankle. I couldn't be active and that forced me to think about my future. Doing graduate work in clinical psychology was not immediately possible. Perhaps I should think about other job possibilities.

WØDBR Logs Air Time

I was not yet ready to return to school or to begin work while wearing a body cast and hopping on a lame foot so I spent most of my time on the air. I received my amateur radio license the year before and was still excited about making contacts with other hams across the country. I set up my station in Pat's old dollhouse in the backyard. Dad built it solidly with enough headroom for an adult. It had four snug windows and a solid door. Insulation in the attic kept it cozy. All of my radio equipment, a bed, and a wood burning stove fit comfortably in the dollhouse. Most nights I slept there even during the winter.

One evening while listening to other hams on the 40-meter band I accidentally bumped my cigarette against the edge of the desk and knocked the burning end off. I looked for it on the floor, but when I couldn't see it I assumed it had gone out. I continued listening to the radio, but suddenly began to feel unnaturally warm around my middle. A little ribbon of smoke began to rise from the front of my body cast and my stomach was getting uncomfortably warm. The cotton and wool padding inside my cast was on fire! I hobbled for the house. I sloshed a glass of water down the opening in the front of the cast. Two more glasses of water and the fire was out. I pulled out the charred soggy cotton and wool and was grateful to find I didn't have any severe burns.

I continued to live in the cast until the last of November. It had been three months and the doctor thought it was time for it to come off. I lay on my stomach while he ran a small electric circular saw up and down my spine cutting into the cast. What a terrifying experience. The noise and vibration gave me cold shivers. What's more I hadn't seen a depth gauge on his saw so I expected he might break through the cast at any moment and cut into my spine. At last he turned off the saw and began breaking the cast apart so I could wiggle out of it. I felt like a chicken hatching out of its eggshell. As he helped me stand up my back felt like limp spaghetti. The doctor said that was normal and fitted me with a corset contraption to wear for the next two months. That support helped to stiffen my limp spaghetti spine. Without the plaster cast I could once again fit behind the wheel of a car.

Job Hunting

Now I needed a job. The lady at the State Employment Service office said she had two openings that might interest me. She sent me to see Donald Peacock Director of Personnel Services with the State Department of Social Welfare. Mr. Peacock looked over my resume and asked if I'd thought about working as a social welfare worker. I hadn't, but the way he explained it I thought it was something I could do. "I have two openings – one in Dickinson County and one in Marion County," he said. I decided to apply for the Marion County job since that was closer to Des Moines.

Social Welfare Office

The next day I drove to Knoxville and found the welfare office in the basement of the Courthouse. It smelled musty like most basements. In a disagreement with the Board of Supervisors the previous director had resigned and had persuaded all the social workers to leave with her. The Board hired Al Figgins to replace her and now he was actively recruiting the three social workers the office needed.

Mr. Figgins was a chubby, middle aged, jovial man with graying hair. Originally he was from the Afton, Iowa area, but most recently had been with the American Red Cross in the Army. His friendly manner made me feel at ease. As the interview progressed I felt that he was a man I'd enjoy fishing with and someone I'd like to work for. He hired me to begin as soon as possible. My wages were $125.00 per month plus a $25.00 a month cost of living increase.

I had a job and now I needed a place to live. Les Jelsma, the office manager, suggested that Irene Mott had a large house a few blocks southwest of the square. She took in roomers and just might have a vacancy. Les phoned her and she had a room available. I went down to see her, looked over the room, and rented it.

On December 1, 1948 I moved to Knoxville and began work as a social welfare worker. This was my first permanent full time job. The welfare office administered the ADC (Aid to Dependent Children) program, the OAA (Old Age Assistance) program, and the county General Relief program. Mr. Figgins assigned me the northern part of the county. That included Pleasantville, Pella, Harvey, and Swan. There were two other new social workers at that time Phyllis Somerville and Howard Spain. Phyllis and Howard served Knoxville as well as some of the other towns like Melcher-Dallas, Marysville, Pershing, Attica, and Bussey. In addition to Les Jelsma and Mr. Figgins the office had two secretaries.

Since wrecking my 1936 Plymouth in the accident coming back from Independence I did not have a car. But the county had a 1939 V-8 Ford assigned to the welfare office and I could use it for getting around my territory.

The Office Christmas Party

The month of December was rushing on toward Christmas. Mr. Figgins decided that the office should have a Christmas supper and party. In this way everyone could become better acquainted.

He made arrangements with a lady in town who opened her house for private parties. She would provide supper for the staff and her living room was available afterward for socializing. Each of us could bring a spouse or guest. I didn't take anyone.

The food and conversation was good and the evening seemed like a large family holiday celebration. Marguerite Knox one of the secretaries brought her roommate Gladys Courtney as her guest. Gladys worked in the sheriff's office in the courthouse. I don't recall talking much with her during the evening, but I thought Gladys was someone I'd like to get to know better.

In the days that followed I was absorbed with learning my job and my territory, however, once or twice I dropped into the Sheriff's office to talk with Gladys. My conversation focused on their two-way radio system. Among other things I wanted to know its frequency thinking I could monitor their conversations on my short wave receiver in my room. I also frequently saw Gladys eating lunch at the Little Cafe on the north side of the square. Several times I wanted to eat lunch with her, but she was always with two or three other women.

Finally one day in April I managed to talk with her alone long enough to ask her to go to a movie. She accepted and we saw "On A Sunday Afternoon." I enjoyed my time with her, but it was several weeks before we got together again. On many of our next dates we went to the river and fished. Some times Bob and Verna, older friends of Gladys, went with us. One night the fishing was so good that the four of us didn't want to leave. We boiled a pot of coffee over our fire and that helped keep us awake. Before we knew it the sun was coming up. We left and when we got to the courthouse square Gladys took the fish we'd caught across the courthouse lawn and handed them in through the window to the sheriff who already was at the office. He looked puzzled. We each hurried home, washed up, and got to work. Somehow we managed to stay awake until quitting time.

Those Wonderful People

As I covered my territory I met people that I really liked. Most were the sort of folks you wanted to get to know better and have as friends. Often when I called at a house to review the amount of assistance the client would need for the coming year I got so interested in visiting that I was reluctant to leave.

Many of these folks had been farmers during the Great Depression and had lost everything. When the economy improved they were too old to make a comeback. Now they were dependent upon an "old age pension." Most had the usual medical problems like high blood pressure, heart trouble, arthritis, diabetes, but seemed determined not to let health problems dominate their lives. Instead almost all of them maintained an active interest in their community, their neighbors, and their relatives.

Life on Iowa's farms and in small towns was new to me. It amazed me that everyone seemed to know everyone else. They knew how many kids each family had, where these kids were living now, and what problems the family might be having. Not only did everyone know all about everyone else in the community they genuinely cared about one other. This interest in one another's welfare leads neighbors to come and assist a sick or injured farmer with his fieldwork, harvesting, or chores when he's unable to do it.

Community oneness was even more cohesive in Pella. Immigrants from Holland settled this small town and they were determined to carry on their heritage and language. Some of my elderly clients had lived in this country all of their lives yet could not speak English. But it really wasn't necessary to know English to get along in Pella. It seemed to be a closed community and it did not readily welcome non-Dutch people. If a Pella boy or girl married someone who was not Dutch the community grudgingly accepted the spouse yet I heard of one Pella boy who married a non-Dutch woman and his church excommunicated him.

On the other hand I was an outsider, but I did not feel the businessmen I had contact with or the clients I saw made me feel any less welcome. While language was a problem with some of my older clients they seemed to know why I was there and we communicated adequately. Once or twice I asked Les Jelsma to act as an interpreter with a client when there were special problems.

I Meet Some Dirty Dutch

Most homes I visited in Pella were spotlessly clean, but there is a saying that, "You have not seen a truly dirty house until you see the house of a dirty Dutchman." One day one of my community contact people suggested I investigate a house where two sisters and their brother lived. All were elderly. The older sister, who had looked after all of them, was ill and the neighbors feared the other two were unable to care for her or to manage the household.

The clutter in their house astonished me. Newspapers were stacked waist high in every room. Narrow pathways between the stacks allowed you to shuffle from room to room. Clothes and rubbish littered the floor. Their beds were nothing more than piles of dirty clothes and rubbish. I don't know what they ate. There was no eatable food in the house. Mr. Figgins and I arranged to have the older sister hospitalized and the two younger siblings taken to the county home for care and keep. We went to court and petitioned to have a guardian appointed for all of them. Now I had seen a truly "dirty Dutch home."

We Find A Client Dead

Another time I accompanied a coworker to the old mining town of Pershing. We were investigating a report from a woman who said she had not seen her elderly neighbor for a day or two. She feared the neighbor might be ill. We went inside her small mining town company house where she lived alone and found the elderly client sitting on a high stool in front of a large wood burning cooking range. She had collapsed forward onto the top of the range resting her forehead and hands on the stove's cooking surface. The flesh on her forehead and hands had burned away exposing the bones. Because the stove now was cold we thought she'd probably been dead for a day or two. The autopsy determined she died of a heart attack.

It was lunch time when we returned to Knoxville, but neither of us had an appetite. The image of her burned head and hands remained with me for several weeks.

A Race With the Stork

One night when I returned to my rooming house after a fishing trip to the river I got a phone call from a local doctor saying that one of our clients was going into labor and needed to get to the hospital. Phyllis Somerville, her caseworker, had made arrangements for her to go to the University Hospitals at Iowa City for her delivery. Unfortunately the hospital's car would not pick her up until the following week. For some reason Phyllis was not able to take care of her case and asked for my help.

"Do you think she can make it to Iowa City?" I asked the doctor. He said he thought so, but I suspected he primarily wanted to shed all responsibility for her care. I grabbed a pair of scissors and some string just in case I had to cut and tie an umbilical cord somewhere between Knoxville and Iowa City. Her mother planned to go with her and I welcomed all of the support I could get. But in a crisis I wasn't convinced that the mother would be much help. She was mentally retarded, blind in one eye, and had poor vision in the other. I helped the mother and daughter into the back seat of the County Ford and we raced off for Iowa City 113 miles away.

It was about 10:00 at night and traffic on the highway was sparse. The Ford had a V-8 engine so I assumed it could go fast. We were running between 75 and 80 mph when the daughter began moaning. I stepped down harder on the throttle. The mother leaned over and squinted at the speedometer for several seconds with her one relatively good eye. "Wow! Ninety miles an hour. That's awfully fast!" Just then the daughter gave a more urgent moan. "But that's ok. Just keep going," the mother advised.

As we drove into Washington, Iowa, the daughter said she wanted to go to the bathroom. I wondered if that was a bad sign. She might have the baby right on the stool. Maybe I'll keep racing toward Iowa City. But the mother insisted that we stop so I reluctantly pulled into a service station. While mother and daughter were in the restroom I tried to think what I should do if she delivered in there. Shortly they both walked out and got in the car. Now we were off again with only thirty miles to go.

When we got to the hospital the daughter was moaning continuously and loudly. A nurse put her in a wheelchair, registered her in, and I left the mother and daughter to handle everything from then on. We had covered the 113 miles in 120 minutes with one rest stop. I collapsed into the Ford and drove back to Knoxville much slower. Later that day I learned the daughter delivered a healthy baby around 4:00 am that morning.

County Ford Hits The Race Track

Periodically the state Social Welfare Department brought staff together from county offices in our part of the state for a day of training. One day three of us from the Marion County office attended a training meeting in Centerville. After the morning's dry session we ate lunch with other social workers at a local restaurant, but the conversation over lunch was no less boring. After eating the three of us left the restaurant for a change of scenery to get our minds off the dry discussions of the morning.

Centerville is not a large town. We drove the County Ford leisurely through it to see whatever there was to see. At the Appanoose County Fair Grounds we drove around the far side of the grandstand and noticed that the gate to the racetrack was open. We interpreted this as a distinct invitation to drive onto the track. We saw no other vehicles on the track and we felt no one would care. We circled the oval at normal city street speed, but remembering how fast the Ford had gone on the Iowa City trip I stepped on the throttle. After all we were on a racetrack where speed is expected. The Ford leaped into action and we were making great time going into the first turn. I didn't know if I could control it should it start to slide and slowed down. Soon I got a better feel for driving the track and we went faster and faster. After several blazing laps we decided not to press our luck and ended our impromptu race. We declared the Marion county Ford the undisputed winner.

The afternoon's meeting was no less boring, but I believe the three of us smiled to ourselves every now and then when we recalled our one car dirt track race.

Chapter 16

COURTSHIP AND MARRIAGE

I Buy Some Yellow Wheels

I used the county Ford for official business, but had no car of my own. I looked for a used car and found one in my price range in Pella. It was a black 1936 Chevy with bright yellow wheels. The body was good and the upholstery not worn or dirty. An elderly couple previously owned it. The engine seemed sound. The only problem was it wouldn't start out in first gear. It had to start in second. I bought it for $250 and was glad to get my own transportation. Starting out in second gear was awkward at first, but I soon got used to it. You just gave it more gas and then let the clutch out ever so slowly. Other than first gear it ran well

Soon after I bought it I found a large Bible printed in Dutch under the driver's seat. I thought the former owners surely must miss it by now. The next time I was in Pella I looked them up and dropped it off. They hadn't remembered leaving it in the car, but were overjoyed to get their family Bible back.

It Gets Serious

Gladys and I dated regularly. We went fishing now and then, but usually went to Des Moines on Saturday nights to visit Mal and Barb Wagner, and Cart and Carolyn Hatch. Mal and Cart were high school and Drake buddies. I had been best man at Cart's wedding. Mostly we talked and listened to classical records. One of our group's favorites was George Enesco's Hungarian Rhapsody No. 1. Mal owned a recording by the Philadelphia Orchestra conducted by Eugene Ormandy. We particularly liked that rapid downward key change toward the middle of the piece and waited breathlessly for it. After listening to a piece of music we often described the scene or activity the piece triggered in our mind. Most of the images in our little game were predictable.

After an evening of conversation and music I drove Gladys to her parent's farm south of Pleasantville where she'd spend the rest of the weekend. Then I drove back to Des Moines and stayed with my folks until Sunday evening. I don't remember the first time I took Gladys home to meet my folks, but now and then we ate supper there.

I gradually decided Gladys was the girl I wanted to marry. I thought the Rose Garden at Greenwood Park in Des Moines would be an ideal place to propose. One June evening we were not in the Rose Garden, but were strolling in the city park on North First Street in Knoxville. We sat on a bench and talked a long time and then I proposed. Gladys said, "Yes," and we considered ourselves engaged. I didn't have money to buy a diamond ring so I did what fraternity guys do in college I "pinned" her. That is I gave her my Sig Ep fraternity pin. She wore it, but I don't believe that many of her friends at the courthouse understood the significance of a girl wearing a fraternity pin. And a Sig Ep pin is not the most romantic pin imaginable since it prominently displays a skull and cross bones.

A September Wedding

It was easy for us to agree on a September wedding. The difficult part was deciding what kind of wedding it would be. Gladys leaned toward eloping. That would simplify everything. Her sister Frances married Andy at the Little Brown Church in Nashua, Iowa. She didn't have to send out invitations or arrange a reception. I agreed we should be married in a church, but I thought immediate family should attend. In the end we agreed on a small ceremony at the Christian Church in Knoxville with immediate family and the people we worked with attending. We set the wedding for Saturday, September 10, 1949 at 8:00 am in the Christian Church with its pastor Rev. Pigg officiating.

On the morning of the wedding Irene Mott, my landlady, was determined I should not be late. She knocked on my bedroom door early in the morning and said breakfast would be ready in fifteen minutes. I washed, shaved, and dressed in a hurry, and then went down to breakfast. When I began to realize how special this day was I got nervous. I drove to the church. My folks and some of the office workers were arriving. Soon Gladys came by in her brother Marion's car. They hesitated briefly at the curb and then Gladys called out, "I've changed my mind." They drove off down the street. It turned out she was going to the bakery to pick up the wedding cake.

With everyone inside the church it seemed like a large gathering after all. Carter Hatch was my best man and Ardith Pink was Gladys' matron of honor. Gladys was dressed in a satiny golden tan dress. It seemed a perfect color for autumn. I wore my best suit.

I don't remember much about the ceremony itself, but I do remember when the pastor pronounced us husband and wife and said I could kiss the bride I did it with gusto. The reception with the cake gave the relatives from both sides a chance to get acquainted. Finally it was time for us to leave. As expected some of the guys had decorated my yellow-wheeled Chevy appropriately. It even trailed a long line of oilcans that Gladys' brothers got from the Shell station across the street. We headed north on Highway 14. Several people followed blowing their horns. When they turned back we pulled off on a side road and I undid the tin cans.

I had arranged to meet my folks in Des Moines and pick up their 1940 Dodge for our trip. It was more reliable than my Chevy. It seemed to me that we waited a long time before they arrived. They helped take the wedding presents to our apartment in Knoxville. With Gladys' folks and relatives they decorated the apartment. We weren't sure what to expect when we got home.

Our Honeymoon Trip

We left Des Moines traveling east on Highway 6. Neither of us had planned where we would go. Primarily we just wanted to be together. Where we might go was of secondary importance. By noon we reached Grinnel and ate lunch in a restaurant downtown. For our first meal as husband and wife I had spaghetti and Gladys had oysters

We drove on at a leisurely pace. When we got close to Iowa City it seemed a good idea to get a motel room for the night. The clerk at the Pines Motel in Coralville, Iowa, assigned us room number seven. We drove on into Iowa City and looked around the campus. Then we ate supper at one of the nearby hamburger places.

The next day we drove to Davenport, crossed into Illinois, and took the scenic river road north to Galena, Illinois. This old Mississippi River town was the home of General U.S. Grant. In the early days there had been many lead mines in the area. The style and age of most of the houses and buildings there was impressive. Several of the streets seemed like terraces carved into the hillside. Every few blocks a street ran up and down the hill to connect with the terraced streets. We stayed in a tourist cabin a short way out of town.

The following day we drove around the area and eventually crossed back into Iowa. As we approached Dyersville with its impressive twin spired Catholic Church the sun broke out of the clouds for the first since we'd been married.

Late that afternoon we arrived at our apartment in Knoxville. It was on the second floor of a large house on Montgomery Street. The McConvilles owned the house and lived on the first floor. Our apartment had its own entrance and stairway. We both were anxious to see what our relatives had done to our place to welcome us home. We were pleased to see they hadn't done any real damage. They draped our clothing, towels, and books over the furniture to create a cluttered look. Further we found that for the next several weeks it was hard to get into our clothes because they had sewed the sleeves shut.

We Adjust To Marriage

Now we were married and began housekeeping in our own apartment with its living room, bedroom, kitchen, bathroom, and closets. It was comfortable and it was ours to share. We found that a major part of marriage involved learning to share our space and our lives with one another. While it is immensely satisfying to be living with someone you love it is also necessary to have time for yourself. Each person in a marriage needs to sense when closeness is desirable and when the other person needs a little space.

I don't believe we ever had any arguments about that, but I do remember one of our first disagreements. It didn't involve a heated exchange of harsh words. It was more like a teasing that simply got out of hand. One Saturday afternoon we were in the kitchen washing dishes. I was drying and kept singing "Rag Mop" a novelty song that was popular at that time. Gladys didn't like the song and repeatedly told me to stop. Finally she told me to stop and gave me a shove. I stumbled back into the window and broke it. That stopped "Rag Mop," but I had a new problem.

It was cold outside so we couldn't leave the window without glass. I measured the opening and bought a new pane. Fortunately the window was above the roof of the back porch so I didn't need a ladder to reach it from the outside. I simply climbed out the window onto the porch roof and puttied in the new glass. From this experience I learned Gladys will take just so much and then she'll likely boot you out a window.

The Police Chief Cuffs Us

Since we both worked at the courthouse our hours were the same. We drove back and forth to work in our 1936 Chevy. When I was in town we ate lunch together at the Little Cafe across the street from the courthouse. Usually the same crowd was there each noon. Andy Rickett, the Chief of the Knoxville Police Department, was one of the regulars. Shortly after our marriage Andy decided to *really* tie us together. One noon he came slyly to our table and quickly cuffed us together. The noon crowd applauded. After we finished lunch he escorted us across the street and into the courthouse still cuffed together. He made it look like he had just arrested Bonnie and Clyde. This provided grand entertainment for everyone on the square that day. He led us to the Sheriff's office where there was a brief discussion about which jail cell to put us in. Andy eventually unlocked the cuffs and let us go, but not before we promised to be on our best behavior forever after.

A House Of Our Own

We settled comfortably into our apartment. With our private entrance and stairway we rarely saw the McConvilles or their children, but we heard them often enough to remind us we were not alone in the house. Just knowing other people lived below us inhibited our laughing, talking, and turning the radio very loud. In the spring we began thinking about a house of our own.

Our resolve to find a house intensified after a doctor's visit confirmed that Gladys was pregnant. We were to be parents! It was a wonderful feeling coupled with a sense that now I surely must settle down, work hard, and prepare to assume the responsibilities of being a father. Neither of us wanted to continue living in an apartment with a baby. We wanted our son or daughter to have their own grassy yard to play in with a swing set and a sand box.

We found a house for rent on north First Street. It was directly across the street from the city park where I'd proposed to Gladys. That alone scored several points in its favor. Mr. Lark the owner had moved out and was building a new house for himself next door. The house was an old one-story place with two bedrooms, living room, dining room, kitchen, bath, and attached storage room and storm cellar. It had a large garden with red raspberry bushes and strawberries.

Gladys' family helped us move from Montgomery Street. Her mother and sister laid new linoleum in the living room. After about two weeks we had settled into our new house. It was wonderful to be in a place by ourselves where we could talk, laugh, and play the radio without disturbing downstairs neighbors. The thought that soon there'd be three of us living there buoyed me up considerably.

Gladys Leaves The Sheriff's Office
Gladys' delivery date was sometime in mid December. She planned to work through September. Meanwhile she grew larger so that getting up and down or bending over was increasingly difficult. But we managed to get out some on the weekends and we tended our large garden in the backyard. When I picked her up after her last day of work she was sad and teary eyed over leaving her job with Sheriff VanHemert. He was a good man to work for and she'd liked her job. Now she had to look forward to the hard job of giving birth and becoming a stay at home mother. It would be a transition for both of us.

One day Gladys phoned to say that she could feel contractions and thought it was time to make the trip to the hospital in Oskaloosa 35 miles away. She phoned Dr. Ralston her physician and found he already was at the hospital. His office planned to let him know Gladys was on her way.

I left work and we headed for Oskaloosa. It was a sunny day with no snow or ice on the road. I drove our old Chevy at the speed limit, but really could have pushed it much faster if necessary. I'd heard it often takes hours to deliver especially with first pregnancies so I believed there was no reason to hurry. A nurse admitted Gladys to the hospital and Dr. Ralston examined her. After a couple of hours without further activity he decided this had been "false labor." He felt certain that Gladys wasn't going to deliver today. We drove back to Knoxville.

A Wintry Race With The Stork
Ten days later around 4:00 o'clock in the morning of December 6, 1950 Gladys woke me and said she was sure she was in labor. She'd had contractions for the last two hours, but didn't want to wake me up until she was certain.

The weather was much colder and it had been snowing for about 24 hours. Our old Chevy was a bit cranky in cold weather so the first thing I did was try to start it. It refused. I phoned Dr. Ralston and was relieved he was at home and not at the hospital in Oskaloosa. He said he would come down to pick us up. He drove a big Buick that he kept it in his heated garage. It'd be warm for the trip.

As we left for Oskaloosa it was still snowing. The road was covered and there were no other tracks on the highway. The big Buick was breaking the trail. Gladys and I were in the back seat where I was trying to make her as comfortable as possible. As we blew past Tracy her contractions were coming every two minutes. The snow lay in an unbroken layer across the shoulders and roadway. It was falling fast and blew in huge sparkly waves in front of the headlights. There were times I wondered how Doc kept us on the road. "The power from above is looking after us," he said. "I often feel God is protecting me and this is one of those times." Finally we reached Oskaloosa safely and wheeled up to the emergency entrance at the hospital. Gladys got into a wheelchair and out of the storm.

After Gladys was given a sedative Dr. Ralston took me aside and said, "I didn't want to mention this in front of Gladys for fear of alarming her, but the baby's going to be breech." I wasn't sure what a breech birth was, but it sounded ominous.

The nurses wheeled her away to prepare for the delivery. Dr. Ralston said that I should come with him. He washed up and got into his hospital clothes. He said I would go into the delivery room with him and stay for the delivery. The nurse cautioned me, however, that should I feel dizzy and want to leave I should sit down in the hallway outside and not try to go downstairs. They had a stool for me at Gladys' head. A large mirror hung on the wall over the doctor's shoulders. This gave me a view of everything as it happened.

The doctor began working and explained what he was doing. At one point he made some small cuts and said that would lessen the possibility of tearing. Afterward he could sew it back together so it would heal faster. Soon the baby's bottom was showing. He explained that from now on he must work fast since the cold air on the baby might cause it to take its first breath. Until its head was outside it would breathe in liquid and not air. That was not a good thing. He reached in around the hips and pulled out the bottom and legs. Then reaching back in he put his fingers in the baby's mouth, drew its chin down, and quickly pulled out one shoulder at a time. Finally he pulled out the head. The baby had arrived and began crying loudly. We had a baby daughter! Tears flowed down my face I felt elated. Emily Lou our first child weighed 8 pounds, 4 ounces. It was now about 8:00 o'clock in the morning.

Now We Are Three

The nurses cleaned up Gladys and Emily. In a few minutes I saw them both in the room. The three of us together gave me the satisfying feeling that our family was becoming complete. It seemed miraculous that we got through the storm safely to the hospital and even though it was a problem delivery nothing had gone wrong. In a silent prayer I thanked God for preserving Gladys and for blessing us with a healthy daughter.

Back in Knoxville I gave the good news to everyone at the welfare office and at the sheriff's office. Later I remember walking home from the courthouse. The snow on First Street was deep and now it was colder. My shoes made a familiar and reassuring crunch, crunch, crunch sound in the snow as I hurried along. The house seemed terribly empty. Suddenly I was exhausted.

The next day my folks phoned that they were going down to Oskaloosa to visit Gladys. Later they phoned me at the office saying they had car trouble and had stalled at the edge of Prairie City. Dad said he was almost certain the fuel pump had gone out. So I picked up a new fuel pump in Knoxville, loaded in my toolbox, and drove to Prairie City. In a short while Dad and I installed the new fuel pump and we all headed to the hospital.

When Gladys was ready to come home from the hospital our old 1936 Chevy was running. I drove it ever so carefully coming home from Oskaloosa. Now with Emily as a passenger I felt the responsibility of driving safely more keenly than ever before.

When we arrived home Gladys' parents, brothers, and sister were waiting to see Emily. Everyone was excited. Walter and Ada seemed pleased to have a third grand daughter. It had been several years since their oldest son, Jerd and his wife Ethel, had their youngest daughter Peggy. After a while Emily became hungry and when Gladys sat down and prepared to feed her I pulled up a chair to watch. I sensed the family thought watching Gladys breast feed our daughter was inappropriate. That embarrassed me and I moved away.

Ada stayed for about a week. It was reassuring to have an experienced mother in the house to look after Gladys and Emily. Follow up examinations with Dr. Ralston confirmed they both were getting along nicely. I felt I had survived, too.

The birth of the first child triggers many changes in a household's routine, but they weren't nearly as onerous as I'd expected. Of course I didn't have to get up several times each night to feed Emily nor was I around most of the day to bathe, dress, change, and feed her. Certainly Gladys was the one who made most of the changes. I thought she quickly become a competent mother.

Work for me went on at the welfare office much like before, but I felt I should be advancing both in responsibility and in pay. I had worked there two years. I knew my territory, caseload, and programs. The added responsibility of a daughter may have heightened my desire to earn more money. I got a chance to advance to casework supervisor and passed the Merit System exam for that classification. Mr. Figgins my boss secured approval from the board of supervisors and reassigned me at that pay level. I began supervision of the three social workers we now had. I liked this work and felt I was a competent supervisor.

Emily continued to grow and develop. In addition to seeing her develop the physical skills necessary for sitting up, walking, and talking, it was amazing to see the infant Emily gradually grow into an individual with her own distinct personality. We often spent weekends visiting my folks in Des Moines. Twice we went on vacation with them once to Chicago and once to Minnesota. In retrospect I believe it was a mistake for us to visit them as often as we did. Even at the time we were doing it I felt uncomfortable. By spending so many weekends with them I felt we were limiting our opportunities to get acquainted with people our own age in Knoxville. What's more it limited the time for just the three of us to be together as a family. We often spent Sundays with Gladys' folks, brothers, sister, brother-in-law, and sisters-in-law on the farm. I enjoyed this immensely for here I was a member of a large close knit family. That was a new and gratifying experience for me. Unfortunately we did not spend as much time on the farm as we did in Des Moines.

We Buy A House

Our house on First Street was comfortable and I was happy there. But it was old, was deteriorating, and gave us many problems. Most of all it was hard for me to pay rent each month knowing we were not accumulating equity in anything. We discussed buying a house. I had inherited $1,000 from Uncle Ernest and Gladys had a small savings account. We wondered if we had enough for a down payment. Sherwood Reality talked with us and he showed us several houses. One of them was a small two-bedroom place on a corner lot. We both liked it and signed papers to buy it on contract. In the fall of 1954 Gladys' family hauled our stuff and helped us move into our new house. I believe we both were thrilled to be living in a house we might eventually own.

Chapter 17

JOB SEARCH AND CAREER CHANGE

I had worked in the Marion County welfare office for about five years. I liked most aspects of the job and my boss and coworkers were wonderful people. But somehow I wanted a job that offered an opportunity for further advancement. I had gone as far as I could in that office unless Mr. Figgins the director were to retire. That was not likely for several years.

I was interested in art – cartooning in particular. In my desperation to get started in this field I entered the "Draw Me" contest sponsored by the Art Instruction Company. Their "Draw Me" ads ran in most of the popular magazines in those days. Some time after I'd mailed in my drawing a representative of the company dropped by and discussed their correspondence course. My entry hadn't won a free scholarship, but after giving it some thought Gladys and I decided it might be worthwhile to buy the course. It cost about $200 that we didn't have. I went to the bank and talked with Eldon Job about a loan. Mr. Job the bank's president was in his usual black suit, white shirt, and plain necktie. He rarely smiled and his demeanor seemed to reflect his no-nonsense view of life.

I felt uncomfortable asking to borrow money, especially from the formidable Mr. Job.

"I'd like to borrow $200," I said.

"What do you want the money for?"

"I need it for some special training I'd like to take," I explained.

That was not good enough and he pressed me. "What kind of special training?" I didn't want to tell him it was an art course by correspondence since I feared he'd think that was a frivolous use of time and money.

After I gave a couple more vague replies it became apparent that he would not consider making the loan unless he knew exactly what I intended to do with the money. I finally told him that I wanted to take the Art Instruction correspondence course. To my surprise and relief he granted me the loan, shook my hand, wished me the best of luck, and I believe he even gave me a rare smile.

In a few weeks a drawing board, T-square, triangles, pens, pencils, paper, ink, and the first lesson book came in the mail. My enthusiasm carried me through the first few assignments rapidly. I completed a lesson, mail it, and after a short time the instructor returned it with notes, suggestions, and criticisms.

One day when I was in Des Moines I stopped at the Meredith Publishing art department to get their opinion of the Art Instruction correspondence course as preparatory training for working in their department. Two of the people there seemed to feel it might be helpful. That was encouraging and we talked further. Next they introduced me to Maynard Reese the wild life illustrator. He was a nationally know artist and we talked briefly. He, too, seemed to feel that the course might be useful. I left this meeting feeling elated and vowed to work diligently at my art. As it turned out, however, my interest waned over the months and I gradually stopped sending in my lessons. To successfully complete a correspondence course of any kind requires tremendous discipline, drive, and focus. Unfortunately I was deficient in such qualities at this time in my life.

In my efforts to improve my job opportunities I took the Merit System exam for Welfare Director IV. Such directors worked in smaller Iowa counties. I passed the exam and placed on the list of available candidates. The starting pay was about the same as my casework supervisor pay, but it had a higher top end. Openings did not occur often, but I did get an interview with the board in

Audubon County. I was not favorably impressed with them and apparently they were not impressed with me since I never heard from them.

Mal Wagner my old high school and college buddy worked at Employer's Mutual Insurance Company in Des Moines. One day he phoned to let me know there might be an opening coming up in their personnel office. I arranged an interview, but once more I was not impressed with what they described and nothing further came of it.

I'm Asked A Blunt Question

Dow Armstrong the Voc Rehab counselor who served our part of the state stopped by the welfare office periodically to discuss any disabled clients we wanted to refer for service. Often we had a client to refer for job counseling, possible job training, and selective job placement. After discussing the clients Dow usually called on them to offer them a chance to apply for services.

One day after Dow and I discussed the clients I wanted to refer he pushed back from my desk and said, "Are you going to do this kind of work the rest of your life?"

His abrupt question startled me, but I answered that I didn't intend to and had been searching for other opportunities. He said, "How'd you like to work for Voc Rehab?"

I answered that from what I knew about the agency, it just might be the kind of thing I was looking for. He said I should phone Howard Benshoof the director for an interview as soon as possible. He gave me some literature so I could familiarize myself with some of the services the agency offered. He also said that if Howard offered me a job he'd probably offer a starting annual wage of about $2,500. He advised me not to accept that, but to hold out for $3,600. I was excited since $3,600 was twice what I earned at the welfare office.

Howard Benshoof's office in the old Bankers' Trust Building had been the operating room when that suite was the medical office of Drs. Pierson and Snyder years earlier. I had awakened in this room after having my tonsils taken out at age five. I remembered how sore my throat felt. Although wood paneling now covered the white tile walls the small white tiles of the floor were unchanged. I even imagined the odor of ether remained in the room.

Even though the room held unpleasant memories for me I thought the interview went well. Mr. Benshoof offered me a job at the lower salary Dow warned me about. I held out for more and he offered me $3,600. I accepted and we agreed I would begin work on December 1, 1954. I was thrilled thinking about the new, more challenging job, and the higher salary. I believe Gladys was excited, too. At least I hoped she shared my enthusiasm.

I Begin With Voc Rehab

The first few weeks with Voc Rehab was considered an orientation period. Mario Barillas began work as a psychologist the same day as I did. We were given space in a spare room where we were to study operations manuals, case files, forms, and anything else the director thought might be useful. Whenever any of the supervisors had free time they dropped by to discuss the work, but I believe I learned as much from the informal coffee break discussions with the Des Moines area counselors.

I was to work out of the Des Moines District office and would commute from Knoxville. My territory was an eleven county area north, east, and south of Des Moines. This included Marshall, Jasper, Poweshiek, Marion, Mahaska, Keokuk, Monroe, Wapello, Jefferson, Davis, and Van Buren counties. Tony Daminani the previous counselor had been gone several months and there were over 200 cases needing attention. On a typical week I was to be in the Des Moines office on Monday then leave home Tuesday morning to work my caseload in the territory not returning home until Friday afternoon.

This required a major adjustment for Gladys as well as for me. It was the middle of the winter and we heated our house with a hand fired coal furnace in the basement. She had to shovel coal and haul out ashes. Also she had to shovel snow as well as take care of herself, the house, and Emily now an energetic four year old. To complicate matters Gladys had no way to get around town when I was on the road with our car. On top of all of this she was pregnant and due to deliver in March. Fortunately a new district office would open in Ottumwa by June or July with Dow Armstrong as supervisor. We would have to move to Ottumwa, but I would serve a smaller territory from that office and would not be away from home overnight as often.

After a month of orientation Tommy Thomsen the Des Moines District Supervisor asked me to go through the caseload and plan a four day itinerary to meet with as many of the clients as possible and to cover as much of eleven county territory as feasible. We left Des Moines on a snowy Tuesday morning in my Chevy. During our four-day road trip we worked with many clients, met with state employment service office staff, and contacted social welfare office personnel. We stayed overnight in Marshalltown, Grinnell, and Ottumwa. The roads were snowy all week, but we were stuck only once and that was in a client's driveway. Late Friday afternoon I was glad to drop Tommy off in Des Moines and head home to Knoxville. Since everything about the work, the clients, and the territory had been so new and different the week was especially stressful. Driving on the snowy roads while trying to keep on schedule added to my stress.

After that week with my supervisor I was on my own. I set up appointments with the clients I wanted to see, made hotel reservations, and handled correspondence related to the casework. I wrote case notes in the field books during the evening in the motel after meeting with the clients during the day. Our secretaries transcribed my notes into the case files while I was in the district office on Mondays. I'd also submit the plans worked out with the client for their rehabilitation. Voc Rehab authorized all funding needed by the client for tuition, supplies, etc., at that time.

All field counselors developed their travel itineraries at least three weeks in advance listing the towns they would be in and the clients they planned to see. They also listed other resource people, such as employers, they would contact, and where the counselor would stay over night. This was a helpful planning tool for the counselor and it allowed the home office to know where he could be found if the need arose. Of course winter storms sometimes made the roads treacherous and fouled up the schedule. But they followed their itineraries as closely as possible.

As the winter of 1954-55 drew to a close it was important that my office and Gladys know where to find me. She was due to deliver in March. As the time got closer I became more anxious, made an extra effort to let everyone know where I'd be, and I frequently checked in by phone. Whenever I was in a client's home or in a resource person's office and heard a phone ring I expected it to be Gladys saying she had gone into labor.

Then There Were Four

When Gladys did go into labor it was a Monday morning before I left home for work. So there was no problem trying to locate me somewhere in my territory. We both were grateful I was at home.

Dr. Ralston was to deliver Gladys again, but this time he was using the Mater Hospital in Knoxville. This meant we didn't have to make a dash for Oskaloosa as we had for Emily's birth. Nor did we have to battle through a snowstorm. It was a mild spring day. The grass was green already and we'd had a thunderstorm that morning. We drove the few blocks to the hospital and Gladys checked in. I was to stay with her during delivery, but not in the same room. There was a seat for me in the hallway where I could observe some of what was going on.

It didn't seem to take long before Cynthia Ann was born weighing 5 pounds, 4 ounces. The thrill of being there when my second child was born was an awesome experience. Once again I choked up and tears of joy flooded down my face. I silently thanked God for His kindness in giving us a healthy child and for preserving Gladys through the delivery.

Cindy was born on March 14th. This was also Elizabeth Courtney's birthday. She was Gladys' paternal grandmother. It didn't strike me at the time, but it would have been appropriate to name Cindy, Elizabeth – at least as a middle name. I'm sure it would have made grandma Courtney very happy. But again I was insensitive to the feelings of others and I still regret we did not do that.

The three or four days that Gladys and Cindy stayed in the hospital following her delivery were not happy days for Gladys. This was Dr. Mater's hospital and she observed that the staff treated Dr. Ralston's patients poorly and made remarks that upset her so much that she felt she would be unable to nurse Cindy properly. I felt much better after she came home where Ada could take care of her and Cynthia.

We tried to prepare Emily for the arrival of a brother or sister and now we tried not to neglect her or to make her feel that she must take a back seat because of the attention given the new arrival. I don't believe Emily resented her baby sister and we were a family – a family of four.

At this stage in my life I began to face a question that millions of other men probably have tried to answer. "How can I be an energetic, upwardly mobile employee, striving to establish a career, while at the same time be a strong, nurturing, father to my children, and a caring, loving husband to my wife?"

In addition a man most likely is a son, a brother, an uncle, and a neighbor. These roles also entail duties. Certainly the many responsibilities we all carry are not mutually exclusive. It is possible to be an energetic employee, a nurturing father, and a caring husband all at the same time. It seems to me that it's a matter of balancing ones energy among these many roles. A man must not focus on his career responsibilities, for example, so intensely that he neglects family responsibilities. Neither should be spend so much of this time and energy on his family that his career suffers and he ultimately loses his job or fails to advance.

This concerned me as our family grew and as I tried to advance my career. I did not develop any wisdom-laden guidelines then nor have I since been able to arrive at any clear-cut ideas. But I have tried to remain sensitive to my various roles and have tried to give proper energy to each of them. I was not always successful.

Plans For A District Office

Voc Rehab planned to serve most of my territory from a new district office in Ottumwa. Dow Armstrong served counties to the west of my territory and also would work as the district supervisor.

These plans now moved forward and the Ottumwa office would open in July or August 1955. We put our Knoxville house up for sale and in a few days we had a buyer who was willing to pay our price, but wanted possession sooner than we'd intended. Certainly we didn't want to move out until we had a place to move into in Ottumwa. Yet the price was much more than we thought we'd be able to get. Actually we were selling the contract we had with Sutherlands and making a good profit at it. In the end we accepted the offer and began making plans to move out. We arranged for the Mayflower movers in Ottumwa to take our stuff to Ottumwa and put it in storage.

We took what clothes we needed and moved in with Ada, Gladys' mother, in Pleasantville. From here I commuted into my territory. It seemed to me that every house in Ottumwa was for sale. Several real estate agents showed me houses, but none seemed suitable. I became desperate. Even though we paid Ada

$40.00 a month to live there and bought most of the groceries we did not want to impose upon her hospitality any longer than necessary. Further my commute into the territory was tiresome.

The Ottumwa District Office opened. Now instead of working out of Des Moines I was to work out of Ottumwa where my case files and desk were located. The office was on the second floor of the Medical Arts building downtown. With no elevator it was not accessible to people with ambulatory disabilities, but Howard Benshoof the agency's director thought that we could go downstairs to meet with anyone who was unable to climb the stairs. I thought his solution was ludicrous.

Our suite on the second floor had been a dentist's office. The x-ray equipment had been in my room. Because of that my office was probably the only counselor's office in the state shielded by lead from radiation. Now that we had an office the agency encouraged me to move to Ottumwa as soon as possible. The agency reimbursed me for my hotel, travel, and meals when I stayed overnight in Ottumwa, but soon discontinued that. That added additional pressure to find housing quickly.

The Naval Air Base Becomes Home

Since we were unable to find a house to buy or rent and the agency made it clear I should get to Ottumwa without delay we looked at an apartment in the hospital building at the old Naval Air Station. This World War II airbase trained Navy pilots. The landing strips and operations building were now the municipal airport for Ottumwa. Private aircraft owners rented most of the hanger space. Boards covered the windows and doors of the other buildings not in use. One exception was the former base hospital. The Good Samaritan Nursing Home used it for patients, but rented a few rooms as apartments.

The rehab office secretary lived there with her two children and she suggested this might be a place for us until we found more permanent housing. We checked it out with Mr. Shore the administrator and decided it was the best we could do just then.

Since we intended to move as soon as we could find a more suitable place we thought we could make do with some of its inconveniences. We had our essential furniture delivered from storage and finally we became residents of Ottumwa although the base was five miles out of town.

We weren't able to find an existing house in Ottumwa that suited us so we considered Housing Plan B – build a new house. Mr. Long one of the real estate agents we worked with suggested we look at lots a homebuilder named Swartz was developing on the north edge of Ottumwa. If we liked the development we could have him build the type of house we wanted. The lots were along the two blocks on the north end of Marilyn Road. Houses built on the two blocks at the south end of the road had been there long enough for the grass, shrubbery, and trees to be established. They looked nice. The school district planned to build an elementary school near the middle of this four-block street. A grocery store was about six biocks away and a church about eight blocks. I could be downtown to the office in no more than five minutes. Everything about the area seemed positive.

We selected a lot and looked through house plans wherever we found them. Finally we found plans for a two-bedroom house that suited both of us. We ordered these plans and gave them to Mr. Swartz for a cost estimate. His estimate seemed within our capability and we had papers drawn up so work could begin. Gladys and I saved money by becoming the subcontractor for all of the painting and varnishing of the house inside and outside. We would buy the materials and do the work. The only exception was we would not finish and varnish the hardwood floors. The house and lot cost \$10,500 less \$1,500 credit for our painting work.

A House Begins To Grow

On March 1, 1956 only a few patches of wilted snow remained among the weeds on our lot and the frost was less than an inch deep. A bulldozer began to dig the basement. It was a grand feeling to see the beginnings of our house. Over the next few days the workers poured the footings and the cement block foundation began to take shape. Each day that I was in Ottumwa I stopped to look at the building site as I went home to the Air base. It didn't take long before the framing was finished and they closed the house to the weather. Before the roof was finished we had a snowstorm. Fortunately it was not one of those furious March storms with several inches of snow. The little snow that fell melted quickly. It did not hinder the work nor did it damage the exposed wood.

The Painting Subcontractor Begins Work

Soon enough of the house was finished so that we had work to do. Now we had to stain the cedar shakes covering the outside a barn red. We had to paint the window trim and other outside trim white. I began painting mostly on the weekends. Emily now five years old wanted to help. We gave her a can of stain and a brush so that she could stain all the shakes she could reach. I quickly discovered how satisfying it is to have your child working at your side. It didn't matter whether she stained a lot of shakes. Just working together was satisfaction enough. As it turned out even at five years old Emily was a good painter. She worked diligently, and stained a lot of cedar shakes.

When we'd finished the outside painting and staining we began on the inside. We had to varnish all the windows, doors, woodwork, and built in bookcases. We'd specified that all of the walls were to be plastered with tinted plaster so they did not need to be painted. The varnishing was slow work, but Gladys and I worked as rapidly as we could.

One Sunday afternoon Frances and Andy, Gladys' sister and brother in law, drove down to help us with the varnish. Both were experienced painters and they accomplished a lot that day. We were glad for their help.

That Famous DC -3 Vs. Dodge Race

Dad decided to take a week's vacation to come down and help us. But the plan was not that simple. First we were to take Emily to Des Moines where she would spend a week visiting my folks. At the end of the week Dad and Emily were to fly down to Ottumwa. Dad would spend the week working at the house and we'd drive him back to Des Moines the following weekend.

We delivered Emily to Des Moines. During the week we went on with our usual responsibilities while Emily enjoyed all of the attention and treats her grandparents gave her. On Saturday morning my mother delivered Dad and Emily to the Des Moines Airport so they could catch their flight on an Ozark DC-3 airliner. At the scheduled time Gladys, Cindy, and I went to the Ottumwa Airport to meet their plane. We were anxious to hear what Emily thought of her first airplane ride.

When we heard the plane slipping down for a landing we walked to the passenger gate. It was then I heard someone's heels clicking rapidly on the terrazzo floor as they ran across the terminal lobby. We turned around and were stunned to see my mother racing toward us so she could meet the plane, too. After she delivered Dad and Emily to their plane in Des Moines she decided she wanted to spend the day with all of us. She had driven their 1953 Dodge from Des Moines to Ottumwa and arrived at the same time as the plane. She would never divulge how fast she had driven.

Dad stayed at the house all day and worked. After I got off work I took him out to our apartment at the base for supper. Then back to the house where he spent the night. During that week he finished all of our subcontracted work. The house was nearly ready for us to move in.

When the contractor finished his work the Mayflower Moving Company hauled what we had in the apartment at the Air base to the house and delivered the rest of our stuff from storage. Finally all of our possessions were in one place and we were living in Ottumwa in a house that suited us just fine. Over the next several months Gladys began making the house a home. I worked on the outside. I planted grass seed and we contracted for some trees and shrubbery. Gradually the place began to look and feel more like home. I was not on the road overnight all week like before and had more time for working around home and enjoying Emily and Cindy.

Emily Begins School

Emily was to begin school the following fall. Work on the new school on Marilyn Road had not started so she would attend a rural school building two blocks from home. That building housed all eight grades. The summer before she was to begin school we bought her a bike so that she'd have transportation if necessary. She learned to ride, but I don't recall that she used it for going back and forth the short distance to school.

Cindy was now an active youngster. There were several other children in the neighborhood for our girls to play with. It was a source of continual wonder and satisfaction to me to see how both girls grew physically and intellectually.

Our Life In Ottumwa

In the five years we lived in Ottumwa I believe we thrived as a family, but we didn't put down roots there or become involved in the community. We didn't attend church or socialize with anyone in town nor were we involved with the school PTA or any civic club or group. Of course we knew our immediate neighbors and often talked with them, but that was the extent of our socializing. Although my office was in Ottumwa my work was primarily in the surrounding counties. I was better acquainted with some of the people in these counties than I was with people in Ottumwa. Our major activities were with our family. We went rock hunting, camping, and very often went downtown to the public library together.

Chapter 18

ROCK HOUNDS AND CAMPERS

When we lived in Ottumwa we got interested in rock hunting. Several local sandbars on the Des Moines River were productive spots for agate hunting. And once Gladys found a well-shaped arrowhead. We also discovered a place along the river near Eldon where quartz crystals lined the fissures and cracks in limestone rocks. But our most fruitful searches were in the gravel pits near Muscatine. Usually we came home with at least a small bag of keep-able rocks. We washed them and stored them in coffee cans hoping some day to work them into jewelry.

Finally we thought we could afford a small lapidary machine. We'd heard of a rock hound supply store in New London, Iowa, and planned a Saturday excursion to check it out. We packed a picnic lunch and set out, but before going to the store we drove to nearby Geode State Park to explore. Certainly with a name like that it ought to be a good place to look for geodes. We walked along some of the trails and trooped out across brushy, rocky, and wooded areas where there were no trails. Nowhere could we find a geode. At noon we ate our lunch then went to the rock hound store.

The store was awesome. They displayed equipment for doing rock cutting, drilling, faceting, or polishing. The store also had a large collection of fossils, geodes, agates, and other semiprecious stones.

We wandered around the store looking at everything and picking up rock-hounding tips from the owner. One showcase held a large collection of rattlesnake rattles. I asked, "Where did you get all of these?"

"They all came from rattlesnakes people killed in Geode State Park," the owner replied. "That place is full of rattlers. Awesome, aren't they?"

Gladys and I looked at each other and shuddered as we thought how we'd been stomping through a park full of rattlers with our two girls.

We Become Lapidary Workers

We selected a small machine with a four-inch diameter diamond saw, two four-inch grinding wheels, and a buffing wheel mounted on one spindle. As we drove back to Ottumwa I believe we all were excited thinking about how much fun we'd have using our new lapidary machine. I believe that Gladys and I were also thankful none of us had stumbled across a rattler in the park.

In the weeks and months that followed we began to learn how to cut and polish our rocks. We sat the machine on a workbench in the basement. Working on it became a family affair. We began cutting and polishing our stones into cabochons. Emily could easily reach the grinding and polishing wheels, but Cindy was not tall enough. She pulled up a chair to stand on and it was gratifying to see she did good work at her age. We visited the rock shop in New London many times for supplies and to sort over the specimens they had for sale. Several times we returned to Geode State Park, but we strayed on the trails and watched closely for rattlers.

We met several other rock hound families while looking for agates at one or another gravel pit and we decided that it might be beneficial to form ourselves into a rock hound club. Our club became an affiliate with the national organization. We met once a month and usually had a program or demonstration. At one of these meetings a member told about hunting Thomsonite along the north shore of Lake Superior. Based on his directions we would later hunt with some success in the same general area while on one of our camping trips. During the warm months the club tried to arrange field trips to likely agate hunting spots.

Several times the club went to a large gravel pit near LaGrange, Missouri. Other times we went to Muscatine, Iowa, and worked the pits on the "island" where gravel had been extensively mined.

We Take To The Woods

Our rock of choice was Lake Superior agate. It occurred to us that perhaps we'd have better luck finding them if we went north to be closer to the source. About the same time we became interested in camping and decided to buy a tent. We saved our dimes until finally it looked as though we might have enough. We looked at the tents at the Army/Navy Surplus Store in Ottumwa and decided on an eight-foot square umbrella tent. We also bought a single burner propane stove, a lantern, a few blankets, and some other things we thought we'd need. As the clerk emptied our can of dimes onto the counter and began counting we hoped there'd be enough to cover our $90.00 total. The clerk counted ten dimes to a stack and put them in a row. We watched the row grow longer until there was enough to cover our equipment. There were even a few dimes left.

We were eager to use our new equipment and planned our first camping trip to Guttenberg, Iowa, where we'd stay in the state park. We chose Guttenberg since we'd heard there was good agate hunting in the gravel pits north of town and it was far enough away so that we'd be reluctant to pack up in the middle of the night to return home if we didn't like it or the weather turned foul.

It was mid afternoon when we got to the park and began setting up the tent. Before long our campsite looked as though it belonged to seasoned campers although I had doubts about how well we'd get through the night.

We hiked around the park and then began supper. After supper we built a fire and roasted marshmallows. At bedtime it was a long time before the girls settled down and went to asleep. Gladys and I lay on our air mattress listening to the wind and watching the distant trees bordering the campground. The wind kept the treetops in constant motion. As they swayed in the wind they assumed different shapes. I imagined I saw a ship under full sail, an angry giant's head, and a team of oxen. One particularly vivid image was a knight in full armor galloping through the night on his horse. Watching these treetops reminded me of watching images in clouds floating overhead on a sunny day.

Gladys and I watched in silence for a long time. It was peaceful and relaxing, but we were excited about our family's first camping adventure. Because of our excitement we couldn't get to sleep. Now and then I looked at the girls sleeping soundly and envied them. At last we both decided we'd just lie there relaxed and not worry about falling asleep. And I don't believe we slept the entire night.

The next morning we fixed breakfast on our propane burner. Surprisingly the food and the coffee weren't half bad. In fact everything tasted better just because we were eating outdoors.

We took down the tent – or as experienced campers might say – we broke camp and headed into downtown Bellevue. It looked the part of an old river town, but not much was happening on Main Street just then. We went north out of town and found the gravel works where agates were alleged to abound. We grabbed our cloth rock bags and began hunting. We had good luck finding agates, but at lunchtime decided to quit. So far our first camping trip had been a great success. We didn't want to press our luck and headed home.

Our Family Grows Again

Once again Gladys was pregnant. Getting up and down became increasingly difficult and getting in and out of our 1958 Volkswagen Microbus was almost impossible. I liked the Microbus better than any of the cars I'd owned partly because it was the first car I bought brand new, but I also liked the amount of room it had for hauling people and equipment. It was ideal for taking our camping trips. But the immediate problem was Gladys could not get in and out of it without pushing on my part and straining on her part.

The Volkswagen dealer sold us a step to mount directly onto the frame. This would surely make it easier to get her in and out of the bus. On a cold winter evening Emily and I laid on the driveway under the Volkswagen bolting the step to the frame. I needed her help to hold the step in position while I pushed the bolts through their proper holes. It wasn't a job we could do while wearing gloves so we held onto the cold metal with our bare fingers. When we finished handling the icy bolts and parts we felt stiff and frozen. We hobbled on cold and stiff feet to the house to thaw out. It was a cold job and I was grateful for Emily's help. Now Gladys could get in and out of the bus with less strain.

Ada Comes To Help

As the time for Gladys' delivery approached Ada agreed to come down and help out with the girls and with the new baby. Labor began for Gladys in the late afternoon on March 19th. I was especially glad to have a step on the bus as I helped her in for the short ride to the Ottumwa General Hospital. At the hospital a nurse helped her into a wheelchair and took her away. I stayed behind answering a clerk's questions to complete her registration.

In the labor room I offered Gladys whatever comfort I could, but it wasn't long before the doctor decided she was ready to deliver. This time the doctor sent me to the waiting room where one or two other expectant fathers were passing time.

It was frustrating not knowing what was happening. Before long a nurse came to the waiting room called my name and said, "Well, Gladys delivered just fine."

"How is she? Was it a boy or girl?" I asked.

"Which did you want?" She must have sensed that I was in no mood to play her guessing game so she added, "You've got a nice healthy boy."

Mark Edwin Perkins was born the evening of March 19, 1960 and weighed seven pounds four ounces. Once again tears flooded my cheeks as I walked into the room where Gladys was in a bed cradling our son. Being a part of the process of creating a human being was overwhelming. Mark was healthy and Gladys had survived another delivery without complications.

With the arrival of each of our children I felt, "Now our family is complete." With Mark's arrival I once again had that feeling of completeness. I felt blessed with a wife, and three healthy children. I just prayed I would be able to assume the awesome responsibility for our family of five.

After two days in the hospital I brought Gladys and Mark home in our frigid Volkswagen. The 1958 Microbus heaters were notoriously feeble. A weak flow of tepid air is the best they could manage. A snowstorm the day before made our driveway impassable. I parked at the end of the drive and we waded through the drifts to the house where Ada and the girls were waiting.

Now We Are Five

With the arrival of our third child I felt like an old pro. Both of us were more competent and less anxious about caring for a newborn. We quickly settled into a comfortable domestic routine. Of course Gladys again had major duties as she had to get up at night to feed Mark as well as care for him during the day. The girls welcomed their brother and I saw no evidence of jealousy.

Most of our activities involved the whole family. The first summer following Mark's birth we did not take a vacation, but stayed home doing fix up chores. Often for a change of scenery we explored the countryside in our Microbus. One Sunday morning we drove south into Missouri just to see what it was like. At that time you could buy at least three things in Missouri that you couldn't buy in Iowa: colored margarine, five percent beer, and fireworks. Since we were there and a store was close by we bought those forbidden items – two pounds of colored margarine, and a six-pack of beer. We didn't buy fireworks.

Back On The Road Again

The following summer Mark was almost eighteen months old. That was old enough to go on a camping trip. This time we worked our way north camping in state parks through Wisconsin.

Rib Mountain State Park, Walsh, Wisconsin. This huge mound of rock, earth, and trees, stands prominently above the rolling hills of central Wisconsin. At 1,924 feet it is the highest point in the state. The campground located on its summit gives a spectacular view of Walsh, and the surrounding countryside.

We set up our 8' x 8' umbrella tent, unpacked our stove, cooking utensils, blew up the air mattresses, and laid out the blankets. With that we had made camp. We explored the park on foot. Several tall radio and TV transmission towers on the mountain took advantage of the altitude to increase their range. We found a few hiking trails, but we did not take those going down the mountain since we didn't want to think about the climb back up. We stopped to take photos at several of the overlooks with their magnificent views.

After cooking supper we sat around the fire enjoying the out of doors. As the sun went down it got cooler. When we went to bed each of the girls had a blanket, Gladys and I had blankets, and we folded a blanket into sleeping pouch for Mark. We put him in the center of the tent. After dark it got chilly and as the night went on it got cold. The moisture from our breath gathered as frost on the tent walls. Several times during the night we awoke to find Mark had crawled out of his blanket and was sound asleep with nothing covering him but his pajamas. Surely he couldn't be that warm. We feared he'd catch a cold so we tucked him back into his blanket/pouch hoping he'd stay snuggled in. He did not so we tucked him in again and again. Although we worried that he'd catch cold he survived his first camping trip just fine.

Other Camping Trips
Our goal was to take a camping vacation each year. This got us around the country to see new sights, gave us a chance to rock hunt, and let us experience nature up close. Our early tent camping trips were into Minnesota, Wisconsin, and Michigan. Later after moving to Mt. Pleasant and getting a canvas top fold down trailer we camped again in many of the same states, but also camped in Indiana, Ohio, and New York on our trip to visit my sister Pat and family in Bound Brook, New Jersey. And we once took a camping trip to the Black Hills, in South Dakota.

Panora State Park, Minnesota. We camped on two separate trips at this small campground at the base of the bluffs along Highway 61 adjoining Mississippi River Lock & Dam 5A. We spent several days there while we looked for agates at a nearby gravel pit. A conveyor belt carried gravel from the dredge to the storage pile. In those days the owner allowed rock hounds to stand next to the belt and grab agates as they sped by. Each newcomer took his place at the end of the line furthest away from the dredge. As people in front left you could move up. Of course the prime spot was to be the first person in line for that gave you first chance to snatch an agate as it raced toward you on the belt. The only chance people down the line had for an agate was when everyone in front of them missed it. Even though there might be seven or eight people in front you could still catch enough agates to make it worthwhile. When you looked away from the speeding belt after watching it for several minutes the ground, trees, and everything appeared to be moving away. This dizziness was annoying, but it never lasted long.

The park gave us an interesting view of the three major modes of transportation along the upper Mississippi – road, rail, and river. Highway 61 ran next to the campground. Along side the road was the railroad and then just beyond that the locks on the Mississippi. A pedestrian bridge ran from the campground over the railroad to the locks. There was a lot of river and rail traffic at that time of year and we had front row seats. Several times we raced across the pedestrian bridge to watch as a tow locked through. Once while we stood on the bridge over the railroad a train streaked by underneath.

We noticed surveyor stakes stuck in the ground throughout the park. I asked the ranger about that. He mumbled something about, "Dammed crazy engineers. They want to widen the highway." His park would lose a lot of its space. As he walked through the grounds every morning he angrily jerked the stakes from the ground in protest and gave them to us for our campfire. I suspect the engineers finally won that battle.

Wyalusing State Park, Wisconsin. This is one of most scenic state parks anywhere. The campground follows the top of a high ridge overlooking the Wisconsin River where it joins the Mississippi. Pikes Peak State Park lies across the river on the Iowa side. At the base of the bluffs the park includes several bayous of the Mississippi.

I enjoyed sitting and looking out over this great scenic valley with its two rivers as we ate supper in our camp. The next morning when I crawled out to start the coffee I was startled to see the valley completely covered by white clouds. We were in sunshine on a ridge of land above the clouds. Here and there the peaks of other bluffs stuck through the clouds as well. Far across the valley the sun shone on Iowa's bluffs. It was as though I was on a mountaintop above the rest of the world looking out at a few tall peaks.

After the fog burned away we descended to the bayous and launched our canoe. These ponds or bayous flow one into the other eventually emptying into the Mississippi. Tall trees, willow thickets, and brush border the water. Cattails and water lilies are abundant. Herons patiently fished in the shallows while turtles sunned themselves on logs. I felt adventurous as we paddled slowly through these areas. Just when I began to imagine that we could be the first white people to canoe these backwaters we'd come upon a cast off auto tire or old tennis shoe – jarring proof that we weren't far from civilization.

Hinckley State Park, Hinckley, Minnesota. Covering about 32,000 acres this heavily forested park was the largest state park in Minnesota when we camped there. It has several camping areas, a swimming beach, and miles of trails. This area was the site of the great Hinckley forest fire in September 1894. A St. Paul and Duluth train carried many people out of Hinckley to safety in a swamp called Skunk Lake. In another daring rescue two trains of the Eastern Minnesota railroad hooked together and backed out carrying its passengers, crew, and 476 refugees from Hinckley to Superior, Wisconsin. In all the fire burned 350,000 acres and killed 418 people.

One morning as I started breakfast I saw the campers adjoining us scrambling around their area retrieving bread, breakfast cereal, canned food, and other litter. The father called over, "Didja see the bear in here last night?" I said that we hadn't seen or heard anything.

"Yep, a mother bear and a cub got into our food."

It looked to me like the bears had torn up, messed up, eaten, or carried off everything they had. They made the mistake of leaving groceries on their picnic table giving the bears easy pickings. We always stored our food in the Microbus overnight. I checked our bus to see if bears had tried to get our food, but the only evidence of a bear was a paw print in the dust on one of the doors. It took only a few minutes for our neighbors to throw their tent, the remnants of their groceries, and their clothing into their car. They left the campground in a hurry. That night I took a hatchet into the tent with us just in case the bear came back. Fortunately we didn't hear or see anything to interrupt our sleep.

Wild blueberry bushes grew almost everywhere in the forest. The berries were ripe and ready for picking. We noticed that the tourists had picked clean the bushes closest to the road. We walked fifty yards or so into the forest before we found bushes with berries on them. Deeper in the woods the bushes again were picked bare. I was sure bears had picked these berries. Our most productive picking, then, was in a narrow band about twenty yards wide running parallel to the road. That was as far as most tourists wanted to venture into the woods and about as close as the bears cared to come to the road. We ate and picked blueberries, but kept a close watch for bears. Emily thought she spotted one, but it didn't move toward us. When we finished we had a couple of quarts of berries. Gladys whipped up blueberry pancakes for supper and had enough berries left for several day's snacking.

Wildcat Den State Park, Wisconsin. This small park lies along the Kickapoo River in the rolling wooded hills of southwestern Wisconsin. Although this is primarily dairy cattle country many farmers put out small plots of tobacco. Since tobacco requires a lot of hand cultivation it is not unusual to see a farmer in his tobacco field hoeing weeds by hand. As we drove through one valley we heard singing and saw a family in the field singing and hoeing their way through their tobacco field. A mother, father, and four children swung their hoes in time to their tune.

The Kickapoo River is a small, clear, sandy bottom stream that meanders through the area. We waded in the stream and thought it would have been fun to float leisurely on inter tubes down the river. In later years I believe several enterprising people began renting tubes for just such an adventure.

Copper Falls State Park, Wisconsin. This park lies further north and seems much further from civilization. It abuts the Bad River Indian Reservation on the north. There is more forestland here and far less land suitable for growing crops. Most of the soil in the area is reddish-tan. The river has several falls, but one year it was so dry that the river was just a scant stream. The falls showed none of their usual splendor. We had a comfortable camp, but deer flies were a minor problem.

Pattison State Park, Wisconsin. This park is perched on the south escarpment of Lake Superior near Superior, Wisconsin. A small river running through the camp crashes down the escarpment in a spectacular 165-foot waterfall known as the Big Manitou Falls. Above the falls a dam across the stream forms a swimming pond with a clean sandy bottom. The water was red-brown a color it picked up from iron in the rocks and soil. Because of its color we spoke of it as swimming in root beer.

I enjoyed camping here. We used it as a base for day trips to the railroad gravel pits near Clouqet, Minnesota. At those pits I stumbled upon one of my largest agates. It was right underfoot as I stepped out of the bus.

The highway back from Clouqet had many hills and curves. It seemed ideal for a road race so each time we traveled that stretch we became competitors in a Grand Prix. Although conscientiously keeping to the speed limit I shifted gears more than necessary to rev the engine giving the illusion of great speed. I also gave a running commentary on the progress of our race. We always faced stiff competition. Competitors often passed us, but we always squeaked out a victory. The kids enjoyed our races and I know I did.

Itaska State Park, Minnesota. The outflow from Lake Itaska is the beginning of the Mississippi River. Several large rocks serve as stepping-stones across the outflow. Or if you're adventuresome you can wade across since it's only ankle deep and about fifteen feet wide. Either way you can truthfully say you have walked across the Mississippi.

After walking across the river we drove to the boat landing on the lake hoping to take a boat ride. Along with about a dozen other people we took seats on the boat and prepared for a ride in the sightseeing launch. Unfortunately the captain could not get the engine to start. We were disappointed, but I felt truly sorry for Emily since she was extremely disappointed.

Gooseberry Falls State Park, Minnesota. We've camped twice at this park on the north shore of Lake Superior northeast of Duluth. The camping area is comfortable, but for me the most appealing aspect of the park is its wonderful beach and it closeness to Split Rock Light House.

We looked for agates on the beach and then went swimming in the Gooseberry River. Just before the river empties into Lake Superior the water is comparatively warm, but as you work your way toward the river's mouth it becomes increasingly cold. Finally the waters of Lake Superior are uncomfortably cold. I found it too cold to swim there.

One night fog moved in and the Split Rock Lighthouse foghorn bellowed all night. It was eerie and not a sound we hear in Iowa. Apparently it intruded into Cindy's dreams because the next morning she related a confused tale of a bride and a froggy. Was the foghorn the froggy? Who knows, but it must have contributed to her dream in some way.

North Shore Prospecting
We left Gooseberry Falls and went up the north shore. Just before Grand Marias I began looking for the landmark highway cut through the bedrock that one of the club members back home told us about. He said Thompsonite was in this bedrock. We found the highway cut and began prospecting. Sure enough there were deposits in the rock. The holes had been steam bubbles when the rock was magma. Minerals seeped in later to form the Thompsonites. We began hammering the magma from around them. This is tricky work since Thompsonite itself is soft and a direct blow will shatter it.

We had been working at the highway cut for a while when a beat-up car pulled up. The driver was unshaven, wore ragged clothes, and seemed grubby. "Ya lookin' for Thompsonite?" he asked. We said we were.

"Follow me."

I wasn't sure I wanted to follow this man anywhere, but we got in our bus I hid our money and reluctantly followed him half-mile down the road. He parked, got out, and said, "Come on."

The forest grew right to the edge of the road on both sides. There was no sign of a trail, but he pushed a bush aside and we saw a well-defined footpath. We followed him into the woods. We hadn't gone far when I heard someone hammering on rock. Soon we walked into a clearing where the base rock was exposed. Three or four people were at work chipping out Thompsonites. They welcomed us and we got busy. We worked with these folks most of the afternoon and took away several nice specimens. Although I initially had doubts about following our host I believe he was just trying to be helpful to some out of state fellow rock hounds. Later I learned he was a recognized geological authority on minerals of the north shore.

We Leave The Country
When we planned this trip I felt adventuresome because we were going so far north that on the map it looked isolated and sparsely settled. We packed enough food and supplies to last the entire trip in case there were no grocery stores. I feared running out of pipe tobacco so I packed an ample supply of Model tobacco.

Now we were on the north shore of Lake Superior and getting close to that region in Canada that I thought looked so desolate on the map. At Grand Portage we looked at the reconstructed fort and trading post. I could imagine we were back in the days of the Voyagers and that nothing much had changed. Across the lake stood Isle Royale. We could take a ferry to the island and camp there, but I thought it might be too primitive for us with small children.

On the way up we'd stopped at a rock shop in Duluth. When we said we planned to head north the owner urged us to go to Isle Royale. "You can find green stone there. I'll pay you top dollar for all you bring back," she promised. Now at Grand Portage we learned there are green stones on the island, but the Government won't allow you to take them. No doubt that was the reason she offered to pay us top dollar. We'd have to steal them. We didn't go to Isle Royale.

Provincial Park, near Thunder Bay, Ontario. We continued on and crossed through customs into Canada without difficulty. We were out of the country!

Our road map showed a park with camping nearby so we drove there. The park covered an entire peninsula jutting into Lake Superior. In turn the campground was on a peninsula that jutted out into a small lake on the larger peninsula. Trees and brush surround each campsite on three sides giving the illusion you are in the woods by yourself.

We sat up camp and were relaxing from the day's drive when we found we weren't so isolated. We heard yelling and running sounds. All at once a black bear cub broke through the brush on one side of our camp space and ran across our area followed by several kids. The cub climbed a tree to escape. The kids tried to climb after him, but called it off and left the cub alone when they couldn't climb high enough to reach it. Or perhaps this was at the urging of their parents. For the kids' sake it was probably a good thing the mother bear hadn't joined the chase.

White Lake Provincial Park, White River, Ontario. The next day we continued on around Lake Superior stopping and stretching at every place the road came close to the lake. Most of the rock was huge and we found few gravel beaches for our kind of rock hunting.

Our next camp area was beside a small lake. Although we were in the woods it did not seem like dense woods. Many of the trees were white birch and that gave us a scenic view. We sat up camp and changed to our swimsuits for a short walk to the beach. I stepped into the lake and was surprised at how cold it was. It seemed colder than Lake Superior. It was impossible to relax and swim. We all took one quick dip then ran for our camp to dry off and warm up.

A middle-aged couple was the only other campers in the area. They played their radio loudly during the evening and it continued long after we went to bed. I tolerated this as long as possible and finally stuck my head out and shouted, "Turn down that radio!" Fortunately it worked. The next morning we met the couple with the radio. They seemed like nice people, but it was clear that he was hard of hearing.

We drove on and after a mile or two came to the little town of White River. An igloo painted on a billboard on the edge of town announced, "White River, the coldest spot in Canada...72 below." A painted Eskimo stood next to the igloo holding an oversized thermometer that read 72 below. After trying to swim in their lake we could easily believe this indeed was Canada's coldest spot.

We drove into Sault Ste. Marie and got lost looking for the road across into the United States. I asked a couple of times, but either these people didn't know or perhaps they only understood French. After searching for an hour we found the right road and then headed through customs. Here we were more closely questioned and scrutinized coming back into the country than we were when we left.

Because there were no state parks close by we selected a private campground on the ship canal connected Lake Superior with Lake Huron. The campground had no natural scenic beauty, but gave us a view of the parade of ships passing day and night. It had a sandy beach so I tried swimming. I quickly discovered, however, that large ships create strong currents as they pass. As a ship approaches you feel yourself pushed toward the shore. As it passes the current reverses and pushes you toward the center of the channel. That was much too hazardous for any of us to do any swimming. We had to be content wading in no deeper than our ankles. Several times during the night the low rumble of a ship's engines approaching woke me. As I watched the ship's lights slipping by I wondered what it carried, where it had been, and where was it going.

While in the area we rode a tour boat through the Soo locks that link Lake Superior and Lake Huron. The natural connection between these two great lakes is a stretch of wild rapids unsuited for large ocean going ships. Two locks offer safe passage around the rapids. One lock is on the American side and the other is on the Canadian side. Our tour boat took us up through one lock, turned around, and brought us back down through the other. The entire trip took perhaps two hours and gave us an experience we couldn't have in Iowa.

Porcupine Mountain State Park, UP Michigan. Our camping trip onto the Upper Peninsula of Michigan was another time when I felt we traveled into wild territory. This park came close to being as isolated as I had imagined.

We drove into a fine looking camping area beside a beautiful beach on Lake Superior. I saw no tents, vehicles, or people there. We had our choice of campsites and selected what we thought was the best one, sat up the tent, and unrolled our sleeping blankets. While eating lunch at our picnic table we realized we were under attack by scores of black flies. They bit any exposed skin and often drew blood. They even bit through our socks. Mosquito repellent did not deter them they just continued biting.

After a quick lunch we loaded our food into the Microbus and headed back to the ranger station. "Isn't there any other camping area where there aren't any black flies?" I asked.

"Well, there's another area, but you'll have to drive sixty miles on an unimproved road to get there. And I have to tell ya, the flies will be just as bad up there," he warned. "Why not spend the day exploring the higher elevations around here then come back down to your tent around dusk. The flies are less active then."

That was good advice because we found no flies up on Porcupine Mountain. According to the story Indians gave the mountain its name because from the lake it looks like a crouching porcupine. The mountain is perhaps 2,000 feet high and from its summit there are wonderful views of the lake and the woods.

We ate supper at a picnic table on the mountain and then started down to our tent. It was almost dark as we drove slowly into the campground hoping we wouldn't arouse the black flies. Ours was still the only tent in the whole camping area. We ran into the tent without being bitten and settled down for the night.

Next morning the sun was shining on our tent when I woke up. I had forgotten the black flies, but as I looked up there they were. You could see their shadows as they swarmed on the outside of our tent waiting for us to come out. We dressed quickly then bolted from the tent to the bus carrying as many blankets and mattresses as we could. The flies descended and began biting viciously. I took down the tent as fast as possible and flung it into the bus without bothering to fold it. Then we sped off.

When we reached Ironwood, Michigan, I said, "Maybe we've outrun those darn flies by now. Let's stop and fix breakfast." We cooked breakfast in the city park, but kept watch for black flies. We didn't see any. After breakfast we could relax and stow our gear away neatly.

Warren Dunes State Park, Bridgman, Michigan. This is another state park where we have camped more than once. The dunes are spectacular, but difficult to walk across. Several dunes stood between the campground and the swimming beach. We took the road down to the beach several times, but one time the kids decided they'd like to be adventurous and walk over the dunes to camp. It was not far and shouldn't have taken long, but as time dragged on and they hadn't arrived at the tent Gladys and I got worried. We drove to the beach watching the dunes as we went. We didn't see them so we went back to camp. They had just arrived. The sand was much looser than they expected and that made it difficult to walk. We were just thankful they made it.

The farms in this part of the state appealed to me. There are many peach and cherry orchards and several vineyards. We enjoyed our tour through the area.

One Sunday we decided to attend the Lutheran Church services in town. An elder greeted us at the door and recognizing us as visitors he said, "You know, don't you, that this service will be in German. Our regular English service is scheduled in an hour." We hadn't known that so we waited for an hour and then returned for the next service.

The church was old and had architectural features we hadn't seen before. The pulpit was elevated so the pastor seemed almost at the same level as worshipers in the balcony. When he ascended his stairs, scowled down from the pulpit at the congregation on the main floor, and began chastising his members for their lack of enthusiasm for supporting the Lord's work, I imagined that God's voice thundering down from on high might sound exactly like that.

Chapter 19

OTHER CAMPING TRIPS WE HAVE KNOWN

Our Trip To New Jersey
One year we drove to Bound Brook, New Jersey, to visit my sister Pat, her husband John, and their boys Don and Jim. On the way out we camped at Tippecanoe River State Park in Indiana, and a park in Ohio. On the way home we camped at Beaver Kill State Park in New York State.

We also camped at **Letchworth State Park, Castile, New York.** This park encloses the spectacular gorge of the Genesee River known as the "Grand Canyon of the East." There are three major waterfalls along this stretch and in places the gorge is 600 feet deep. The camp ground is at the edge of the gorge and even with a protective fence it was a bit unnerving to think we were camping with children just 75 feet from its brink. From here we made a day trip to Niagara Falls and crossed over into Canada. It was worth the effort to see the falls in person after seeing only pictures of them for so many years.

After that we hoped to make camp that night at a park we selected on the map. When we got there it was crowded, dirty, and didn't look inviting. So we drove all night and arrived at Warren Dunes State Park, Michigan, about 4:00 in the morning. We joined the line of cars waiting for camping spots to open up when other campers left the park. We rested at this park for a couple of days before driving home.

One Stinker Of A Park
For a change in scenery we went south one year for our camping vacation. We'd heard about the Lake of the Ozarks in Missouri and that became our destination.

We set up our tent at the **Lake of the Ozarks State Park.** I was disappointed to learn the beach was a couple miles away so we drove there. We paid a fee to camp at the park, but now they charged us an additional fee to get onto the beach. Once on the beach we found it as pleasant as sitting on a muddy sandbar on the Des Moines River. It was not a place to enjoy a swim. We were disappointed and upset.

The view of the lake from the campground was far less spectacular than the grand views shown in brochures promoting the Lake. The Lake looked like a collection of flooded creeks and hollows without broad vistas. But the toilets were the worst part. These pit style privies were overdue for cleaning. Finally it was sweltering. We managed one night then left the next morning headed north to look for cooler weather.

Back in Iowa we stopped at **Lake Wapello State Park, Drakesville.** What a pleasant change. The campground was spacious, the restrooms clean, and the lake was imposing. It was even much cooler. We rented a boat and nosed around on the lake.

That night a thunderstorm blew in. Now crashes of thunder heard from inside a house can be loud, but outdoors with only tent fabric separating you from the elements it is deafening. The metal tent pole of our umbrella tent went straight up the middle of the tent. I realized it was too much like a lightning rod. But after several minutes lightning hadn't struck us. I began to relax and listened appreciatively to the storm. Paroxysms of thunder reverberated off the surrounding hills and when they were almost dead a new spasm erupted. As the storm moved closer thunder grew louder until it seemed to be booming directly above us. Each blast shook the ground and the tent as well. After several ground shaking minutes it retreated and grew faint. But just before dying it would regain its vigor and again light up the sky and shake the ground. This became one of the most protracted storms I have been a part of. The thunder crashes approached and retreated most of the night.

Other Notable Camping Trips
When I fantasize about an ideal camp the sky is always a brilliant blue. If clouds appear they are always small white and fluffy. The temperature is mild and the humidity is low. No black flies or mosquitoes pester us. Cool clean sand covers the beach. The water is always just right for swimming. The campgrounds are spacious and quiet with clean restrooms and showers. And all fellow campers are helpful and friendly.

A surprising number of times it has been like that for us, but a few trips were far less than idyllic.

Our Quest To See The Stone Presidents
We decided to camp in the Black Hills of South Dakota the last week of June 1968. The first day we got as far as the Gavin Point camp ground at **Lewis and Clark Lake, Yanton, South Dakota.** We picked a campsite and set up our canvas top fold down trailer. Other than a small museum at the dam displaying a live rattlesnake in a Lucite cage there was not much to see in the area. But that didn't matter since this was to be just an overnight stay. In the morning we planned to be on our way to the Black Hills with more interesting attractions.

After supper it began to rain. Gently at first then worked itself to monsoon level in a short time. The trailer was reasonably snug, but water began to drip in a spot or two. We corralled those drips and felt confident our little shelter would keep us dry. It was well suited for sleeping five people, but it was not suited for five people who were wide awake and moving around. There was little room for that so we read or played cards. Finally since there was not much else to do we went to bed hoping to leave early in the morning.

It rained all evening all night and the next morning it was still raining as though it could not stop. It was hard to make coffee and cook a hot breakfast in the rain, but we did it. It began to look as though we weren't going to get an early start for the

Black Hills. As the day wore on it became clear that we were not going to be able to leave at all.

From time to time some of us moved to the van to relieve congestion in the trailer. The ground got soggy, the canvas of the trailer looked soggy, and we all felt soggy. For me there was a major bright spot in all of this sogginess. All I had to do was think how fortunate we were we hadn't set up at the first camping area we looked at. It was above the dam and down a dirt road to a bluff overlooking the lake. It was a beautiful spot, but with this rain the road would be impassible. Here we had a surfaced road to leave on.

Somehow we managed to get through the rainy day without getting too upset with each other. And after another meal in our cramped sleeping trailer we went to bed. While our sleeping bags were dry they felt damp. The rain continued to drum on the canvas top as we settled in for the night. Sometime in the early morning I woke up and realized that the steady drumming of the rain on our canvas roof had stopped. It wasn't raining any more! I drifted back to sleep knowing we'd finally be able to be on our way to see the Black Hills and its "Stone Presidents" as Mark called them.

The next morning we packed away soggy gear and drove across southern South Dakota through the Pine Ridge Indian Reservation to **Angostura Recreational Area, near Hot Springs, South Dakota.**

The drive through the reservation was particularly depressing. Most of the houses were ill kept shacks that usually had two or more broken down cars in the yard. The few villages we passed had boarded up buildings, a cluttered gas station, and invariably a gaudy looking tavern. A collection of people, mostly men, loitered in front of the gas station and tavern. In a few places we saw small frame houses had replaced the shacks. All of these houses looked as though they were mass-produced somewhere else then hauled in on a flatbed. All the houses were barn red and probably had the same floor plan. Certainly these new mass produced houses gave their residents much nicer living quarters.

The Angostura Recreational Area looked new and was comfortable. After two days of confinement in the rain-drenched tent it was good to stretch our legs and dry out in the warm sun.

After a night's sleep we packed up once more, drove to the **Blue Bell Camp Grounds,** and set up the trailer. We left it there and drove to the Wind Cave became tourists and walked through the cave listening to the guide's explanations of the formations.

Next we headed for Mount Rushmore. I thought the highway was extremely rough. It felt like the Van was going over a washboard. Then it dawned on me. It wasn't the road it was our universal joints. We turned off the road to Rushmore and headed for the Frontier Ford Company in Rapid City hoping the joints would hold together until we got there. It was amazing. We made it to the dealer; he had replacement parts in stock, and got us back on the road in about an hour – not much longer than it takes to change a tire.

It was clear we had run out of time and would not see the Stone Presidents today. On the way back to our trailer Mark suddenly began to holler in pain. A honeybee got in the van and stung him. I pulled over and got some ice out of the chest to put on the sting. By the time we got back to the campground he felt better.

The campground was beside a fast moving stream that made soothing splattering noises as it swept over the rocks. With the Van repaired and no rain forecast for tomorrow I believe everyone except Mark relaxed. I believe he began to think he might never see the Stone Presidents.

The next morning we finished breakfast and started for Mount Rushmore. It was a thrill when we caught sight of the monument while still many miles away. When we got there I hoped Mark was impressed and felt that it was worth his worry.

After a couple hours at the monument we left for the campground. On the way back to camp we saw a place offering horseback rides. Cindy was especially excited about a chance to ride a horse. We all got our own horses and the trail guide lead us out. The trail took us on a scenic tour through wooded hills, across some fast moving streams, past several mule deer, and up a few narrow canyons. Mark's horse tried to pass Cindy's horse on a narrow stretch of the trail, but Cindy's house wouldn't let that happen. For a time I thought Mark and horse might tumble down the hill, but we all managed to get back safely and walk stiffly to our Van.

When we left the Black Hills heading home we decided to go through the Bad Lands. We took a scenic drive through the Needles then on into the Bad Lands. What a desolate looking place and yet there is sufficient vegetation for wild burros, coyotes, possibly antelope, and other animals.

As we left the Bad Lands it looked stormy. The radio reported strong winds and a possible tornado moving in. It might be best not to stay in a campground, but to spend the night in a motel. We checked into Graham's Best Western Motel in Murdo, South Dakota. Then as predicted strong winds and rain began, but no tornado hit near us. As the rain pelted the motel windows and the thunder crashed I was glad we weren't out somewhere in a campground. The next day we arrived home after driving 1,599 miles for the entire trip.

Another Soggy Trip

The last part of an earlier camping trip was another soggy experience, but the earlier part was pleasant. On August 1, 1966 we bought a canoe and went to **Pine Lake State Park, near Eldora, Iowa.** We camped in our fold down canvas top trailer and launched the canoe for its maiden voyage. The next day we drove to **Wyalusing State Park in Wisconsin** and again put the canoe in the water.

The following day we camped at **Mayflower Lake Resort, near Birnamwood, Wisconsin.** This was a fine lake where I thought I could teach the girls canoeing skills. Emily, Cindy, and I paddled out to deep water and then deliberately upset the canoe. I demonstrated how to bail most of the water out by sloshing the canoe back and forth. Then showed them how to get back into the canoe. We practiced until I felt the girls knew what to do should they ever capsize. We paddled to shore to pick up Mark who had waited for a canoe ride. He was unhappy that he wasn't with us when we upset the canoe. It made no difference to him that he was only six years old and did not know how to swim.

Next we drove to **Forest County Park near Crandon, Wisconsin,** and the soggy part of the vacation. It began raining while we were driving to the Park. When we arrived and opened the trailer water covered the floor. It had splashed in around the wheel well covers during the drive. Our sleeping bags were stored on the floor and got soaked. We had a kerosene heater that we used to heat the trailer on cold nights so Gladys draped our sleeping bags over it to dry them. To prevent further trouble I used some of the kids' modeling clay to caulk the seams where the wheel well covers met the floor. They looked classy with a bead of red modeling clay around them. Now I felt we could drive in the rain and the water would not splash in.

We were in a thick forest. Nothing looks, feels, or smells damper than a rain soaked forest. The trees oozed moisture. Wherever you walked water squished out of the pine needle mat covering the ground. The air hung like a cold fog dripping water as rain continued. It was cold. Even had the sun been shining it couldn't have penetrated and warmed this dense wood.

We spent most of the first afternoon and evening drying our sleeping bags. Gladys moved them around the heater so that by bedtime they were reasonably dry. All night long the rain beat steadily on our canvas top. When I stuck my head out the next morning the forest was as dismal as the day before. We passed time as best we could, but that night went to bed with rain drumming on the roof. The next morning, it was still raining, and continued all day and into the night.

The third morning the rain slackened and we decided to get away as quickly as possible. We packed up and drove through light rain to **Baraga State Park near Baraga, Michigan.** Our trailer, sleeping bags, and clothes still felt damp as we set up in our new camp. We found this forest was as soggy as the one we'd left. It continued to rain and turned cold. The one bright spot was that during our drive in the rain no water came in around the wheel wells to soak our sleeping bags again.

The next morning we were ready to move on. We thought almost anywhere else might be drier than where we were. After our one night in the Baraga State Park we moved on to the **Cheppewa River** campground in the **Chequameon National Forest.** Unfortunately it was just as rainy cold and soggy as what we'd just left. As before at the other soggy campgrounds we explored some of the trails during those brief periods when the rain slackened, but without sunshine we were damp and cold most of the time.

We stayed one night at the Cheppewa River camp and the next morning when it didn't appear as though the rain would stop we packed up and headed south. Even if it was still raining it might be warmer.

We pulled into **Merrick State Park, Fountain City, Wisconsin.** The rain was gone and the sun was shining. By the time we set up camp I began to feel warm again. Merrick State Park is on the Mississippi River up stream from Fountain City. The area is not strikingly scenic nor is the park on a breathtaking bluff. It was simply a good place to relax, dry out, warm up, and enjoy the nearby rock hunting. Without the constant drumming of rain on our canvas roof we were able to get a night of refreshing sleep. We put the canoe in at the bayou and explored the backwaters. After a while we got adventuresome and paddled into the Mississippi. When I saw how well we were doing we paddled on down stream to Fountain City. It felt good to dock the canoe and stretch on shore. For a reward we bought ourselves a round of soft drinks.

As we paddled back up stream it was awesome to look across that wide river toward a towboat near the opposite shore nudging its string of huge barges. Even at that distance we could hear the low rumble of its powerful diesel engines. And here we were an entire family relying on a few square feet of fiberglass to stay afloat and our own muscles to move us along sharing the river with this powerful giant. Although we weren't in the same class we held a common goal – getting upstream.

Chapter 20

MEANWHILE BACK AT VOC REHAB

I thought my work in the Ottumwa District Office was developing nicely. Voc Rehab now served southeastern Iowa better than ever. One category of disabled that had not been well served, however, was the mentally ill and mentally retarded. These disabilities are as vocationally handicapping as any physical disability. In addition the public attitude about mental disabilities further hinders the employment of these folks.

Voc Rehab decided to move aggressively to work with these disabilities by assigning special staff to the four Mental Health Institutes and the two Hospital Schools for Retarded. Until now these institutions were visited only occasionally by the counselors covering regular caseloads in the area.

The central office asked me if I'd accept a transfer to the Clarinda Mental Health Institute to set up a vocational rehabilitation office there. I was interested in working with mentally ill people and responded that I would consider it. Dow Armstrong, my Ottumwa Supervisor, suggested I consider going to the Mt. Pleasant MHI instead. That would keep me in the Ottumwa District and he would still be my supervisor. That suited me and also pleased the central office. I arranged a visit to the institute and met Dr. Brown, the superintendent, Keith Klynn, the chief social worker, and several other staff. They seemed excited about the prospects of establishing voc rehab as another treatment discipline at the institute. Fortunately Gladys was willing to pack up and move.

I began to travel to Mt. Pleasant and work my way into the hospital. I was trying to get acquainted with the staff, learn how they provided services, and tried to determine how voc rehab might fit in. I was also trying to explain to them just what our agency was all about and how we could assist their patients.

We listed our Ottumwa house for sale, but no potential buyers wanted to see it. It became clear we'd likely have to move to Mt. Pleasant before the house sold. I contacted realtors in Mt. Pleasant and they showed me a few houses that for various reasons I thought were unsuitable. I advertised in the local newspaper for a house to rent. There was just one response to this ad. I talked to the landlady. She asked what line of work I was in and when I told her I'd be working at the Mental Health Institute she quickly responded, "Sorry, the apartment is no longer available." I later found out that in the eyes of many residents there is a stigma associated with working at the MHI.

A few days later I received a phone call from Mr. Morrison in Mt. Pleasant. He erected prefabricated houses and said he was finishing one and asked if we would like to see it. We looked it over and it seemed just right. We bought it and moved in. That left our Ottumwa house vacant. After several months we rented it to a new secretary who worked in the Ottumwa Voc Rehab office. That helped us financially as it was difficult making mortgage payments on two houses. After a year the secretary and her husband moved on and again the house was vacant. We listed it for sale, but it stood vacant for another year. Finally we received an offer for about the same amount as we'd initially paid for it. We accepted the offer so we'd no longer have two mortgage payments.

Mt. Pleasant Becomes Our Home

Now we had to get accustomed to a new house and get acquainted with new neighbors, new schools, and a new town. The grade school was two blocks away and was one of the newer schools in the district. Our neighbors included the school superintendent, the high school principal, other public school teachers, a college professor, and a psychologist at the Mental Health Institute.

I planted grass seed in the yard. At the rear of the yard I started to spade up ground for a garden. I soon unearthed old bedsprings, fence wire, tree stumps, and other junk buried under just a few inches of soil. Apparently the contractor buried any junk left on our lot when construction ended. I was upset with him and said I wanted all of that junk hauled away. He sent down a dump truck and they filled the truck with the junk. I finished the garden space and eventually enclosed it in a wooden fence. With grass seed, flowers, some paint, and a lot of work we began to get our house and yard looking as though someone lived there who cared.

Emily went to junior high school, Cindy began elementary school two blocks north of home, and we gave Mark some exposure to "school" by sending him to Mrs. Zenor's preschool in her home a block away. After my election as chairman of the elementary school P.T.A. I felt even closer to the school. A couple of years went by and Mt. Pleasant really did begin to feel like home. We became a part of the community in ways we had not done in Knoxville or Ottumwa.

Voc Rehab At The MHI

The MHI staff accepted me and I participated with the other professional disciplines in patient staffings and treatment programs. I worked with patients prior to their release and kept their cases after their discharge. Our agency decided that the MHI voc rehab counselor should serve clients originating at an MHI after discharge rather than transferring their cases to a field counselor. Most field counselors felt unprepared for working with mentally ill patients and preferred not to. Follow up in the field with these clients took me away over night about once a month. Ordinarily the only times I needed to stay over night was when I called on my clients in Davenport and Clinton. I handled the other cases with day trips.

Many of the patients hospitalized at the Institute were women who were housewives before their admission. Of course they received psychiatric treatment but no guidance or training to help them resume their homemaker duties once they returned home.

Voc Rehab considers homemaking as legitimate an occupation as a job outside the home. I felt that we could institute a homemaker training program within the hospital where women patients could practice their meal planning, do the necessary grocery shopping downtown, cook the meal, and perform housekeeping duties before they were released. By planning a meal, shopping for the food, preparing it, and serving it to fellow trainees, a woman could feel confident that she would be able to provide for her family when released back home.

Dorcas Wheatley, the wife of one of the hospital's social workers, was a trained home economist with a degree from Purdue. She was looking for work. I hired her to head up the unit. The hospital cooperated by remodeling part of the central building into apartment-like living quarters. In addition to paying the instructor's salary Voc Rehab set aside a budget to purchase food and other supplies.

We found that many of the women needed training in nutrition. Some typically served potato chips and soda pop to their children for lunch and thought that was an adequate meal. And we discovered an unanticipated benefit to our homemaker training. In the homelike setting of the apartment the women felt more comfortable discussing their emotional issues than they did in the clinical atmosphere of their therapy groups. Our operations soon became an important part of the hospital's services. I was pleased to hear the superintendent and other staff brag about **their** homemaker unit. Eventually we were able to establish similar units at the other three Mental Health Institutes.

Family Activities

We continued to be a rock hunting family. We often drove to the gravel pits near Muscatine to look for agates. On one trip we met an elderly couple and chatted with them while we all hunted agates together, but when it began to rain everyone retreated to their cars hoping it would soon end. When it became apparent that the rain would likely continue for the rest of the day the couple invited us to their home in Muscatine to show us their rock and mineral collection. We were amazed to see the delightful museum they had created in a storage building behind their house. Obviously they spent many hours hunting in the field and then hours cutting and polishing many of their specimens. We warmed ourselves with hot chocolate and cookies while admiring their work. We kept our small collection in coffee cans, but some day hoped to display it properly.

We discovered other rock hounds in Mt. Pleasant. Two of the most avid were the pharmacist at the MHI and the other was the owner of the Gamble Store. We eventually organized ourselves into a rock and mineral club and affiliated with the national organization.

Because southeast Iowa was new to us some weekends we drove through the countryside to get acquainted with the area. Burlington, Iowa, was not far and we often went to its parks and scenic spots overlooking the Mississippi. It also seemed adventuresome to leave the state and cross the river into Gulfport, Illinois. At that time Iowa laws forbid the sale of liquor by the drink. With its many taverns Gulfport was willing to meet this need for thirsty Iowans, but we weren't interested in the taverns. Instead we drove a few miles to the Henderson State Forest. To us this pine forest seemed huge. The trees stood in neat rows like fields of corn. There were several different stands of trees and each stand covered perhaps forty acres. The groups ranged in height from thirty or forty feet down to seedlings just getting started. The taller stands reduced sunlight to twilight. As we wandered through the woods in this dim light all the rows looked the same and it was easy to feel lost. That increased our sense of adventure.

Other times we drove down river to Ft. Madison, Montrose, and Keokuk. Often we'd cross the river at Keokuk and drive up the Illinois side through Nauvoo. The drive on either side of the river held many grand views, but I liked the Illinois side better since it gave broader views of the river.

A country road runs inland from Ft. Madison toward Houghton. We dubbed it the Bluebird Road. There always were many bluebirds in the area and we rarely saw them anywhere else. Continuing west the road went to Salem, Iowa. Quakers established the town and it had been a stop on the Underground Railroad. We enjoyed the area because of the dam on the Skunk River and the sandbar below it. It wasn't the best rock-hunting site, but we found several Montana type agates there. One Sunday afternoon with our kids we searched that sandbar thoroughly. The next morning I learned that some people who were there just after we were stumbled across a live rattlesnake. I was glad that we hadn't seen it.

I brought my old balloon tire bicycle down from Des Moines and cleaned it up so that it was once more ridable. Each of the girls had bicycles, but Mark did not. I bought a bicycle seat especially made for kids and attached it behind my seat. Now we could ride around town together. Although we enjoyed these rides Gladys could not ride a bike and did not go with us. The girls were in Brownies and the Girl Scouts at various times and Gladys participated in some of those activities with them.

Emily began flute lessons and was in the junior high school band. One Memorial Day the band marched in the parade downtown. The band had uniforms and their marching and playing sounded good to me for I was a proud father after all. As I stood listening it suddenly dawned on me that the band was playing and marching to "Mary Had a Little Lamb." I had never thought of it as a march, but it sounded just fine.

One time I wanted some homemade bread. I thought it would taste better than commercial bakery bread and without preservatives it might be healthier, too. Gladys gave me a recipe and I baked the bread. We liked it so much that for a time bread baking was a regular Saturday chore. Cindy wanted to sell bread to the neighbors. She helped me bake several loaves then took them around to the neighbors and sold them. She did this every Saturday for a few weeks.

I Meet Rev. Koch

I often saw a minister visiting patients at the MHI. He smiled warmly as we passed in the hallways. When visiting with patients or staff he always was able to find something to laugh about. His infectious laugh bounced off the walls and you found yourself smiling or laughing with him. One day he stopped to introduce himself. He was Rev. Alton Koch the volunteer Lutheran chaplain at the hospital and the pastor of the local Lutheran parish. His church, Faith Lutheran, was on the edge of Iowa Wesleyan College campus just a few blocks from where we lived. Over the next several months he often stopped in my office to just say hello. If I weren't extremely busy we'd chat for a while. One day he asked about my church background and wanted to know if we were attending church in Mt. Pleasant. I said we weren't. He invited us to come to Faith Lutheran and worship with them.

Several weeks later we visited his church. The small building had been a chapel on a military base during World War II and was hauled to its present site just a couple of years before. There were pews on either side of a center aisle. On a slightly raised platform in the front stood the altar and pulpit. Behind the altar a large cross hung on the wall. An electronic organ sat off the platform to the right. A door on the left opened to the pastor's office. The basement had a social room, kitchen, and several small cubicles for Sunday school classes. I thought it was a snug little church for this congregation of 120 people.

The worship service was different from what I'd grown up with at First Federated. This was a liturgical service and the music was new to me. Also most of the hymns in the hymnal were unfamiliar. With so many differences I listened closely as Rev. Koch began his sermon wondering what theological differences there might be. The message he gave, and his explanation of his Biblical text sounded familiar. It was the kind of sermon I might have heard at my old boyhood church. After service many people in the congregation shook my hand and made us feel welcome. They hoped we'd be back next Sunday.

The following week Rev. Koch stopped by my office at the hospital to ask what I thought of the service. "It seemed to me that your interpretation of scripture is very close to what I've been taught," I replied. "But I was taught it is sinful to drink any kind of alcohol." For that reason our church used grape juice rather than wine for communion. Our church forbids card playing, dancing, and most movies. I asked his stance on those issues.

He replied that Lutherans follow scripture as closely as possible, but do not make a rule where there is no Biblical basis for the rule. He said such issues are peripheral. "They are not considered sinful unless they interfere with a Christian's worship," he said.

In the weeks that followed Rev. Koch visited us at home for further discussion of the practices of the Lutheran Church, Missouri Synod. Gladys and I agreed that we wanted to get involved with a church. We had not attended church or participated in any way since our marriage. Rev. Koch gave us study guides and came down once a week for ten weeks to give us adult instruction. At the end of that time we could decide whether or not we wanted to become members of Faith Lutheran Church. We decided to join. On February 19, 1961, we became members. Rev. Koch baptized Emily, Cindy, and Mark, but did not baptize Gladys and me. Our parents had us baptized when we were children.

From then on our family was active in the church singing in the choir, teaching Sunday school, and serving on various boards and committees. On May 17. 1964, Emily completed confirmation instruction at Faith Lutheran. After we moved to Des Moines Cindy and Mark took confirmation instruction at Mt. Olive Lutheran. Cindy's confirmation was May 18, 1969, and Mark's was April 7, 1974.

Backyard Rabbit Breeder

When I was a child my father built a rabbit cage to raise a pair of rabbits. Perhaps he thought caring for them would be an educational chore for me and the off spring would help supply meat for our table. This was during the depression so a supply of inexpensive meat was welcome. I was perhaps five years old and probably too young to assume such duties. Shortly after he got them one of the rabbits wiggled out of my arms as I took it out of the cage. It fell to the ground breaking a leg. It became meat for our table. I suspect we ate its mate shortly afterward since I don't recall that we had rabbits long.

I don't believe this childhood episode had anything to do with it, but I became interested in raising rabbits. I read everything I could find about their care. I studied the diagram and instructions for building a hutch in an Extension Service booklet. Since Gladys didn't object I bought the lumber, hardware cloth, and roofing to build a first class hutch following the design shown in the booklet. When it was finished I looked through a rabbit magazine to locate breeding stock. I ordered a pair of New Zealand white rabbits from a breeder in Missouri. They arrived by express and I put them in their new home, gave them water, and Purina rabbit pellets. I stood back to admire them. They were fine looking animals, the hutch looked serviceable in its spot at one end of the garden, but as I stood there I suddenly felt, "What in the world have I gotten myself into now?"

But looking after them did not take much time and I quickly got into the rather pleasant routine of doing the chores for my livestock. After a few months I got them to breed. As the gestation period drew to an end I put a nest box into the doe's cage. The nights were getting cold so I rigged a heating wire under the bottom of the nest box. One cold night I plugged in the heater before I went to bed feeling that if she kindled that night the newborns would be nice and comfy.

During the night a neighbor beating on the back door suddenly awakened me. The electrical heat unit had caught the nest box on fire! The fire spread through the straw bedding in the female's cage and engulfed her half of the hutch in flames. I quickly unplugged the electric cord and rescued the male from his cage adjoining the female. It was apparent that it was too late for the female. She was dead. I threw water on the fire and quickly had it out. In just a few days I repaired the burned area of the hutch as good as new. But it took me much longer to get past the anguish and guilt I felt over causing the death of the doe and her unborn bunnies.

Later I bought a replacement doe from a dealer who was showing at a rabbit show in West Chester, Iowa. She was a good New Zealand white, but in my mind couldn't compare with the doe lost in the fire. Ultimately she kindled several bunnies that survived. Earlier she had kindled twice and then stomped them to death. Later Cindy wanted to raise Dutch rabbits so we bought a pair. They are a smaller breed than the New Zealands, but are showy with their black and white markings.

Magazine Columnist

I gleaned much of my rabbit raising information from articles in the *Small Stock* magazine published in Lamoni, Iowa. Despite the magazine's name it focused almost exclusively on rabbits. Most of the articles dealt with large-scale rabbit raising. Few discussed the special problems facing the small breeder raising a few rabbits in his backyard. I didn't consider myself an expert on rabbit raising, but I thought I could write an article for each issue discussing some of the trials and tribulations I was experiencing as a backyard breeder. I planned to relate the humorous and ridiculous things I'd done.

I sent a letter to the magazine's editor outlining my ideas and was surprised to hear back that he was interested. He said he would be happy to print all the articles I could supply. I don't remember exactly what I said in my first article, but I sent it off and anxiously waited for the magazine's next issue to see myself in print. When it finally came I was pleased to see my little piece laid out nicely and covering two pages. “The Backyard Breeder” became a regular feature of the magazine.

When I sent the second article I suggested that it might provoke greater interest if it had an illustration or two. I drew a couple of sketches to illustrate the article. I intended for the sketches to show him what I had in mind and assumed he would have an artist do the actual drawings. But when the article appeared I was surprised to see he had used my unretouched sketches to illustrate it. From then on I sent illustrations with each article, but drew them more carefully than my first rough sketches.

I don’t remember what I said in most of these articles, but I do remember telling how disappointed I was when I attended a rabbit show. My article didn’t mention the town by name. My article said the promoter and participants were unfriendly. Everything seemed disorganized. None of the judges discussed their reasons for picking the winners they chose. It seemed to me that such attitudes would not promote rabbit raising nor serve to enlighten anyone about the standards breeders should strive for in developing their herds. This article sparked more letters to the editor than any of my other articles. Most of the letters made the point that “...the backyard breeder’s experience is not typical of most rabbit shows.” I was reassured.

After several months I wrote a resignation letter to the magazine’s editor. I had enrolled at the University of Iowa and would start classes for my master’s degree. I felt that I no longer had time to continue the “Backyard Breeder” articles.

Chapter 21

BACK TO SCHOOL AT AGE FORTY

Decision Time Again

I had worked as a counselor with Voc Rehab for perhaps ten or twelve years. Most of what I knew about counseling I had learned on the job, but there were vast gaps in my knowledge. If somehow I could fill these gaps then I was sure I'd be more effective. It was becoming clear to me that returning to college and completing a master's degree in vocational rehabilitation counseling was the only way to do this. But was this realistic? "I've been out of college fourteen years. I have a wife and three kids to support and a job to do. How can I take time out for school?" I wondered.

During a Voc Rehab staff-training meeting at Clarinda I talked with George Allen, one of our central office staff, about the University of Iowa's program. I wondered how I might be able to take advantage of it. He encouraged me and thought perhaps I could qualify for either a federal or state stipend to complete the training. I arranged a visit with Dr. John Muthard, the director of the University's program and he, too, encouraged me to apply for graduate school. I discussed this with Jerry Starkweather, our director, and he was receptive.

I began commuting from Mt. Pleasant to Iowa City to take Saturday classes. I continued to work full time on my job and Voc Rehab paid my tuition and books. It was daunting going back into a classroom after fourteen years, but it was also exhilarating. Although it seems corny I remember the first time I walked into East Hall to begin classes I actually heard Brahms' "Academic Festival Overture" playing in my head. Such background music somehow seemed appropriate. I took all the Saturday courses relevant to my degree the University offered. One semester I took some relevant late afternoon and evening classes. Finally it was clear I'd have to go for at least one summer session to finish my degree. I made arrangements with Vic Nielsen, in our Ottumwa office, to cover my hospital cases when he passed through on his regular trips to Burlington.

Statistics, a required course, was at 7:00 am that summer. Iowa City was on daylight savings time while Mt. Pleasant was not. The commute took a little over an hour so to get to class I had to get up around 4:30 am. I had classes all morning and used the afternoon for library work. Usually when I got home there was more studying to do. I tried to spend some time with Gladys and the kids, but I know that most of the time I was a crabby bear warning everyone, “Be quiet so I can concentrate!” Somehow we all managed to live through that summer and the only remaining requirement for my degree was my thesis.

Developing A Thesis

I wanted to do a study at the hospital that would have a practical application for Voc Rehab’s work with mentally ill clients. I discussed this with John Muthard the department head who also was my advisor, but he seemed indifferent to everything I came up with. His response to one of my study proposals was, “You might as well just count the number of blue cars driving out of Mt. Pleasant on highway 34.” He did not warm to any of my ideas yet offered no suggestions for my study. At this point I became one of those graduate students known as an “**all butter**.” That is a student who has finished **all but** the thesis.

And so I remained an **all butter** for a year or two until Dr. Muthard left to take a similar position in Gainesville, Florida. Len Miller, assistant chairman, replaced him. Shortly afterward Len contacted me and said, “Let’s get you off your butt and get that master’s finished.”

Len typically used earthy plain language and that was refreshing in the oh-so-serious and staid academic setting of the University. He taught some of the courses I’d taken. I liked him as a professor and as an individual. His lectures were bold, brash, and sometimes profane, but always informative and pertinent. I discussed my idea with him and it seemed that in a short time we had the study outlined. I was trying to answer the question, "How can you predict which hospitalized mental patient will be able to successfully obtain and hold a job back in the community?"

I planned to apply a scale that rated certain medical, employment, and age factors to a sample of the hospital's patients during their first 30 days of hospitalization. Then I planned a follow up twelve months later to determine their employment status. In the end I found two characteristics or behaviors that significantly correlated with successful employment after discharge. These were: 1) The patient seems to know why he/she entered the hospital and does not claim he/she has no need for psychiatric help, and; 2) The patient reports promptly for all scheduled interviews with doctor and other staff members. The *Personnel and Guidance Journal* published my article in their January 1969 issue. There – such as it was – I had done my bit and contributed to the vocational rehabilitation body of knowledge. And I learned a few things, too.

After I took my written and oral comprehensive exams the department certified me as having met all the requirements for the degree. On February 4, 1967, I was graduated. By then we lived in Des Moines. We picked up Mom and all drove down to Iowa City. After the ceremony we celebrated with lunch at the Amanas. Earning a master's degree was a goal I had for years and now that it had happened I felt extremely satisfied.

Gladys Gets Treatment For Her Hearing

Gladys' hearing had been deteriorating. Finally it was so poor that she missed much of our conversation at home. At church or in a noisy place she heard practically nothing. Everyone had to talk loader and she depended more and more on lip reading.

She decided to go to the University of Iowa Hospitals for an evaluation and possible treatment. During her day of evaluation she had time off at noon so we ate lunch together. It was a pleasant surprise to find she could hear me even when I didn't raise my voice. The doctor found perforations in each eardrum and glued thin paper patches over these holes. With the paper functioning as temporary eardrums they did more testing to determine whether her loss was a conductive or a nerve loss. The final recommendation was to patch these perforations permanently with pieces of a vein taken from the back of her hand.

An Unexpected Development

Gladys decided to have the surgery done and an appointment was scheduled. The doctors would do one ear at a time. Ada came down to stay with the kids while we were in Iowa City. Everything was set, but early in the morning the phone woke us up. It was my uncle Jim Greig calling from Des Moines. He said he and my mother were at Methodist Hospital where an ambulance had rushed Dad due to a heart attack. Gladys and I were preparing to leave for Des Moines when Uncle Jim called back sadly to report that Dad was dead. He was dead on arrival at the hospital.

I suppose everyone wonders what it will be like when a parent dies. If that parent is in ill health I assume you frequently think about him dying, but if the parent is healthy then you may not think about his death at all. My father was not seeing a doctor for any illness. His death was sudden and certainly unexpected. Just five months earlier he retired at age sixty-five from the Iowa-Des Moines National Bank where he worked for forty-six years. After retiring he built a shop in the backyard using the lumber salvaged when he tore down the small house my grandmother Bowlsby had lived in on 53rd Street. He planned to pursue his woodworking hobby in this shop. Both he and my mother were looking forward to his retirement.

I was overwhelmed with sadness and disbelief. Dad had always been a source of guidance, encouragement, and wisdom. But I was angry, too. He received so little time to enjoy his retirement. It just didn't seem fair that Dad should be dead at age 65. "Isn't a person entitled to at least 'three score and ten'," I thought.

In addition to my sadness and anger I was puzzled. The night of his death I dreamed that we were together on the river near our old fishing spot. The water was frozen and as we walked out onto the ice it suddenly broke and Dad fell through. I saw him looking up at me as he floated downstream under the clear ice. I ran along on the ice above him, but couldn't break through to free him. He kept floating downstream away from me. At that moment Uncle Jim's phone call giving me the sad news of his heart attack woke me up. What should I make of this dream? Was it just a coincidence or something more profound? I can't explain it, but believe it could have been something more profound.

Gladys and I drove to Des Moines. Mom's grief was so intense that she couldn't make even simple decisions. I phoned Pat and she said she'd fly out. I also talked with the coroner who asked permission to do an autopsy. He said it was necessary since Dad was not under the care of a physician at the time of his death. Later the coroner reported it was a "massive heart attack" that killed him. "His coronary arteries were filled with plaque and looked like those of an 80 year old man," he said. Prior to his heart attack Dad had experienced no symptoms.

The day of the funeral was one of the coldest days of that winter. We did not linger long at the cemetery. Pat stayed for a few days to help Mom out and finally she was on her own trying to adjust to being a widow.

Chapter 22

OUR MIGRATION TO DES MOINES

Jerry Starkweather our agency's director asked if I'd like to replace Tommy Thomsen as District Supervisor in Des Moines. Tommy was my supervisor when I began with Voc Rehab, but was now retiring. Of course Gladys and I would have to sell our Mt. Pleasant house, find a house in Des Moines, pack our stuff, and transfer Emily and Cindy to new schools. Neither of us wanted to leave Mt. Pleasant and I don't believe the kids were crazy about it either. We now had roots in Mt. Pleasant. But this job would be an advancement. Also it would move the kids into a better school system. We decided to move.

We listed our house for sale with Bill Keefe in February 1965. Bill suggested we set a price that was considerably higher than I thought it would fetch. He said we could always come down, but when it ultimately sold we received our asking price.

Friday February 19th was my last day at the MHI Branch office and the following Monday I began work in Des Moines. We could not move until our house sold and we found a house in Des Moines. We also thought it best that the girls finish the school year where they were. I had to begin the new job right away so I rented a room at the downtown YMCA. The Y was inexpensive and only five blocks from the office. I lived in Des Moines during the week and commuted back to Mt. Pleasant Friday evenings. I hated being away from the family so much, but we kept telling ourselves it would be only until school was out. I used my evenings to familiarize myself with my new job and territory. The Des Moines district covered eleven countries in central Iowa with a combined population equal to all of the rest of the state. When I got tired of doing homework in the evenings I played polkas on my accordion. I don't know if other residents at the Y liked the music, but no one complained.

House Deals

When we began thinking about moving to Des Moines I checked out the location of the Lutheran churches. I was pleased to see that one church, Mt. Olive Lutheran, also had a school. I thought it would be fine for the kids to have the advantage of attending parochial school. I targeted my house hunting to a six-block radius around Mt. Olive. This would place them within easy walking distance of school. And this area was in the Roosevelt High School district so they also could have the advantage of attending Roosevelt when they reached high school.

After touring several houses I pared my choices to two. Gladys came to Des Moines on the bus to look at them and we decided on the house at 1708 - 59th Street. On Saturday March 27th we made a bid of $13,500. The sellers made a counter offer of $14,250 that we accepted, however, the lenders insisted that it be lowered to $14,000.

On April 1st we accepted an offer on our Mt. Pleasant house. The Faith Lutheran congregation gave us a farewell picnic lunch at McMillan Park. After finishing the paperwork for selling our house we were almost ready to move. Mark had come down with the mumps and stayed a couple blocks away with Mrs. Miller, one of the Faith Lutheran members, while the movers loaded the truck. On Tuesday, June 1, 1965 we moved into our Des Moines house. I was glad to move out of the YMCA and have our family under one roof again.

Des Moines District Supervisor

When I became district supervisor Bill Herrick was designated the assistant district supervisor. Although Bill had worked in Voc Rehab for a few years I scarcely knew him and had no idea whether we could work together effectively. As we got acquainted I was pleased to find we held similar views about rehabilitation. I liked him as a coworker and I felt there was such a rapport between us that indeed we could lead the office to a higher level of performance. This became one of my most enjoyable and productive periods in Voc Rehab.

From its beginning the district office shared office space with the state office in the old Bankers Trust Building. It was crowded, cluttered, and gave counselors no privacy for interviewing clients. A standard office joke was that your client could become so distracted by the closeness of an adjoining counselor's desk and client that he'd often answer questions asked by the other counselor. Although I had not seen this happen I felt it could happen.

Our first priority was to move into our own space. We sold this idea to Merrill Hunt, the director, and set about looking at office space in the downtown area. We wanted to relocate to a mall or some other outlying area where parking for staff and clients would be convenient, but Mr. Hunt insisted that we remain downtown.

We found space in the old Plymouth building owned by the Coppolas. They were willing to create private office space for each counselor. The paper work was completed and we moved. I believe all of the staff immediately felt better about having suitable work space and being away from the constant intrusion of state office personnel. Probably the state office staff was just as pleased to see us leave.

Each counselor had at least 200 clients in his or her caseload. It was just fantasy to believe that any client could receive timely service when his counselor was spread so thinly. My second priority was to hire more counselors. I bargained with the state office for as many new positions as possible and was successful in getting a few authorized. I did not get as many as I wanted, but any increase in staff helped. I partially achieved my second priority. Later we could press for more staff.

Mean, Lean, Rehab Team

My third priority was to help staff become more efficient and effective. I frequently mentioned that I'd like to see us become a "Mean, Lean, Rehab Team." Certainly I did not want us to become an impersonal, unfeeling rehab mill. Rather I wanted to convey the idea that we were dedicated, determined, rehabilitation professionals working effectively and cooperatively on behalf of our clients. I instituted staff meetings every Monday to disseminate information and to discuss casework problems or questions. I encouraged counselors to bring their particularly difficult cases to these meetings and we could staff the cases. Hopefully the thoughts and suggestions of fellow staff would be helpful.

As a part of my continuing orientation to the district and to the staff I scheduled time in the field with each counselor. Seeing counselors in action in their territories helped me to better understand them.

We Have A Problem

Through this activity and from other things that happened I sensed I had a problem with one of the counselors. The itinerary he filed each week was vague making it difficult to find him in the field or to know what he intended to do there. He missed appointments he scheduled with clients and was not producing much. I discussed my concerns with him and he promised to do better.

Unfortunately his work did not improve. Together we developed a plan of action. It specifically listed those things he would do over the next three weeks. A deadline was set for each activity. We met at the end of each week to review his progress. Soon it was apparent he was going to meet few of his goals. I felt I'd given him every possible chance. I gave him three weeks to meet his goals or lose his job.

He had a good educational background, had done good rehab work in the past, and was a likable guy, but it was obvious that he was not contributing to our "Mean, Lean, Rehab Team." This was the first time I had to fire an employee. It seemed to me it might get complicated since he might appeal. I believed we did everything possible to help him. I documented his problems and the remedial steps taken. We met on the final day of his three-week work period. I found he had accomplished almost none of his goals. I told him that he was through at the end of the day. He asked, "Can I leave right now?" I agreed.

During the next couple of days I sensed the staff was more accepting of me as their supervisor. I asked and learned that everyone was waiting to see how I handled the problem counselor. Had I not fired him I would not have received the acceptance that I was now getting. "He hasn't been doing his job for months," a counselor said. "Should have been fired a long time ago." Nobody told me my first test would be to fire that counselor, but I felt as though I'd passed.

Motorcycle Mania

In the 1960's lightweight motorcycles from Japan invaded the country. Names like Suzuki, Honda, Kawasaki, and Bridgestone became familiar. More and more of them buzzed around town sounding like angry mosquitoes. Since high school I had wanted a motorcycle and now the urge to buy one resurfaced. Shortly after we moved to Des Moines I felt that I could get one without encountering too much opposition or jeopardizing our budget.

I bought a bright red Suzuki K10. It was much like the time I got my first bicycle. I rode it everywhere. I even rode it to work. It must have been unusual to see me driving to and from work wearing a big white helmet, necktie and suit coat tails blowing in the wind, and a brief case strapped on behind.

Merrill Hunt, the Voc Rehab director, believed anyone who rode a motorcycle was automatically a member of Hell's Angels. To him all cyclists were unshaven, worthless ruffians up to no good. When he learned that one of his district supervisors not only owned a cycle, but was riding it to work as well he was scandalized.

One day he phoned to say he needed to meet right away with several central office staff and Bill Herrick and me across town at the Voc Rehab Center near the State Capitol. Bill had not driven to work that day so he did not have a car to drive us over. That left my cycle as our only transportation. So off we went through the downtown business district with neckties and coat tails flying to Merrill's emergency meeting on the east side next to the State Capitol. You can imagine Mr. Hunt's consternation when two of his supervisory staff roared into the Center's parking lot astride a bright red Suzuki. Clearly he was disgusted, but he managed to conduct his emergency meeting without saying anything nasty about our cycle riding.

Promoted To Chief

About the time I began to feel comfortable with the progress staff was making in the Des Moines District office our director reorganized the agency. He intended for us to become more active in the state's mental health, mental retardation, and prison facilities. Most of us welcomed these changes.

I began work in the Central Office in 1966. After working as the supervisor of the Des Moines District office for about a year I would now work as the Chief of Mental Health Services covering the entire state. I was chosen for this position because of my interest in mental health and my experience setting up the Voc Rehab program at Mt. Pleasant a few years earlier,

In this newly established post I felt free to define its goals as I went along and one of my first goals was to establish a Voc Rehab department at each of the four mental health institutes. It required developing plans with administrators at the institutes, hiring staff, as well as developing programs. This was the beginning of another rewarding and satisfying period with the agency. Unfortunately I had to be on the road again and away from home overnight once or twice a week.

In four years we developed active and productive units at each institute. Usually we had two or three counselors, a secretary, and a supervisor. The institution assigned some of their instructors or therapists to the unit to augment our staff. With combined Voc Rehab and Institute staff each unit had fifteen to twenty people. The services offered by these units became a part of the institution's treatment program.

Chapter 23

A HOBBY LURCHES OUT OF HAND

Like most girls our daughters Emily and Cindy had a dollhouse when they were young. Most of its plastic furniture pieces were passable replicas of full-size furniture, but I thought I could make more realistic pieces out of wood. I built a table, chairs, benches, and a hutch cabinet. The girls seemed pleased and I enjoyed building them so I worked on other pieces trying to include as much detail as possible.

The mother of one of Cindy's playmates saw some of my work and asked if I had considered building some to sell. I hadn't thought that anyone would want to buy them, but I liked thinking that perhaps I could earn money this way. My mother said she'd like to show a table and chairs to a lady she often visited in a retirement complex who collected small stuff. The lady liked my furniture and bought those pieces.

My Miniatures Sold in Gift Shops

This first sale in 1969 encouraged me to look for a shop willing to stock my work. The owner of the Artistic Gift Shop in Beaverdale was interested so I put a price on them and left an assortment of pieces there. Almost every time I checked back he'd sold something and paid me seventy-five percent of my sale price. It was satisfying and encouraging discovering people would buy my work. I used most of this money to buy additional equipment for my workshop.

Living History Farms in Urbandale was preparing to open a gift shop and advertised for handcrafts made by Iowans. I submitted several pieces to the jury who would decide what the shop would carry. They accepted my work and also gave me helpful suggestions for improving some of the pieces. This, too, was a consignment shop paying the same as the Artistic Gift Shop.

I began to receive inquiries by phone and by mail saying they had seen my work at Living History Farms and wanted to buy other pieces. Often the caller wanted a piece of furniture I did not build. If it was something I wanted to add to my line I'd build it. Some inquiries came from miniature shops. These were not consignment sales and it got my work into places like Cold Spring Harbor, New York, and Anchorage, Alaska.

Living History Farms invited artisans to come and demonstrate their crafts during weekend festivals in the spring and the fall. I usually attended and demonstrated weaving rush seats in ladder-back chairs. Gladys and I showed my other pieces and sold enough to encourage us.

In early December 1974 Living History Farms held an all-day pre-Christmas event in Beaverdale. This time we artisans were scattered among the stores in Beaverdale and sat in their store windows facing the street surrounded by our work while we demonstrated our craft. I was assigned a window at the Iltis Lumberyard. Artisans doing their craft in a store window created enough interest that the sidewalks seemed crowded all day. Many of the viewers came into the store to have a closer look, to talk, and to buy.

For a brief time I had my stuff in the Village Peddler consignment gift shop in West Des Moines. They sold a number of pieces, but I pulled out after seven months. The store clerks did nothing to protect my work and I felt rough handling by their customers damaged too many pieces. Four years later I returned my work to West Des Moines. This time Bazaar American had my miniatures and safely displayed them in a glass case.

Although my miniatures sold well in consignment shops I saw this as only an interim step. I believed my work was now good enough that shops ought to be willing to buy it outright. I wanted to discontinue all consignment sales except to Living History Farms. I would continue with them because they were a non-profit organization.

Our First Miniature Show

Possibly another good way to sell our miniatures was at a miniature show. Gladys and I began planning to do a show. I built a lighted display case and we bought plastic shoeboxes to carry the miniatures on the road. About this time the Wee C Miniature Club in Chicago sent a show contract inviting us to be a dealer in their November 1980 show in Oak Brook Terrace, Illinois. We returned the contract with our table fee and worked hard to beef up our inventory.

The show was in the ballroom at the Holiday Inn. Tables lined the room and many dealers were arranging their wares on these tables when we arrived. The show chairperson gave Gladys and me nametags identifying us as "Perkins Miniatures." We found our assigned table and began carrying in our things from the Van. I noticed that most of the dealers and their helpers wheeled their miniatures into the room on handcarts. I decided for the next show Perkins Miniatures would also have a handcart.

Gladys and I fussed over the arrangement of our miniatures on the table. We hoped to achieve such an attractive display that customers would instantly be enticed into buying. When the doors of the salesroom opened people flooded the room. I was excited and reached for our sales book. They began strolling past our table and they asked questions, but when the evening ended we had used few pages of the sales book. I was disappointed, but the dealer next to us said, "Don't worry. Nobody sells much on preview night. People are just looking then, but just wait 'til tomorrow and Sunday."

That dealer was right. We used many pages of our sales book on Saturday and Sunday. Then it was time to pack up. As we left Chicago we both were tired, but the excitement of our first miniature show buoyed us up for our 330-mile trip home. We sold a lot of furniture and that was the best affirmation of our work we could have. Somewhere between Chicago and Des

Moines I thought, "Maybe we **are** ready for the big time. From now on we will do as many shows as possible."

We Go On The Road

Early in 1981 there were several new beginnings. Ronald Reagan was inaugurated President, the American hostages were released by Iran, and Perkins Miniatures got serious about miniatures shows. Two of our shows brought us little or no sales. Both were arts and crafts shows in shopping malls. I discovered few people strolling through a shopping mall are there to buy miniature furniture no matter how appealing your display is. Based on these two shows and a disappointing mall show a year earlier I decided we would do no more such shows. We did six regular miniature shows in 1981: One in Omaha, three in Chicago, and one in Hyannis, Massachusetts. We also sold to individuals and shops by mail.

Perkins Miniatures had taken off and I was busier than I intended to be. I worked at Voc Rehab at least forty hours a week, spent almost every weekend working on our thirty-acre farm in Union County, and served on the school board at Mt. Olive Lutheran School. Finally I built miniatures in the evenings and whenever I could find an extra five minutes. At times I felt as though I had a tiger by the tail and dared not let loose. It was clear a change was necessary. I could not continue such a schedule. Should I leave Voc Rehab and work full time building miniatures? Was that realistic? Could I really make a living doing that? It was decision time.

Decision Time

The Apostle Paul writes in Corinthians that opportunities are like open doors. God had opened a door allowing me to enter and work in voc rehab for almost twenty years. But now the opportunities to continue using my skills in that agency were fading.

It is said that God doesn't close one door of opportunity unless He opens another one at the same time. Could it be that building miniatures was that second door for me? I was not convinced that it was. It seemed irresponsible to jump from a stable job with generous benefits and a large salary to chancy work with no guaranteed benefits or salary. One of my bosses said, "Going off to make doll house furniture is the craziest damn thing I ever heard of. You're going to starve!"

I believe that God gave each of us certain skills and talents and that He leads us into different experiences for our education. He intends for us to use our skills to help others and to earn a living. He has a plan for each of our lives.

For several months I prayed asking God what His plan was for my life from here on. Was I to stay where I was, go to another job in the counseling field; or did He want me in miniatures. Of course I didn't expect an answer by phone, post, or email although that would have been nice, but I believe He began to show me by further restricting opportunities on my old job. And He nudged me toward miniatures. It was as though He was saying, "Use the interest and talent in art, woodworking, and antiques that I gave you."

I would sell a few pieces and I'd say, "Thanks Lord, but this is not a living. I have children in school and need more."

And He'd seem to say," Just trust me – you'll see."

Once I got a phone call from a store in New York ordering a lot of my furniture. And I said, "Thanks Lord for this sale, but this is not a living."

And He seemed to say, "Don't worry – it'll work out."

I sold more furniture at miniature shows and the shop in New York phoned to order more stuff. I said, "Thanks Lord, but I'm not yet convinced."

And the Lord seemed to respond; "You'll make it just fine."

Finally when my furniture was selling as fast as I could build it I began to trust and to believe that a door of opportunity had opened. It seemed I could work full time in miniatures yet I was still skeptical. The thought of leaving a secure job and stepping out onto thin air to a job with no guaranteed salary, medical coverage, sick leave, or vacation benefits was daunting. So in January 1982 I took only a baby step and cut back to three days a week at Voc Rehab. I thought that would allow me to firmly establish our miniature business yet still give us some reliable income. My co-workers and friends thought I was crazy, but if Gladys and the kids thought I was crazy or irresponsible they kept it to themselves and encouraged me.

In January 1982 we flew to San Diego to a miniature show. This was the first time we'd flown to a show and the first time either of us had been in California. Freezing rain made the streets slick and caused our van to slide, lurch, and spin its wheels as we drove to the Des Moines airport. We boarded the plane. The ground crew deiced it twice before we could leave.

In Denver we changed planes. From my window on the plane I watched the last of the baggage move up the ramp and the workers prepare to close the hatch so we could take off. I hadn't seen our trunk of miniatures. Without them we couldn't do the show. Just then an airline baggage tractor raced up and deposited our trunk on the ramp. I could rest easy now. The baggage hatch closed and we were off to San Diego. It was a thrill to go from the cold, ice, and snow of mid-winter to the summer-like temperatures in San Diego.

We sold a good amount of furniture and it gave Perkins Miniatures its first west coast exposure. In our off hours we toured around San Diego in a rented car and then after the show we drove back to the airport for our return. The sky was clear as the pilot flew over the Grand Canyon. Even from 35,000 feet it looked impressive. Back in Des Moines it was still winter and we had to scrape ice off our van for the trip home.

A month later we flew to Orlando, Florida for a show. It seemed almost obscene to bask in the warm Florida sunshine while cold and snow continued at home. After the show was over we drove down to visit my sister and brother in law, Pat and John, in Safety Harbor. We stayed there for a couple of days before returning to the winter cold in Iowa.

During the rest of the year we did shows in Troy, Michigan; Wichita, Kansas; the Spring Festival at Living History Farms; Hyannis, Massachusetts; and Chicago. At the time of the Chicago show Gladys was in Dike helping Emily following the birth of our second granddaughter Jessica. Mark planned to help me do the show. To get ahead of a snowstorm that was moving in we got up and left for Chicago at 3:30 am hoping to beat it. The only snow we drove through lasted about fifteen minutes near Iowa City. I thought it was great fun to be on the road and do a show with Mark.

Many customers wanted to have a hand in making their miniatures and asked about kits. I built a child's ladder-back chair kit and printed instructions for completing it. Everything needed to complete the chair was included in the kit.

I introduced this kit at the Wichita show and gave a workshop using it. This was the first of scores of workshops Gladys and I did around the country. Mostly we gave workshops on the ladder-back chair, but we also taught how to build a child's table and chairs, a marbled top table, a French provincial fireplace, and several other pieces.

Usually we had from two to twelve students in a workshop, but in 1990 Gladys and I were asked to teach 150 students all in one class how to weave a rush chair seat in a ladder-back-chair. These students were members of the Midwest Miniature Guild meeting in Minneapolis. The Guild's officers selected fifteen members to work as table instructors. Before the workshop I showed this group how to weave the chair seat and they finished their chairs. When the workshop began the 150 members sat at tables in the hotel's large meeting room. Each instructor joined a table. After I gave a few general instructions from the podium Gladys and I circulated among the tables helping out where needed. The workshop went surprisingly well and the students wove excellent miniature rush chair seats.

And Now Decision time Again

I had now worked three days a week at Voc Rehab for a year and during that time God convinced me that building miniatures was the work I should be doing. I submitted my resignation indicating my final day on the job would be March 10, 1983. As I left the building for the last time it was a little frightening to think I would no longer receive regular paychecks. However I would begin receiving a small check each month from my State retirement program. "Here I am at age 58 starting a new career," I thought. It felt good.

That year we drove to Orlando, Florida, in February to do a show and then a week later did a show in Kansas City on our way home. Later that year we did shows in Troy, Michigan; Omaha, Nebraska; Dallas, Texas; Cleveland, Ohio; Peoria, Illinois; Hyannis, Massachusetts; Oklahoma City, Oklahoma; Minneapolis, Minnesota; Southfield, Michigan; and Elizabeth, New Jersey. We did twelve miniature shows and taught several workshops in my first year of retirement During this time I continued building miniatures for Mary Sternberg a miniatures dealer who did shows all over the country.

For nineteen years we traveled to miniature shows and conducted workshops at many of them. Ordinarily we drove our Dodge van, but did fly to three shows. In addition to those places already mentioned we did shows in Denver, Colorado; Hunt Valley, Maryland; St. Louis, Missouri; Tucson, and Phoenix, Arizona; Davenport, Iowa; Belleville, Illinois; Harrisburg, Pennsylvania; Columbus, Ohio; Fenton, Missouri; Des Moines, Iowa; Atlanta, Georgia; Elk Grove Village, Illinois; Mt. Kisco, New York; and

Rockford, Illinois. Usually we returned to these towns for shows year after year although we went to some of them only once.

Oh The Joys Of Entrepreneurship

Developing and running our miniature business was satisfying in several ways. It allowed me to express my creativity, challenged my organizational skills, and offered me an opportunity to promote and sell our products. But what I liked most was that Gladys and I developed a closer emotional relationship as we worked together developing the business. Also the sales trips around the country gave us a chance to see many attractions we had not visited. Places like: Cape Cod; Florida and Arizona in the winter time; the Ford Museum in Dearborn, Michigan; Old Sturbridge Village, Massachusetts; the battlefield at Gettysburg; Valley Forge; Strasburg Pennsylvania railroad tour; Hancock Shaker Village, Pittsfield, Massachusetts; Old Tucson; St Xavier Mission; the Petrified Forest and Painted Desert; several glassworks in eastern Ohio; and the industrial concentration around Elizabeth and Newark, New Jersey.

We Come In Off The Road

In June 1999 we once again went to the Spring Fling Show in Westmont, Illinois. Each year we looked forward to seeing our customer friends and our dealer friends at this show. It was as enjoyable as previous years and we sold a large part of our inventory. At the time we did not know this would be our last show. Three months later the doctor found a malignant tumor in Gladys' cheek and removed it. Radiation treatments followed for many weeks. Gladys' health came first and we could not sign a show contract not knowing if we'd be able to do the show. This seemed a good time to get off the road. We both were finding it harder and harder to do the lifting and carrying required for setting up and tearing down at a show.

Not doing shows did not mean we were out of the miniatures business. We continued to receive orders and we supplied two or three dealers with pieces. It seemed, however, that we were slowing down. I'd been building miniatures for thirty-four years and Gladys and I were on the road for nineteen of those years. As I think back I remember some high points as well as some low points.

Two shows stand out in my mind as our best shows. In 1989 we had a table at the NAME (National Association of Miniature Enthusiasts) National Houseparty in Minneapolis. We sold almost everything we took with us. Even though it was one of our most lucrative shows the weeks of preparation wore me out so that I didn't enjoy it.

The other outstanding show was a NAME Regional Houseparty in Naperville, Illinois, in 1993. A year earlier the promoters contracted with me to build 350 half-scale rockers with rush seats. These rockers were one of the items participants received in their bag of souvenirs. While I was building the rockers we lost our drinking water for almost three weeks and our electricity for a couple of days because of the record flooding in the upper Middle West. I had to weave many of the chair seats by the light of a kerosene lamp. The participants liked the rockers and I was pleased that I'd been able to complete the order despite the flood. With my sales at the show and the sale of the rockers this was a high gross show where I enjoyed myself.

On the other hand there were two shows where we barely made enough to buy supper and get out of town. In 1985 we took in only $123.93 at a show in Ohio. At an Illinois show in 1992 we struggled carrying our display cabinets and merchandise up a flight of stairs and down a hallway to reach the sales room. When the show began we discovered our table was directly beneath the public address speaker mounted in the ceiling. Throughout the show the promoter kept up a barrage of commercials for her table and her charities. It was difficult to have a conversation with our customers. And finally one of the promoter's charities gave away samples of gooey candy at their table next to ours. More than once a potential customer with sticky candy fingers wanted to handle our furniture. We did not do that show a second time.

Two shows stand out as unusual because the person in charge publicly recognized God. At one the promoter got on the loud speaker just before opening time and asked everyone to be silent for a moment of prayer. She asked for God's blessing on all of us and on everyone visiting the show. She asked that we all have a safe and enjoyable show and a safe trip home. At the other show the lady in charge gave a prayer of thanksgiving before we began eating supper together. I appreciated these public expressions of their faith.

I like the challenge of building a large number of the same piece and have received several contracts for large orders. I built thirty-five ladder-back chairs for a NAME Regional Houseparty in Greensboro, SC. The chairs became a part of their banquet table centerpieces.

Another NAME Regional Houseparty contracted for 350 half-scale Victorian style tables. Earlier I built 350 half-scale rockers. Of course I had to build the 150 ladder-back chair kits we used in the Minneapolis workshop. Another time I built kits for 32 settee rockers, 30 high chairs, and 52 hutch cabinets all in one order. I once turned 500 Shaker sewing spools for a private customer in New Jersey.

Publicity is important in establishing a business of any sort and I believe we received helpful publicity over the years. The *Des Moines Registe*r once published an article and photos telling about our miniatures. Another time the *Skywalker* (an alternative newspaper in Des Moines) ran an article and photos.

One of the national miniature magazines printed two articles about our work. Other articles have referred to our work. Perhaps the most gratifying print media coverage was a feature article published in the June 1996 issue of *Better Homes and Gardens WOOD* magazine Afterward we received almost six hundred letters requesting our catalog or asking for information. This expression of interest in our miniatures led to the most costly bonehead business decision I ever made. I was convinced that we should take an ad in the *WOOD* magazine for at least three months. The ad cost $3,600 but I believed we would earn that back and much more through the sales of plans and instructions for building our furniture. Unfortunately we had few inquiries and sold only two plans.

One of the local TV stations interviewed me twice about miniatures and the Public Television station did a segment for their weekly "Living In Iowa" program.

Giving talks and demonstrations is another way to publicize miniatures. The superintendent of miniatures at the Iowa State Fair asked me to demonstrate and sell our miniatures one day at the 1984 Fair. I didn't expect to sell much, but it was enjoyable meeting and talking about miniatures with so many people. Paxton Lumber invited me to their store three times to demonstrate my miniature lathe with its duplicating attachment. These spectators were predominantly wood workers and asked some penetrating questions. In addition to enjoying these demonstrations Paxton Lumber paid me for my time.

The Senior Group at a local church invited me to talk about miniatures at one of their meetings. I took along several pieces of my furniture and a dollhouse I'd built. After telling about how I designed and built my pieces I opened it up for questions. Only one or two people asked questions. A week later I talked to second graders at an elementary school. They asked many more questions than the seniors had. I was surprised how focused, insightful, and imaginative their questions were.

In 1994 the old *Nutshell News* miniature magazine hosted a tour to visit miniature shops, collections, and museums in the Midwest. They would spend one night in Des Moines. The promoter invited Gladys and me to have supper with them and then talk about building miniatures. She encouraged me to bring along any pieces I wanted to sell. Gladys and I enjoyed our supper then I talked for about twenty minutes. After that we put out our miniatures. It was gratifying to see the interest these people displayed and when the evening was over we had sold almost everything. People from South Africa, South America, Europe, Canada, and Australia bought our stuff.

The magazine has changed its name to *Dollhouse Miniatures.* They hosted their second Midwest tour in 2004 and again invited us for supper, presentation, and sale. This time there were not as many participants from overseas, but we sold twice as much as ten years earlier.

Conclusion

I no longer build miniatures for us to sell at shows, but I do build pieces to fill occasional mail orders and for a few wholesale accounts. It appears I may have come almost full circle. I began building miniatures as a hobby, moved to building and selling miniatures as a business, and now I'm back building miniatures mostly as a hobby again. Once again my work has been way too much fun. Now I want to see what door opens next.

Chapter 24

WORK IN IOWA'S DRUG ABUSE PROGRAMS

Change Is Blowing In The Wind

In the psychedelic 1960's most college age kids let their hair grow, dressed in odd-looking clothes, and hung strings of beads and peace symbols around their necks. New words and expressions invaded their vocabulary. Words like "Crashed," "Bummer," "Bad trip," "Far out," and "I'm cool," became common.

Music changed, too. The lyrics seemed to lament social inequalities or the war in Viet Nam. Along with their passionate protests against the war these kids expressed concern over the degradation of the environment. They rejected corporate excesses, racial segregation, and many mainstream values. Some rejected traditional churches as "irrelevant" and dabbled in Far Eastern spiritual beliefs. Drug use and abuse blossomed to frightening levels. "Turn off, turn on, and drop out," became the words many chose to live by.

The willingness of these young people to question and reject many of society's values and practices appealed to the rebel within me. Surprisingly I felt a kinship with and sympathy for much of what they said. However I did not condone the violent methods they sometimes used when trying to bring about changes or their rush to discard many traditional religious values.

In 1971 Governor Bob Ray appointed Dr. Philip Levine, a professor from Drake's College of Pharmacy, to head a Drug Abuse Advisory Committee to study the problem and to make recommendations to the Governor. Representatives from the major departments of state government, private groups, and individuals with an interest in drug abuse prevention came together to investigate. As Chief of Mental Health Services with Voc Rehab I thought I should cooperate with these departments in the state's drug abuse efforts. My boss encouraged me to help in whatever ways I could.

Over the years I've discovered that new challenges excite me. I relished diving into this uncharted area of drug abuse prevention, education, and treatment and in the end my work in this area was yet another satisfying chapter in my career with Voc Rehab.

Our state advisory committee tried to get a feel for the type and extent of Iowa's drug problems. We sought information from whomever we thought could supply it. Often I traveled with some of the Drug Abuse Authority staff to contact individuals or small groups around the state. One day Fred Brinkley who now was the permanent Director of the Drug Abuse Authority and I flew to Spencer. The director of their mental health center met Fred and me at the airport. He had arranged our itinerary for the day, but we didn't know what he'd included. He whisked us off to the local radio station.

"I've arranged an interview for you both with the manager," he said as he parked in front. He hurried us into the building and introduced us to the station manager as we sat down in the studio. I assumed the manager wanted information to use later in a news story. The DJ was playing a pop tune of the day. When the record finished the station manager made a few introductory remarks then looked at me and asked, "Can you tell us, Mr. Perkins why you've come to Spencer today?"

Suddenly I realized the DJ had not started another record. Instead we were on the air live. Panic surged from my stomach into my throat. I wasn't sure what was included in the day's schedule so I stammered out a few generic sentences saying we were there to learn the extent of drug problems in Spencer and to discuss ways to deal with those problems. That satisfied the station manager for the moment and he turned his attention to Fred. From time to time he asked me other questions, but after a few minutes the on-air interview was over and the listeners got their pop music back.

After that disquieting beginning I felt the rest of the day just had to get better.

Voc Rehab Tries Training Its Staff
If our agency were to work effectively with individuals disabled by drug abuse our staff had to learn about such problems. Bill Herrick, our training director, and I planned a staff conference in Des Moines for all counselors and their supervisors. We enlisted the help of Des Moines drug treatment center staff as well as staff from the state Drug Abuse Authority and the Alcoholism Commission.

Two of our state supervisory staff were cool to the idea of holding such a conference. It seemed to me their reluctance was partly because they believed alcoholics and drug users were not *worthy* of vocational rehabilitation services. They felt drug abusers were bare foot, unwashed hippies who preferred to lie about and get stoned rather than work. But in the end they approved our conference and it began. We scheduled sessions at two downtown hotels. After a presentation by some of the hippie staff and counselors from the treatment center our counselors made their way to the second hotel. As we walked along I noticed the hippie presentation apparently had an unintended effect on one of our counselors for he had taken off his shoes and walked barefoot through downtown Des Moines. Behind him one of our reluctant state administrators frowned and looked disgusted.

A later staff-training seminar turned into a group therapy session when the training facilitators confronted the entire staff about crude remarks one or two of them made to some of the black counselors. That incident triggered the exploration of personal interactions, tolerance, and respect for others. It also triggered emotional discussions that moved close to physical violence. But this did not discourage us and over the next three years we held several more staff training seminars around the state.

I was fortunate to get to attend out of state training sessions lasting from one to three weeks. I went to the University of Oklahoma, in Norman, Oklahoma; Arizona State University, in Tempe, Arizona; and Washington, D. C.

I attended the alcoholic counseling training summer program at Rutgers University in New Brunswick, New Jersey. This session lasted three weeks. One of the weekends I flew from Newark, NJ, to Syracuse, NY, to visit my sister Pat, her husband John, and their boys Don and Jim for the weekend.

I spent several days at Mills College in Oakland, California, with a group of voc rehab people from around the country to write guidelines for voc rehab staff working with drug abusers. Another time I worked with a group in Chicago, Illinois, to draft standards for insuring that voc rehab should be a component of any drug treatment program.

During a three-day training visit to the NARCO treatment center in St. Louis, I accompanied one of their counselors to an outreach office in a depressed part of the city. As we walked toward the office my guide suddenly said, "Hey, I got to go in here for a bit. Hang loose. I catch you later."

After saying that he disappeared into a building that had no sign to identify it. I was on my own. All of the buildings on the street were old, battered, or abandoned. Beer cans, wine and whiskey bottles, cigarette butts, newspapers, and unidentifiable trash littered the sidewalks and street. Men and women of all ages were on the sidewalks. Some walked along as though they were on an errand, but most gathered in clusters on the curb or leaned against the buildings smoking, laughing, and talking. I didn't know where the outreach office was located, but I walked a short way down the street. Then I stopped next to an abandoned store to wait for my guide to return. Suddenly I realized I was the only white person in a crowd of black people in a black neighborhood in a high crime area of St. Louis. For the first time in my life I was a minority and I felt uneasy. I tried to blend into the street scene to become as inconspicuous as possible.

After fifteen or twenty minutes my guide reappeared and we continued our tour. I wondered why he left me on the street and what business he took care of while he was gone, but he did not want to explain.

"Sir, Your Rug's On Fire!"

I accepted a request to be on a WHO-TV public affairs talk program because I felt informing the public about drug abuse problems was a part of my Advisory Council job. The other participant and I sat down on the set and Professor Dale Miller, the moderator, explained his ground rules. Someone turned on the bright studio lights and the show began.

After Professor Miller introduced us the discussion moved along satisfactorily until a loud pop and brilliant flash from overhead startled us all. One of the large bulbs lighting the studio had exploded. Sparks showered onto the set and landed on the rug. I sensed that the show must go on and we continued as though nothing happened.

Out of the corner of my eye I saw a plume of smoke rising from the carpet and then it burst into flames. Still the three of us continued our discussion trying not to notice our set was on fire. Finally the other participant could stand it no longer and shouted in the general direction of a cameraman, "Hey sir, your rug's on fire!"

Professor Miller continued to ask us provocative questions hoping the show could continue despite the distraction. A crewmember now crawled onto the set keeping below camera level and began beating the fire with a rolled up newspaper. Whomp! Whomp! Professor Miller asked, "And Mr. Perkins could you tell us what the Advisory Council hopes to accomplish?" Whomp! Whomp!

"We hope to alert Iowans about the drug abuse issues in their own communities," I said. Whomp! Whomp! Whomp!

"But isn't drug abuse primarily a city problem?" Professor Miller asked.

"Not really. Every community has its drug problems," I responded Whomp! Whomp! The crewman continued beating the rug and we continued discussing the prevalence of drug abuse throughout the state accompanied to the Whomp! Whomp! Whomp! beat of the rolled up newspaper. Soon all that remained of the fire were a few wisps of smoke floating across the set and the show continued. Professor Miller concluded that drug abuse was truly a hot topic.

I Go To Washington

I was excited when I got a chance to attend a weeklong drug abuse seminar in Washington, D.C. I had never been there, but now I was going to see our nation's Capitol as well as participate in a first-class seminar. My secretary booked my flights and my hotel room.

My flight connections didn't get me to Washington until 1:00 in the morning and landed me at Dulles International rather than at the National airport. I rode a bus downtown along with a number of other late-night travelers. I hailed a cab to take me to my hotel. I assumed it would be a short ride. The hotel reservations clerk told my secretary that the hotel was within walking distance of the seminar's meeting place. The cabbie headed out of downtown and kept driving. Soon we were far beyond walking distance. After a lengthy ride we reached my hotel in northwest Washington near the National Cathedral.

I checked in and hurried to my room thinking how nice it would feel to fall into bed and sleep. I quickly changed to my pajamas and brushed my teeth. I looked around the room for the bed. There was no bed! I called the front desk and asked, "Where's my bed?"

The clerk said, "Try the sofa. It's a hide-a-bed. Pull it open. It's already made up."

The next morning I got up early. The seminar began at 8:00 and I had to get back downtown. I got in the shower, but there was no soap just a sample bottle of shampoo. That had to serve as soap. Downstairs I asked the bell captain if I could get a cab. He said he'd call one for me. I stood outside ready to get in the minute it arrived. After ten minutes the cab had not arrived. At a larger hotel across the street cabs seemed to come and go frequently. I hurried across the street and asked two ladies who were getting into a cab if they were going downtown. They looked surprised, but said they were. "Good, then maybe you'll share your cab with me," I said and got in without waiting for their answer. I may have broken several cab etiquette rules, but I arrived at my seminar on time. Later I found I could take a bus downtown from the hotel. For the rest of the conference I rode the bus.

I saw a few tourist sites while in Washington. One afternoon after the seminar I walked through the National Cathedral. The clear high notes of the boy's choir practicing for Sunday's services reverberated from the chancel and bounced off the vast stonewall of the nave. Their high clear notes were the right accompaniment for my tour.

On my lunch hour I walked through an exhibit of Shaker furniture at the Smithsonian. I studied the chairs and made mental notes how to improve my miniature ladder-back chairs. I walked past Blair House the traditional home of the vice-president. I saw the White House from a distance. And I strolled through Lafayette Park. But the most memorable event of my week happened at the airport while I stood in line waiting to board the plane for home. An Army major in line ahead of me suddenly whirled around and blurted out, "I've never been so glad to get out of any damn place as I am to get out of this crazy Washington, D.C." He summed up my feelings exactly.

It is unrealistic to expect our staff to learn about drugs and how to work with drug abusers in one or two brief seminars. I decided a newsletter might give information to staff as well as respond to questions arising from their work with clients. In 1975 I began writing "Drug Notes" an eight to twelve page pamphlet. It gave counseling tips and suggestions, discussed different drugs, and usually contained a cartoon. Originally I intended it just for our staff, but other agencies asked to be included on our mailing list. Even a college professor in Canada asked to be on the list. He asked for twenty-five copies for his students. I was pleased to learn he was teaching a psychology class and not an English writing class. An English professor might have used it as an example of bad writing. For several years "Drug Notes" was the only newsletter of its kind in Iowa.

Drug Treatment Licensing Board

Iowans gradually realized there were significant drug abuse problems in their communities. They developed clinics and residential facilities. Many were a part of a mental health center, but the standards covering their drug treatment work seemed unclear. It was reasonable to believe that these programs ought to meet certain minimal standards especially if they were asking for state and federal funding. The Drug Abuse Treatment and Licensing Board was established in 1976 and I was appointed as one of its members.

It was the Board's responsibility to develop the standards, review each program, and grant a full license, a provisional license, or deny a license to operate. Typically two or three members of the Board would do an on-site review of the program then recommend specific action by the full board. At these reviews it was always gratifying to see how many communities were running effective programs despite inadequate funding. Their successes happened because of their dedicated workers.

Charleston Conference

As chairman of Iowa's Drug Abuse Advisory Council I accompanied the agency's deputy director to a national conference in Charleston, SC in 1977. After hearing about the encouraging progress many programs in states around the country were making I came home believing that maybe we could get drug abuse under control in Iowa. But what impressed me most was just being in Charleston. This was my first trip to a major city in the Old South. The architecture of its stores, churches, homes, and government buildings inundated me. Whenever I had free time I walked the streets of old Charleston and its waterfront trying to catch and remember the look and feel of the town. I tried to imagine how its streets looked in Colonial times. Except for the automobiles and people in modern clothing I decided it would have looked much like it does today.

One evening another conference participant and I heard music as we strolled through a neighborhood of large old homes. We came to a home sitting behind a brick and ironwork fence. When we reached the main gate we could see a large white awning festooned with wide ribbons and bows in the side yard. An orchestra sat under the awning playing dance music. In front of the orchestra several young couples dressed in formal clothes were dancing. A black maid wearing her starched uniform and apron stood at the gate. I asked her, "What's the occasion?"

She smiled and replied, "Why this is Miss Ellen's coming out party."

So this is what a coming out party looks like. We stood and watched for a few minutes. It was a beautiful and touching sight. I thought how grand it is that this genteel remnant of the Old South is still clinging to life in Charleston. Yet this ostentatious reminder embodies some repugnant elements that are demeaning. We walked on.

There are many historically significant places to visit around Charleston, but the conference agenda allowed little time for sight seeing. Yet I was determined to see Ft. Sumter in Charleston harbor. A tour boat left from the waterfront right after lunch each day for a tour of the harbor including sailing by Ft.

Sumter. I would miss the afternoon sessions at the conference, but at the moment that didn't matter.

I sat on the open top deck toward the bow of the tour boat enjoying the sights, sounds, and smells of the harbor. I watched our dolphin escorts roller-coastering along on our bow wave. Near the town of Mt. Pleasant we passed some navy ships including the Yorktown aircraft carrier anchored in the harbor. After cruising past several points of interest we approached Ft. Sumter. I didn't know what to expect, but I thought the island and the fortifications would be larger. I tried to imagine how the two-day battle in April 1861 and the much longer siege of the fort later must have looked. The initial battle lasted only a little over thirty hours, but it was the beginning of the Civil War lasting four years. When the tour ended I walked back to the conference confident that I had a more enjoyable afternoon than those who attended the scheduled session.

Mental Health Services

While all of these efforts to develop community alcoholism and drug abuse education and treatment programs was happening there was considerable activity in the mental health field. I worked with the Polk County Mental Hygiene Committee. They delivered their services through the Mental Health Clinic at Broadlawns Hospital. Also they tried to coordinate services with the Clarinda Mental Health Institute.

The Governor appointed a state mental health advisory group to review how services were provided and to recommend changes if necessary. I was a part of the group. It was gratifying to see the committee's recommendations incorporated into legislation that passed in 1981. I attended the ceremony when Governor Ray signed the bill.

My work with drug abuse, alcoholism, and mental health spanned ten years from 1971 to 1981. Most of that time I was not doing the traditional things associated with vocational rehabilitation. Nevertheless I felt my work truly contributed to the structure and tools needed to rehabilitate these individuals. Much of the time it felt as though we were working in new, undeveloped, extremely difficult areas. Perhaps it was because it was so challenging that I view this decade perhaps my most enjoyable period in Voc Rehab.

Chapter 25

"WHY ME?"

It was Friday, August 31, 1977. As I laid my notes on the podium and looked out at the dozen new counselors in the room nothing seemed unusual. They took out pens and notebooks like dutiful students ready to capture any new knowledge I might give them. I hoped they would not be disappointed.

For twenty minutes I described how they could work successfully with alcoholics. Then I took questions from the group. When there were no more questions I handed out my pamphlets, put my notes in my briefcase, and closed the lid. Then it happened! Suddenly, severe pain tore through my chest. One or two counselors came forward with additional questions and I answered as best I could, but just then my biggest concern was to get out of the building. "Surely if I go sit in my van I'll feel better in a couple of minutes," I thought.

I tried to relax in the van, but the pain was unlike any I had experienced before and it wouldn't quit. I hoped I was wrong, but I was certain this was a heart attack. What had triggered it? Folklore has it that a heart attack follows some specific excitement or stress. I thought back over the day and the seminar. My presentation had gone well. I was dealing with a familiar subject and wasn't worried about talking to this group. Nevertheless it was happening. "Well, I won't go back to the office. I'll just drive home. Maybe I'll feel better if I lie down," I thought.

When I arrived home early and looking pale Gladys immediately asked, "What's wrong? Are you all right?"

"Just some chest pains. Going to lay down for a while," I said as I went into the bedroom.

It didn't help to lie down. I couldn't get comfortable. Gladys came to the door several times to check on me. "Don't you think you should see a doctor? Do you want me to call 911?" she asked.

I declined her offer a couple of times, but finally I asked, "Can you drive me up to Doc Bell's?"

I told the office receptionist, "I'm having chest pains. I need to see Dr. Bell."

"Sit down and he'll be with you shortly," she replied.

After several minutes Gladys tried to impress on her the urgency. That did not help. After waiting an hour the nurse finally ushered me to the exam room. Dr. Bell listened to my heart then said, "Get over to Northwest right away. I want you in the hospital. I'll be over in a few minutes to check you in."

I was in the admissions office answering the clerk's questions when Doc Bell arrived. He said, "Come with me. Gladys can finish checking you in."

Soon I was in a hospital gown and sharing a room with another patient. My chest pain had now lasted for three hours. It had become overpowering. It felt as though two cement blocks were pressing into my chest making it hard to breathe. The nurse gave me nitroglycerin, but that didn't help.

Before long Doc Bell transferred me to Intensive Care. The nurse stuck monitoring patches on my chest, an IV needle in my arm, pushed an oxygen tube up my nose, and gave me more medication. Another nurse showed Gladys to a lounge area and told her she could come in to see me briefly once each hour. I didn't know until later that Gladys stayed at the hospital all night and looked in on me every chance she got.

"Why Me?"

I remember little about that night except the persistent overpowering chest pain and my intense anger. "Why did this happen to me? It's just not fair!" I snarled.

For the first time in my life I faced a life threatening illness. I was so sad that my cheeks were wet with tears. "I might die," I thought. "Dad died with his first heart attack. I might die, too." That was both sad and frightening.

As I prayed for God to ease the pain a Bible verse from Romans floated into my consciousness. "Whether we live, we live unto the Lord; and whether we die, we die unto the Lord; whether we live, therefore, or die, we are the Lord's." (Romans 14:8 KJV). That wonderful truth gently settled over me. I was no longer angry, sad, or frightened. I was willing to accept whatever the Lord had in store for me knowing it would be for the best.

The next day they transferred me from Intensive Care to a regular room. Dr. Bell examined me daily and had blood drawn for lab tests. I told him, "I think I had a heart attack. I did—didn't I?"

He said, "Let's just wait until we get all the lab work back."

The next morning someone jostled me awake. Only the night light was on, but I could see it was 4:00 am and my visitor wore faded jeans and old cowboy boots. "I'm Dr. Shirk. I'm filling in for Dr. Bell this morning."

He asked how I was feeling and if I'd been able to sleep well. I said, "I feel slightly better and until now I've been sleeping ok. My chest hurts and I feel awfully weak. No energy at all. Dr. Bell hasn't said so, but I think I had a heart attack."

"Hell, no question about it. You did have a heart attack and a fairly good one at that," he said. He listened to my heart and then headed for the door saying, “Got to get some riding done before I go to the office.”

So it was a heart attack. Until a doctor actually labeled it a heart attack I could believe it was something benign. But Dr. Shirk sounded so certain. I had to face the reality that it was a heart attack. Resentment, anger, and fear tried to resurface, but they evaporated when I remembered that I was still in good hands.

Doc Bell transferred me to Methodist Hospital for angioplasty to determine which cardiac arteries were blocked. The angioplasty showed several major blockages and by-pass surgery was recommended.

Next the doctor transferred me to Mercy Hospital because that was the only hospital in Des Moines doing such work at that time. The surgeon agreed that by-pass surgery was the best treatment for me, but he said, “We won’t schedule the surgery for about three weeks. By then you’ll be stronger and better able to tolerate it.”

“Well if you’re not going to operate for three weeks,” I said, “Then I can just as well go home and wait there.”

“Oh no, that wouldn’t be wise. If your heart started to kick up again we’d have a better chance of helping you if you were right here on the cardiac ward. If you were home we might not have that chance.”

I was not pleased, but I stayed in the hospital. Even though Gladys visited every day and I had other visitors as well I became bored, agitated, and slightly depressed. The doctor prescribed a tranquilizer to help me tolerate the confinement and inactivity. It seemed to help, but it also may have contributed to a vivid hallucination. Or was it a hallucination?

One day as I thought about my up coming heart surgery I was startled to see Dad standing in the corner of my room. How could this be? Dad's been dead for fifteen years. He looked concerned, but smiled and reassured me. He said, "It's going to be ok, Don. Everything's going to be all right."

I was too surprised to say anything as he gradually disappeared. His words, however, stayed with me and had a remarkable calming effect. I believed him. Everything will be all right.

On September 22nd the surgeon did five bypasses. Almost at once I had felt better. One day after the surgeon transferred me back to a regular room Gladys wheeled me outside onto a patio for fresh air. It was a sunny fall day. After almost a month inside I looked forward to a breath of fresh air, but I quickly wore out and was glad to get back into bed.

Over the next several days I became stronger. I could walk up and down the hallway and could sit in a chair for longer periods of time. I was ready to go home. The doctor released me on Sunday, September 30th. As promised everything turned out all right.

Cardiac Rehab

It was good to get back home in familiar surroundings. I napped some in the daytime, but walked for thirty minutes every day at the mall. Six weeks after getting out of the hospital the cardiologist released me to return to work half time. This was a giant step forward and I tried to pick up where I'd left off. I still devoted most of my time to drug abuse and mental health issues. After working half time for two weeks the cardiologist cleared me for full time work. He also recommended that I think about beginning cardiac rehab at the YMCA three evenings a week.

I went to the rehab class a couple of times to observe what it was like and in mid December I joined the group. About a dozen of us who had undergone by-pass surgery dressed in our gym clothes and began exercising under the supervision of a nurse, physical therapist, and physician. For the first ten minutes the therapist led us in stretching and bending exercises. After about five minutes of exercising the therapist asked us to sit on the floor and bend forward to touch our toes if we could. As we began this exercise I heard a woman behind me suddenly scream and moan. I looked around and saw she was clutching her chest. "Ohmygawd!" I thought. "She's having a heart attack. I'm getting out of here."

As I started to get up one of the volunteer helpers saw my concern and quietly told me. "It's ok. She's not having a heart attack. She has an adhesion that hurts sometimes when she exercises."

I was still uneasy, but stayed. After ten minutes of exercises we walked, jogged, or did a combination of the two for twenty minutes to get our heart rate up to the level prescribed by the cardiologist. After that we played volleyball for the remainder of the hour.

At the end of the hour I was tired and sweaty, but as I walked off the volleyball court to the showers I felt euphoric. I had exercised, walked, jogged, and played volleyball. I got my heart pumping fast and actually worked up a sweat yet I hadn't fallen over dead as I thought I might. That convinced me that once again I could lead an active life.

Other Health Concerns

I try to remember that regardless of my health problems the important thing is how much I permit them to interfere with the things that I must do or want to do. As I used to tell my Voc Rehab clients, "You must focus on what abilities you have and not on what your disability may have taken away." I have tried to let that influence my attitude about my health issues.

To be sure I have serious problems. I have hypothyroidism and take daily medication. In 1993 I had back surgery to repair damage to vertebrae damaged in an auto wreck 45 years earlier. In 1996 I had a second bypass surgery for three bypasses. And in 2002 I had cardiac ablation and ended up with a pacemaker. But

I try not to let that keep me from participating in life. Overall I believe I'm in good health and try to do those things that a person in good health does rather than focus on my problems and resign from most activities.

In some ways health issues have been like a rollercoaster ride. I've had low periods when they have interfered with my activities or caused considerable pain for a time. But then following surgery, medication, or sometimes for no apparent reason I've soared to highs where I feel good again and have surged forward with enough energy to do almost anything. Often the problems I faced six or eight months ago no longer bother me. Usually I feel good and have a positive attitude. I am optimistic and believe I am still productive in several areas. Who could ask for more?

Chapter 26

MILESTONES

So far I have described milestones where I was the principal player, but there are other milestones that are immensely important to me where I had only a minor role.

Training Young Drivers

Getting a driver's license is an important milestone on the road to growing up. As a parent I worried about the bad things that happen to young inexperienced drivers. When each of our kids reached driving age I chose to spend time with them to help them learn how to drive. They all had a driver's education class at school, but I wanted to augment that with more on the road experience to enhance their chances of survival.

Emily was first to reach drivers' age. Several times we went out together in our 1964 Ford Station Bus. If she did well I gave her a thumbs-up. One day at the State Fair grounds she practiced driving on city-like streets without traffic. She did a good job and was even learning to come to a smooth stop at the stop signs. Next I asked her to practice parallel parking. She lined up the bus and backed toward the curb faster than she intended. There was a bump and a bang as a rear wheel went up over the curb and the tire blew out. And so it was that Emily learned how to change a tire before she learned to parallel park. I gave her a thumbs-up for tire changing.

Cindy and I went for her driving lessons in our Volkswagen beetle. All the driver's education cars at school had automatic transmissions, but our Volkswagen had a stick shift so Cindy had to learn how to shift gears just as Emily had to learn in the Ford Station Bus. Shifting gave her some trouble, but she soon got the hang of it. Several times we went to Camp Dodge where she could experience city-like streets with stop signs and curbs but without much traffic.

Early in her training she was driving an oval around an empty parking lot. Snowplows had cleared off the snow and piled it in high banks around the lot. After maneuvering slowly around the lot several times, I suggested that she try going faster. She stepped on the throttle and we whizzed down one side of the lot. When it was time to turn at the end of the straightway she was going too fast for the corner. We hooked into the snow bank but managed to stay upright. She kept going and made the turn. That was more thrilling than either of us expected. She got a thumbs-up for a hair-raising ride.

Mark also did his practice driving in our Volkswagen beetle. We went out together several times and he earned many thumbs-up, but never for changing a tire or for a thrilling ride.

All three kids became excellent drivers. I would like to think our drives together helped them. At least I claim their driving skills as vicarious mileposts.

Emily Graduates Then Marries

When Emily was home on a semester break during her final year at Iowa State I asked if she'd like a car as a graduation gift or was there something else she'd rather have. It surprised me when she said, "I'd rather have a sewing machine."

She explained she planned to get married in August following graduation in May. She thought a sewing machine might be more useful. How could this be? I hardly knew she was seriously dating anyone much less that she was going to be married so soon. The following day we met Wayne who also was an Iowa State student. He seemed like a fine young man. As we got acquainted I felt confident he could be trusted with our first-born's future happiness.

As father of the bride I had few responsibilities for planning the wedding. It seemed my sole role would be to pay some of the wedding expenses and to give the bride away. We met Wayne's family at the rehearsal. Afterward and they took us all to Babe's Restaurant for supper.

Emily had her wedding at our church Mt. Olive Lutheran on August 11, 1973 with pastor Reinhold Dorman officiated. Our first-born was getting married. I believe I was as nervous as the bride. After the wedding Emily and Wayne left for Cincinnati where Wayne had an engineering job with General Electric and Emily would begin her graduate work at Miami of Ohio.

A Texas Wedding

On the day after Christmas in 1978 Cindy left home and moved to Austin, Texas. I was pleased that she had the job skills and the self-confidence needed to leave home to seek her fortune, but as I watched her drive away in Mom's 1954 Chevy we'd given her I felt sad. Later she moved to Brazoria, Texas. There she took a night school course in real estate sales at the community college where she met Dean. During a lengthy telephone conversation she told us that she planned to marry him. She did not plan to have her wedding in Des Moines, but would get married in Texas.

We took our van and Mark drove his Toyota pickup. The trip went smoothly until we reached the outskirts of Houston during the Friday afternoon rush hour. We weren't sure when our exit highway would come up nor which lane we needed to be in to catch it. Changing lanes would be almost impossible. Then to make driving more challenging it began raining hard like a cloud burst. The spray kicked up by the other cars and trucks on the freeway made it seem like we were driving under water. When we spotted our turnoff we radioed Mark on the CB. I don't know how he did it but he dodged across the rain-soaked freeway in time to follow us off.

We stayed at Cindy's rented house and tried to help with the last minute wedding chores. The best way for me to help was to stay out of the way. A wedding requires a woman's touch. I took my toolbox to the storage shed and worked on miniatures. Em,

Wayne, Andrea, and Jessica flew into Houston then drove down in a rented car. At one point Cindy wanted everyone out of the way and sent us to the beach with Dean.

All the loose ends finally came together and the wedding took place on May 26, 1984. It was a solemn and joyful occasion. Dean's mother arranged the reception afterward in a social hall with a live polka band. Nothing says celebration more emphatically or eloquently than a happy polka. Gladys and I didn't dance, but we enjoyed watching everyone else including eighteen-month-old Jessica who danced on top of a table.

A Memorable Year For A Wedding
We all remember events easier when they happen the same year as another major event. I can easily remember the year Mark and Sharon married because it was the year of the big flood –1993. The water treatment plant was underwater and no one had water for almost three weeks. We had to pick up bottled water at one or another distribution site around town. I collected rainwater to pour into our toilets to flush them. And our electric substation was flooded so we were without electricity for four days.

Mark and Sharon's wedding on September 3, 1993 followed shortly after the flood. The ceremony was at Christ the King Catholic Church. Following the ceremony everyone ate supper aboard the Spirit of Des Moines cruise boat. The boat normally cruises up the Des Moines River while supper is served, but because of the high water and strong current it remained at its mooring near the Botanical Center.

Now all three of our kids were grown, married, and out of the house. Our nest was empty and seemed so different, but we didn't celebrate with wild abandon.

Suddenly We Are Grandparents
Each time I became a father I was thrilled. Now I became a grandfather for the first time and felt the same thrill. I was glad that Emily and Wayne returned to Iowa from Cincinnati when

they decided to start a family. Andrea was born in February 17, 1977. In August that year I had a heart attack followed by by-pass surgery. I remember sitting in a wheelchair in the hospital when Emily came to visit. Andrea was about seven months old and Emily laid her in my lap. I had looked forward to this visit and getting to hold her and talk to her. Suddenly I felt weak and feared I'd drop her. I was disappointed I couldn't hold her longer.

Jessica was born on November 5, 1982. Once again I was thrilled to be a grandfather. Gladys drove up to help Emily with Andrea and Jessica. During this time we had contracted to do a miniature show in Chicago. Mark was available and agreed to help me. I thoroughly enjoyed having him with me and proud to be able to introduce him to our dealer friends. I secretly hoped he'd be so excited doing the show that he'd get interested in miniatures and eventually take over the business.

Mark and Sharon Lose An Angel

In August 1996 Mark and Sharon brought us joyful news. They were going to become parents after months of fertility treatments. After each visit to the doctor they kept us informed. Following one visit they were excited – they had heard the baby's heartbeat. Mark bought a tape recorder so he could record the heartbeat during their next office visit. Not long afterward they came to report that the doctor could no longer hear a heartbeat. Apparently the baby was dead. It was fifteen weeks old.

Seeing two of our kids brokenhearted over the loss of their child was one of the saddest times in my life. Gladys and I choked up and shed tears over the sorrow of our kids and the death of our grandchild. I wanted to say something or reach out and do something to ease their pain and sorrow yet all I could do was stand there, hug them, and tell them how sorry I was. The four of us comforted one another.

In the hospital a few days later I saw my dead grandson's pale miniature body. It would not have covered the palm of my hand.

"I'm sorry you never got to grow and run and play in the sunshine," I thought. "What great things you might have done had you been born?" Mark and Sharon named him Angel. I shared their sad milestone

A Lump To Worry About
It began innocently enough – just a lump in her cheek. But it grew and gave no sign of going away. The doctor did a biopsy. When we went back later to hear the pathology report he said it was a lymphoma – a cancerous tumor – that required treatment. He thought it was early enough that surgery would take care of it. Afterward radiation would give added assurance that it was subdued.

Gladys had a life-threatening illness. I hoped I could give her the loving care and support that she had given me so many times when I was facing treatment.

After surgery in September 1999 to remove the tumor, the oncologists at the Methodist Hospital Stoddard Cancer Treatment Center recommended radiation. From November 1st to December 3rd we went to the hospital five days a week for radiation. Finally the treatment was finished and after several follow-ups the doctor declared her cancer free. She has been cancer free for five years. Somehow five years seems to be a magic milestone. If you are cancer free at the end of five years then the chance of reoccurrence is small. Gladys' cancer and its successfully treatment is a milestone for us both.

A Nontraditional Wedding
It was exactly the kind of spring day I would order, if such things were possible. The sky was incredibly blue, the sun warm, but not too warm, and gentle breezes carried the fragrance of spring blossoms. People of all ages in colorful clothing brightened the streets around Old Capitol and downtown Iowa City, Iowa, where bikers sped past in a centurion race. Periodically cheers rose from the crowd standing behind barricades as the colorful

thread of riders streamed past. Supporters shouted encouragement to their favorites.

I was with a group of spectators clustered on the steep downhill leg of the racecourse. It was clear we had a favorite rider in the women's race. Each time the stream of women sped past we shouted, "Go Andrea! Go! Go!" All of us wore identical yellow t-shirts. Large black letters on the front said, "Lee & Andrea's Wedding, 4.27.03." The back held a stick figure drawing of two bike riders standing beside their bikes and holding hands. A large heart floated in the air between them.

It was clear to the other spectators that we were there for something more than bike races. After Andrea finished her race we strolled to the east walk of the Pentacrest and sat up our folding chairs. Colorful chalk drawings of sunflowers and bike wheels decorated the sidewalk. At one spot an arch made of bicycle wheels welded together and decorated with sunflowers spanned the walk. The atmosphere in the arch area was festive as we talked and laughed with one another and answered the questions of two or three newspaper reporters roaming among us.

Just then without announcement or fanfare the ceremony began when a fetching toddler named Lily made her way to the arch while carrying a basket and throwing flower petals. She wore one of the yellow t-shirts. A slightly older boy wore a silver bike-riding suit and went up the walk to assume his position as ring bearer. Next each of the wedding attendants and Lee rode their bikes up to the arch area, dismounted, and stood waiting. They were dressed in identical silver bike suits and wore bike shoes and helmets. Finally a tandem bike moved slowly up the walk driven by Wayne, the bride's father, with Andrea the bride pedaling stoker. She wore a silver bike suit, bike boots, and a white veil streamed from the rear of her helmet.

A bike race official in his black and white stripped shirt and black pants. presided over the ceremony. He blew the whistle that hung from a lanyard draped around his neck to begin the ceremony. Then he read from his clipboard.

Now most of the spectators became paparazzi shooting pictures as they crowded around the wedding party at the arch. Scattered among the spectators were photographers from TV and the press. With the crush of people and the noise of cameras it was impossible to hear much of what was said, but I gathered the vows had many references to bike racing and were unique to Lee and Andrea. However there was the traditional exchange of rings and the official's closing statement was, "You may now kiss the other person." Lee and Andrea were married.

I had witnessed another milestone. My oldest granddaughter was now a married woman. They rode the tandem bike down the sidewalk followed by the attendants on their bikes. The bridal party took a short victory lap down the block and back. Now it was time for congratulations and best wishes. That evening everyone gathered at the Pizza Ranch in North Liberty for the reception. But before that Lee had one more duty to perform, he had to ride in his scheduled race.

I reflected how life repeats itself. First Gladys and I married and then became parents. Our children married and then we became grandparents. And now the first of our granddaughters was married. Life repeats itself.

Chapter 27

FINAL THOUGHTS

As I close these sketches I remember the day I ended my career at Voc Rehab. When I picked up my briefcase containing the few mementoes I was taking with me my boss walked in to say good-bye. "You made a difference here, you know," he said as he shook my hand.

I thanked him and left. "You made a difference." That was all he said, but that said it all. Can any of us hope for more than that?

When I think about the events in my eighty years I firmly believe God blessed me and guided every step I took. He allowed me to be born in the greatest country in the world, to strict, loving, Christian parents, and He gave me a wonderful sister. He provided me with the fine wife I'd prayed for and gave us healthy intelligent children and grandchildren. He guided my education and led me into the careers I've had. And all along the way I've had *Way Too Much Fun.* But more importantly I hope that when my family and friends think of me they can truthfully say, "He made a difference."